WARRIORS
DIPLOMATS
HEROES

Books By Scott F. Paradis:

Warriors, Diplomats, Heroes:
Why America's Army Succeeds
Lessons For Business And Life

Promise And Potential
A Life Of Wisdom, Courage, Strength, And Will

Success 101 How Life Works
Know the Rules, Play to Win

And Coming Soon:

The Money-Go-Round
Get In On It!

WARRIORS DIPLOMATS HEROES

WHY AMERICA'S ARMY SUCCEEDS

LESSONS FOR BUSINESS AND LIFE

SCOTT F. PARADIS
COLONEL, US ARMY (RET)

Warriors, Diplomats, Heroes:
Why America's Army Succeeds
Lessons for Business and Life

Published and distributed by:

Cornerstone Achievements
Post Office Box 256
Mount Vernon, Virginia 22121
www.cornerstone-achievements.com

ISBN: 978-0-9798638-7-5 (print, soft cover)
ISBN: 978-0-9798638-8-2 (e-book)
ISBN: 978-0-9798638-9-9 (print, hard cover)
Library of Congress Control Number (LCCN): 2012908073

Copy edit by Ms. Stephanie Pierce
Cover design by The Brand4U

Printed in the United States of America

This book is dedicated to the courageous men and women who have donned the uniform to serve. Through their commitment to enduring values, their focus overcoming daunting challenges, and their willingness to act despite the risks we all get to live fuller and richer lives.

A special thanks goes to all the family members of soldiers, sailors, airmen, and marines. Great achievements are made possible by the steadfast support, unwavering encouragement, and shared sacrifice of cherished spouses and children, siblings and parents. No one is alone, and while enduring love, support, and sacrifice are not always acknowledged know they are the motivation that drives all success.

CONTENTS

PREFACE

The men and women serving in the United States Army, Navy, Air Force, Marines and Coast Guard continue every day to accomplish remarkable feats of discipline and daring, both in far-off places and close to home. In this book, when I write of warriors, diplomats, and heroes I could refer to men and women of any military service as all branches have accumulated extraordinary legacies of mission success. Since, however, I have served as a soldier my focus is on America's Army.

Warriors, Diplomats, Heroes, Why America's Army Succeeds is a vehicle to express timeless truths. The military theme is the context to reveal lessons one can apply to improve personally or excel professionally; to set the pace and lead by example or build cohesive, capable teams. Success in any area of life is possible, is achievable for anyone. It's just not for the faint of heart. Soldiers of America's Army demonstrate this fact.

At various times in your life you are called upon to be a warrior, a diplomat, a hero - you must follow and you must lead. When you lead inspire people to act - provide a compelling vision and irresistible motivation. Your success is ultimately the product of a team. Show your team how to do, become, create, something extraordinary.

As the subtitle to *Warriors, Diplomats, Heroes, Why America's Army Succeeds* promises *"Lessons for Business and Life"* lessons are offered directly and indirectly throughout this text. Select lessons are highlighted simply as boxed text:

Lessons for Business and Life

Chapter 19 provides a summary of some of the most important insights for your review. Draw and apply wisdom from the lessons countless American soldiers offer you.

FOREWORD

America's armed forces are the instruments of this great nation, conceived in liberty and forged in the furnace of adversity, specifically designed and intended to address the two most influential elements of the human condition: power and fear. The Army's mission is to fight and win the nation's wars. As the world's premier ground combat force, the United States Army engages enemy forces wherever and whenever circumstances demand. The Army employs national power through the force of arms and the imagination and will of industrious soldiers. The Army manipulates and manages power to achieve national goals - objectives determined by political leadership at the behest of citizens of the United States - a responsibility all members of the society bear.

To accomplish perilous tasks in austere, demanding, and often dangerous environments America's Army must control, suppress, and manage the innate human tendency to fear. The primal instinct, to preserve one's life and one's standing, is a luxury which in combat soldiers subordinate to team and cause - a greater good. Seeking to preserve one's life in the face of a daunting challenge might unwittingly risk the ultimate treasure: ensuring the lives, the liberty, and the happiness of the people soldiers serve.

Freedom is not free and prosperity does not issue forth without first exacting a price. The men and women who serve in America's Army are willing to discipline themselves and sacrifice all. They toil; they stand guard; they risk everything so that others might enjoy full and prosperous lives - lives free from threat, intimidation, and fear. Soldiers do the nation's bidding under the most extreme conditions. They depend upon each other, they support each other, and if need be, they suffer and bear the gravest of burdens.

America's Army has built a legacy of achievement through the dedication and sacrifice of countless men and women. American soldiers have defeated foes, won the peace, and secured the future by overcoming fear, advancing in the face of overwhelming obstacles and employing power in a measure necessary to the task. Power and fear are the domain of warriors, diplomats, and heroes - the province of America's soldiers.

Soldiers' courage and loyalty, duty and honor, selfless service and sacrifice offer varied and vast lessons. Every man and woman who has worn the uniform of this nation has a tale to tell, a tale of commitment, of trial, of overcoming adversity. These hard-won lessons apply to circumstances far removed from the battlefield - these lessons apply just as well to business and life.

Winning - succeeding - whether in battle, in business or in life, are not so different. The principles are the same; only the conditions vary. In the field, on the precipice of battle, there is no mistaking the risks. The soldier is all in. In business and in everyday life people tend to think and act with less gravity. The truth is, however, the stakes are the same.

Learn the lessons millions of American soldiers have sacrificed their lives to teach. Live a life of fealty to principles of the highest order. Embrace each day as the adventure it is. Make the most of your life; focus on what matters, and through your commitment and sacrifice bring joy and happiness to those you share your life with, those you encounter, those you serve.

A soldier's life is ordered, disciplined, and measured, but for a purpose. He or she must be willing to suppress ego and advance under the very threat of death. Your task in this life is no different. Proceed.

ALL IN

Dirt presses cold and damp against my flesh. I lie frozen in place, scanning toward the top of the berm. I know not when I will have an opportunity to rest again. My gaze is fixed and my hands, cold and sweaty, cling tightly to the rifle I have come to rely upon dearly. It is the tool of my craft, an instrument to reduce threats and defend the lives of my closest buddies, my true friends.

As I lie motionless, attentive but self-absorbed, a storm gathers in my mind. I do battle with fear, a struggle I have endured countless times before. On a battlefield, fear seems a constant companion. It lurks around every corner. Soldiers all recognize the same villain, so we pierce the surreal environment with macabre humor, but there is no time for humor now. I console myself knowing the enemy feels the same discomfort, shares the same dread, and ponders the ill fate cast upon those of us arrayed on this godforsaken field.

My unit, my band of brothers, is fixed motionless awaiting a predetermined signal to begin the advance. Our mission is to secure the high ground 1,000 meters ahead. Between us and our objective are hundreds of enemy troops. We will pass through killing zones of artillery and mortars - death raining from the sky. We will breach wire and encounter mines, explosive devices that kill with ruthless efficiency, devoid of the human emotions of war. We will face a wall of lead from rifles and machineguns. If we survive the gauntlet we will engage the intimate weapons of cold, hard steel as we close with the enemy. Only one can be victor.

We know the critical nature of our task. We have prepared for this moment; we have rehearsed every move. We have worked hard in our training, losing sweat then to avoid losing blood now.

The battlefield is eerily silent. The creatures of the night are still. Affixed, they seem to be watching and waiting, anticipating the spectacle, the carnage to come.

I have struggled with and relied upon these men shivering in the cold beside me. Each man now wrestles with his own demons. We have endured countless hardships, celebrated hard-won victories, and shed tears freely for patriots and heroes, soldiers and friends lost. We have marked occasions of anniversaries and birthdays far removed from the pleasures of home and the warm embrace of family. We are family. We hold each other up. We stand together, we fight together, and if need be, we die together. If we do not survive, our legacy will be of lives snuffed out in the prime of youth, sacrificed so that others might live.

The time is nearly upon us to rise, to advance, to risk it all once again.

The earth beneath my body seems both foreboding and welcoming. I know not what beckons over the berm. I have seen it before - the struggle of wills, the tearing of metal through flesh, the stench of death. I love life with every fiber of my being, but in my heart I hold dear a cause dedicated to unfailing principles. In this instant of time I am connected to life and to the men I love; they are counting on me to do my part. Every breath I take is sweet and sure, for I have no way to know how many I have left. I have made my peace with God.

My leader rises to his feet. The stillness breaks. He signals me to advance. I let go of any reservation; I let go of my resistance. I am committed to this team, to my brothers, to this task. I willingly give all that I have so that others might enjoy more life.

I do not seek to leave this earth today, but if my time is up I accept that today is a beautiful day to die.

THERE IS NO GREATER LOVE THAN TO LAY
DOWN ONE'S LIFE FOR ONE'S FRIENDS.

PART 1

SECRETS OF SUCCESS

CHAPTER 1

GUTS & GLORY, THAT OTHERS MIGHT PROSPER

Assembled for our welcoming to the United States Army Infantry School, a full bird colonel, a burly mountain of a man with a booming voice calls out...

Gentlemen, you are here to learn the art of war. Not for some self-aggrandizing purpose. Make no mistake about it; you will be called upon to endure the crucible of combat. Your task at that crucial time, in that austere and perilous place will not be to merely survive. Your task will be to lead with honor, to fight with integrity, and to win decisively.

You are from this day forward called upon to make yourselves tactically sound and technically proficient. You will gain skills with your weapons, with equipment, and most importantly with men. Your task is no less than to fashion yourselves into leaders worthy of commanding the fine sons of this great nation.

This is not a task to be taken lightly. You must uphold and embody the principles of duty, courage, and selfless service. The Congress of the United States has commissioned you to support and defend the Constitution against all enemies, foreign and domestic. There is no greater oath or no greater challenge than to face your fear and lead men courageously into battle. I expect, no I demand your best - physically and mentally. You must be ready to respond when the trumpet sounds to gather the full measure of your strength, to employ your wit and your resources with ingenuity and resolve, and to fight tenaciously and win.

There are only two types of soldiers in this Army, the infantry and those that support the infantry. You are to lead the way. Into the face of any foe, into the gauntlet of death you will advance. Your men, your family, your nation depend upon you.

To effectively lead in America's Army you must know yourself and understand your capabilities. Here at the Infantry School, it is our calling, our duty to ensure you have every opportunity to realize your full potential as soldiers, as leaders, and as men. We will prepare you to survive and stand victorious on the field of battle.

Over the course of the next few months we are going to prepare you physically, mentally, and emotionally. The challenge before you is about you working to your limits and then reaching down in your gut and moving beyond what you thought were your limits. Here at the Infantry School, in this officer basic course, and then for those of you going on to Airborne and Ranger School, we are going to push you like you have never been pushed before. In the end you will count yourselves among the elite - the tip of the spear. You will stand out, not because of riches or fame, but by way of sacrifice for and devotion to a cause greater than yourself.

Gentlemen you are the infantry, you close with and destroy the enemy. Believe me when I tell you - you will be cast into the fires of hell sometime, somewhere; how well you prepare now will determine your fate, the fate of your men, and quite possibly the fate of this nation. God bless -- make the infantry proud.

Now this isn't exactly what was said, but looking back some twenty-eight years later this is assuredly what was meant. Young men report to the "Benning School for Boys" still to refashion themselves into capable leaders, confident soldiers, and self-sure, unbreakable men.

Some of the soldiers in that very auditorium, and men and women in other branch schools (armor, aviation, military intelligence, etcetera) around the Army at that time, led the sons and daughters of this great land into battle. They fought, bled, and died in places like Grenada, Panama, Kuwait, Iraq, Somalia, and most recently again in Iraq and Afghanistan. The legacy of tragedy and triumph continues. The mantle of responsibility, of commitment, of leadership is passed from one generation to the next. The charge rests upon each succeeding generation to bear the burden, uphold the principles, and endure the sacrifice, lest the greatest experiment in self-government crumble and fall.

A nation conceived in liberty and dedicated to the principles of equality, justice, and opportunity will only survive if the people believe these ideals are worth preserving, are worth fighting for, are worth dying for. The soldier displays commitment to those ideals by the uniform he or she wears and the martial discipline he or she bears to ensure the flag continues to fly, opinions continue to be expressed freely, and votes continue to be cast.

The year I first passed through the Infantry School was 1984. Not George Orwell's world of big brother, totalitarian rule, and mind control, but rather a time of a resurgent America. Ronald Reagan was president, and the economy was gathering steam. A newfound confidence was emerging in the nation. America's Army, having been for eleven years an all-volunteer force, was remaking itself, rearming, retraining and projecting power to stare down a determined foe - the Soviet Union.

Hardy, ambitious, and hopeful young men still sought, as they continue to do to this day, to better themselves and serve in a tradition, a lineage of honor, reaching back over two hundred years.

As we sat in those Fort Benning, Georgia, classrooms, in Building Four (Infantry Hall) and around the sprawling installation, as we tested ourselves in forests and swamplands across vast training areas, we found ourselves being transformed. We became part of a culture unique in the American landscape. We became soldiers and leaders - comrades in arms. We learned to build teams and to rely on those teams to achieve seemingly impossible tasks. We became the men we intended to become: men grounded in principles, men of reason, and men of action. The Infantry School welcomed boys and issued forth leaders - to strive, to endure, and if need be to offer the ultimate sacrifice.

I always realized the United States Army was not perfect. No institution, and this includes all human institutions, comprised of flawed men and women could be perfect. The Army collectively, and soldiers individually, fail time and again to live up to the values and ideals the institution as a whole aspires to. I was not blind to the frailties of men - the shortcomings of character, and the weakness of the flesh. I too bore then, and still bear today, my share of deficiencies. But I sought to do better, to become more, to live like the men of action who dared to try. The Army, through its striving, through its focus on ideals of character and ideals of proper action make even the most flawed among us better. America's Army and the men and women who have filled its ranks have forged a legacy of achievement unparalleled in scope and scale in all of human history.

It was the Army that freed the colonists from tyranny and oppression. It was the Army that held together a young republic in times of trial. It was the Army that opened the west and secured a vast, fertile land for settlement. It was countless soldiers sacrificing their fortunes and their lives to set slaves free. It was soldiers who emancipated the inhabitants of Spanish colonies in the late nineteenth century. It was American soldiers who answered the call to end the worldwide threat of despotism not once, but twice in the first half of the twentieth century. It was American soldiers dispatched to stand shoulder to shoulder with the South Koreans and to ultimately stave off the onslaught of Chinese hoards. Soldiers endured the heat of Southeast Asian jungles and the lash of an elusive but formidable adversary. It is soldiers of America's Army that now police the world to promote ever-greater freedom, protect the weak, and destroy those who seek to harm the innocent across the globe.

America's Army has succeeded and continues to succeed like no other institution. The Army trains to win, intends to win, and fights to win. But the Army is much more than a fighting force. Soldiers respond to natural disasters, to human calamities of every conceivable kind. Soldiers win wars, secure the peace, and build nations. The Army and the other military services are the nation's rapid-response force for every imaginable contingency. How is it that the Army continues to amaze, continues to perform, and continues to succeed?

Why America's Army Succeeds

I was one of the younger students in my high school class. I turned seventeen in October of my senior year, the youngest age to enlist in the service. Early on in high school I had briefly entertained the idea of attending one of the military academies. The Naval Academy and the idea of becoming a Marine Officer seemed most intriguing. Eventually, however, I dismissed that notion; I hadn't maintained the grades needed, nor did I want to tie myself down to an extended commitment. To a young person, a few years seem like a lifetime.

As my father had served in the Air Force in the 1950s and many of my uncles had seen action with the Army in World War II, I felt a sense of duty to do my part, but I was college bound. When the phone call came from an Army recruiter, my first and only military recruiter, I had my response ready. I was headed off to college next year. Though I wanted to serve, the track I was on would not allow it. The Army sergeant first class, not missing a beat, responded with the words, "Have I got a deal for you." He went on to explain the benefits and advantages of a new offering called the Simultaneous Membership Program. I could join the Army Reserve, complete basic training in the summer after graduating high school and still start college that fall. In college I could enroll in the Reserve Officer Training Corp (ROTC) and after two years of preparation and instruction I could earn a commission as an Army lieutenant.

It was the best of both worlds. I could fulfill my duty by serving in the Army, complete my education, and pursue a civilian career. I didn't need to waste my time guarding facilities, or watching and waiting for a Russian horde to advance through the Fulda Gap - an unlikely scenario. If anything of any significance on a geopolitical scale happened, something requiring my services, I would willingly and ably contribute what I could. I signed on the dotted line.

A few days out of high school I raised my right hand, swore an oath to the nation, and embarked on my first Army adventure. Traveling with a handful of other fresh recruits, I left the Military Entrance and Processing Station in Manchester, New Hampshire, and boarded a plane. That flight was my first trip in an airplane since I was a toddler - the first flight I remember. The year was 1980. The Mariel Boatlift, the mass emigration of Cubans, who were followed later that summer by Haitians, was in full throes. Upon disembarking at Newark International Airport I thought we had landed in a foreign country.

Lining the jetways of the terminal building were hundreds of Cuban refugees. They had tired, bewildered looks in their eyes. They were anxious and troubled, not knowing what the future had in store for them. We raw recruits had more energy, but we were not unlike those refugees. We had bewildered looks in our eyes, and we weren't sure what the Army had in store for us. Luckily the Army had planned for our arrival. A group of young soldiers and junior noncommissioned officers policed us up along with a score of other recently arrived recruits and put us on a bus. We rode an hour from Newark to Fort Dix, New Jersey. Along the way we sorted out what was happening and cautiously measured the capabilities and intentions of the men and women who journeyed along with us. Regardless of where we came from or what we aspired to, what we had before us was to become competent soldiers, and an effective team ... and that we did.

In assessing why, or how, the Army is able to succeed where other organizations fail, one may be inclined to point to overwhelming resources - the weapons, the remarkable technology and the awesome firepower the Army can bring to bear. That determination, however, would, in fact, miss the fundamental element. The truth is much simpler. America's Army succeeds because of its people - the values they adhere to, the processes they employ, and the grit and determination they exhibit.

Soldiers come from all walks of life. They don't look the same, they don't talk the same, and they don't think the same except in one respect: soldiers intend to win, plan to win, and fight to win. The Army succeeds in achieving virtually impossible tasks, in dangerous, austere environments, because quality people do the necessary things to guarantee victory.

The Army, like the other armed forces of the United States, is an institution designed to confront, manage, and overcome the two most influential aspects of the human experience: power and fear. America's Army is the land force charged with managing national power. The Army applies and manipulates deadly force to achieve the national will. To carry out this charge under extreme duress, the Army as an institution collectively, and soldiers individually, must deliberately and directly rise above - that is overcome - fear.

The Army relies on universal, immutable principles to organize vast and powerful units, synchronize myriad capabilities, and complete complex and formidable missions. To accomplish the most demanding tasks, to succeed in the most severe circumstances, and to triumph over the most threatening of all adversaries, America's Army operates by three indispensable precepts: America's Army is *Values Based, Mission Focused and Action Oriented*. These three cornerstones of Army doctrine and Army exploits are the very same principles employed to achieve success in any and all areas of life. The Army has adopted measures to inculcate these principles into its culture. Soldiers come to understand that the power of a team proceeds from the strength of its foundation. Values based, mission focused, action oriented is the Army's foundation.

Secret of Success - Be values based, mission focused, and action oriented. Do the right things for the right reasons. Do what has to be done.

First, America's Army was established to secure liberty, to unshackle the aspiring citizens of a new nation from the chains of tyranny and oppression. It was built on self-evident truths:

> *We hold these truths to be self-evident, that all Men are created equal, that they are endowed by their Creator with certain unalienable Rights, that among these are Life, Liberty, and the pursuit of Happiness...*

A ragtag contingent, a continental army made up of farmers and artisans, shopkeepers and merchants, men standing together for a common cause, the cause of freedom, overcame the most powerful military force in the world at that time. A sense of purpose, a sense of commitment to one another, and dedication to a cause held the Army together. Despite dreadful losses and atrocious conditions, the Army persevered. Common values and a shared vision of freedom bound those men together. Victory came by way of their ability to focus and apply the limited resources they possessed at the decisive point and time. Ultimate success was achieved by vigorous action when the opportunity presented itself. Values, focus, and action were the keys to winning freedom.

As the new nation formed, the founders conceived of the Army as an instrument of power in the service of ideals enshrined in the Constitution of the United States.

> *We the People of the United States, in Order to form a more perfect Union, establish Justice, insure domestic Tranquility, provide for the common defence, promote the general Welfare, and secure the Blessings of Liberty to ourselves and our Posterity, do ordain and establish this Constitution for the United States of America.*

The Army was an institution of the people. Soldiers swore an oath, and still do to this day, to support and defend the Constitution of the United States against all enemies, foreign and domestic. The words of our founding documents proclaim the ideals, the values, which guide and drive America's Army and its soldiers. It is because of these values and the strength and commitment of countless men and women that the Army has succeeded and continues to succeed.

Building upon these core national values the Army seeks to build a strong, resilient, and reliable culture. To ensure Army teams function under the most extreme conditions and when facing extraordinary threats, the Army imbues standards of conduct and behavior amongst all soldiers. These standards are moral and ethical ideals such as: courage, respect, loyalty, selfless service, integrity, honor, and duty. The men and women wearing Army uniforms are willing to risk their lives for one another and the nation because they believe in these values, they live by these values, and they seek to uphold these values.

Build on a solid foundation of enduring values.

Second, the United States Army, in its two hundred and thirty-seven-plus-year history, has ranged in size from thousands of soldiers in its infancy, to over eight million in World War II. Today the Army consists of some 1.1 million soldiers in three components (Active, Reserve and National Guard). The key to the success of the Army as an institution is its adherence to ensuring that disciplined people employ effective processes to leverage the ultimate power of a massive team.

Given vast resources and control of awesome firepower, leaders in America's Army understand the indispensable tenet of focus. The Army is, and to succeed must remain, mission focused. For any undertaking, of virtually any scale, an Army unit conducts a deliberate decision-making process, considers alternative courses of action, and produces a detailed plan of execution. The key component, the key product of that decision-making process and operational planning effort is a mission statement.

The mission statement is a well-defined task and purpose - an objective to achieve and a reason for achieving it. The mission states clearly and succinctly what is to be accomplished and why. Every soldier, every member of the unit from the commanding officer to the very last private, must understand the mission and understand it completely. Every soldier must know both the task and the purpose. Each soldier then focuses all his or her energy and effort planning for, preparing for, and then executing to achieve the intended outcome. If one soldier remains to carry on the fight, that soldier will act to advance the purpose, even if the task is no longer achievable. The "why" is the driving force. The Army is mission focused. To win, to succeed, whether in battle or in business, requires a deliberate, active focus on the mission at hand.

Focus on the objective, not obstacles.

The third and equally important component of the Army's success is its penchant for action. The Army is action oriented. To manipulate power, to overcome adversaries, to influence circumstances, requires the physical presence and vigorous action of men and women with boots on the ground. War is not conducted from a couch or the comfort of a boardroom. War is a participatory, not a spectator, sport. It is an outdoor sport. The terrain, the elements, the enemy make war unpredictable and unforgiving. Soldiers have to get down on the ground, get dirty, struggle and fight with all they have. Winning, succeeding,

requires getting in the game and taking action, sometimes force-
fully, but always intelligently.

Achieving a mission, great or small, simple or complex, requires the calculated application of a variety of resources ranging from information, to personnel, to technology and weapons
systems. Mission success demands action. America's Army succeeds by taking - vigorous, sometimes violent, but always spir-
ited - action.

Act with enthusiasm, with commitment.

The United States Army is composed of unique individuals.
Recruits and leaders alike join the Army's ranks for various reasons. Some enlist for patriotism, some for adventure, some for
a challenge, some to earn a decent living. Though their intentions vary they come to share a common purpose - to protect
America and, if necessary, fight and win our nation's wars.

Though far from perfect, the U.S. Army has an unequaled
record of achievement. Ordinary men and women accomplish
extraordinary feats due to their grounding in immutable principles and their reliance on each other - the power of a team. We
can learn a lot from the military.

The United States Army succeeds in accomplishing tasks
ranging from winning in battle, to ensuring the peace, to rebuilding nations, to relieving victims of suffering (man-made or
otherwise) because of three main factors: the Army is *Values
Based, Mission Focused,* and *Action Oriented.* These three
features are the enduring principles of success in any endeavor.
They are proven to work in the military, in government, in business, and in life. America's Army succeeds because it has institutionalized the tenets of success and seeks to inculcate these
measures as core processes and disciplined means of executing
every mission.

Guts and glory has an attractive allure for young men and
women seeking to discover what they are capable of, seeking to
challenge themselves, and aspiring to spend their energy and talents in a cause worthy of their devotion. America's Army offers
this opportunity. Men and women join as individuals, but are
soon forged into cohesive teams, teams grounded in principles,

teams focused on accomplishing the nation's missions, teams willing and able to act - and act decisively. The Army succeeds because as an institution it seeks the highest good for mankind. Soldiers fight, soldiers endure, and soldiers sacrifice so that the people they leave behind might have a chance to live free, to grow, and to prosper. Success is a soldier's calling.

Individuals lead and contribute; teams win!

CHAPTER 2

PRINCIPLES ABOVE ALL ELSE

Nothing brings people together like common values and shared sacrifice. The early settlers, the Pilgrims and the pioneers realized this. Disadvantaged groups, outcasts, and soldiers throughout history have accepted this reality as a fact of life. Both wise and noble, and ambitious and self-serving leaders among those set apart, those enduring hardship or extreme tests of fortitude and will, leverage both values and adversity itself to draw people closer together. The more each individual shares in relieving the burden of the group, the lighter the collective load becomes, and the stronger, more capable, and more committed the team.

Shared hardship brings people together.

I was ordered to Department of the Army (DA) in 2001. I reported to the Pentagon in April. Because, however, the Pentagon was undergoing a multi-year renovation, about one-fifth of the personnel assigned to headquarters in the massive and historic building were parceled out to commercial offices nearby. My office, my cubicle actually, was on the eleventh floor of a building in Crystal City - as the bird flies about half a mile from the Pentagon.

It was a beautiful September morning in 2001. The sun was shining, not a cloud in the sky. Since my cubicle was nowhere near a window I couldn't enjoy the sunshine while at my desk, but I looked forward to an early afternoon, lunchtime run - a time to relax and think. My phone rang; it was my wife, Lisa. This was not an unusual occurrence. Lisa was in the throes of a job search so I might hear from her a couple of times during a work week. Her calls were always brief and usually with the purpose of coordinating some important detail. After I said hello, her first words were, "A plane just hit the World Trade Center in New York." My immediate thoughts were that a small, private plane had veered horribly off course and run into the colossal towers. Lisa responded that the crash was no Cessna, but rather an airliner.

As her words sank in and I was gathering my thoughts, I heard, in surrounding cubicles, voices growing louder with anxiety. Someone yelled to turn on the television. I realized this wasn't just an accident. I told Lisa I would call her right back. I rushed into one of the offices with a television; a number of my colleagues had already assembled. We observed the news coverage of the first tower being hit and watched as a second plane struck the adjacent high-rise. Whatever was happening was being done deliberately.

I called Lisa right back. I asked her to go immediately to the store and pick up provisions. We didn't know what was happening, but we had best be prepared. While we were talking, the alarm sounded in my building. Once again, I had to go.

Our leadership had surmised, since we were a military organization occupying the upper floors of an unsecured building, we faced an actual threat, and we had to react. We evacuated the building and accounted for all our people. As we gathered on the street, we began to realize we were in a vulnerable position - open to attacks from passing vehicles. We looked at every truck with suspicion. As a plan was being coordinated a loud explosion erupted from the direction of the Pentagon. As we saw the smoke begin to rise, a few of our team, those with children at the daycare center located on the Pentagon's grounds, started running toward that building.

The rest of us, operating with limited information, speculated that different agencies in downtown DC were targets. Chaos seemed to be the order of the moment. There was no panic, but we knew standing on the street made little sense. Since we had no clear idea of what the threats were, our leaders released the team.

As my colleagues dispersed I saw no reason to rush into what was quickly becoming a commuter's nightmare, so I went back up to my office. From there I watched the gridlock coalesce. I, like much of the workforce in DC, relied on a combination of methods of transportation to get to and from work. Sometimes I took the train, sometimes the Metro (the subway), sometimes the bus, but most often I slugged. "Slugging" is a term used to describe a collective carpool unique to DC. Three passengers are required for commuters to use the high occupancy vehicle (HOV) lanes leading into the city (like the one running up route 95/395 from the south). To comply with the HOV restrictions drivers stop at designated lots and pick up riders. The system amounts to a carpool without having to coordinate pick up times, a mutually beneficial system. Since I had slugged in that morning, I was without a car. My trip home proved to be its own adventure; an escapade that paled in comparison to what so many others endured that fateful day.

Now DA focuses primarily on resourcing the Army and on developing and refining Army policy. It is not a war-fighting headquarters. After the events that had just unfolded, however, we anticipated shifting from a peacetime to a wartime footing very quickly. The plan was to get home, ensure our family members were all accounted for and safe, and then to tie back in to await instructions. We saw the first blood being drawn, and as had happened countless times before, the immortal words of Thomas Paine rang true:

> *These are the times that try men's souls. The summer soldier and the sunshine patriot will, in this crisis, shrink from the service of their country; but he that stands now, deserves the love and thanks of man and woman. Tyranny, like hell, is not easily conquered; yet we have this consolation with us, that the harder the conflict, the more glorious the triumph. What we obtain too cheap, we esteem too lightly: it is dearness only that gives every thing its value. Heaven knows how to put a proper price upon its goods; and it would be strange indeed if so celestial an article as FREEDOM should not be highly rated.*

Chapter 2: Principles Above All Else

We knew the trumpets were soon to sound. The Army was ready.

Life presents challenges,
prepare yourself and your team
to endure hardship.

On the morning of September 11th, 2001, the United States was clearly surprised. Terrorists had struck a blow against a mighty power, believing that a morally bankrupt nation would crumble. They fundamentally misunderstood the American people and clearly miscalculated. While we do suffer from the very same weaknesses that have ravaged civilizations from time immemorial, namely greed and power-lust, and we have wandered from the noble path, the American spirit still lives in the hearts of men and women across this great land. The American people can and will come together to oppose any foe to assure the survival and success of liberty.

Surprise is one of the principles of war enumerated by Carl von Clausewitz, a professional Prussian soldier and German military theorist who lived during, and endured, Napoleon's conquests of Europe. The surprise of that aerial assault and the psychological impact of its fallout were felt around the globe. The attacks of September 11th were reason to employ the remaining principles of war, yet we first had to invoke other, more sacred principles - tenets of unity, fidelity, and justice, to set our course. America rallied to conduct a measured and appropriate response.

Our political servants, realizing their responsibility to defend the United States, sought to take action against those responsible for the horrific attacks of September 11th. They charged the military with the mission to deliberately and decisively contain, capture, and destroy the men and organizations responsible for the calculated acts of aggression against innocent people.

U.S. intelligence agencies quickly identified the culprits responsible for the devastating attacks of September 11th. With the dust of collapsed skyscrapers still settling, fires still burning at the Pentagon, and charred wreckage of an airliner littering a Pennsylvania field, the United States military responded. American forces deployed to neutralize the threat.

A Revolution for Ideals

America's Army, as an extension of the people - all the people - is an apolitical organization. Its allegiance is to the Constitution and the people of the United States. It is a tribute to the men who have led America's Army, beginning with George Washington, continuing through a series of Civil War generals, and on into the 21st century, that civilian control of the military has endured. The exigencies of politics aside, America's Army stands ready to serve the people of the United States. America's Army upholds the rights of all citizens while simultaneously relying on - and counting on - their support and backing.

America's Army is an army of citizens. The Army is an instrument of the people, by the people and for the people. Without young men and women willing to step forward and serve, the unbroken line of defense would falter. Men and women who still believe in and adhere to American values of service and sacrifice, of duty, loyalty, and commitment to a cause greater than self, compose the Army's ranks. It is the values that soldiers hold dear that give the Army strength.

The United States Army rests firmly on the unyielding declaration:

> ...it is the Right of the People ...to institute new Government, laying its Foundation on such Principles, and organizing its Powers in such Form, as to them shall seem most likely to effect their Safety and Happiness...with a firm Reliance on the Protection of divine Providence, we mutually pledge to each other our Lives, our Fortunes, and our sacred Honor.

The founders, men speaking for the people, called on a higher power and pledged everything they held dear to an attractive ideal. These men vowed to stand united unto death for an honorable cause - a cause of liberty and justice. They cited the preeminence of natural law, the divinely inspired moral principles which order society, as justification to demand the status of free men. Appealing to the supreme judge of the world and in the name of, and by the authority of the good people they declared these colonies to be free and independent states. Disposed to assume a station among the free nations of the earth, Americans fought for, secured, and then specified their rights. They established and still maintain an army to secure those rights.

The rights America's Army secures are, as Alexander Hamilton put it:

> *The sacred rights of mankind... not to be rummaged for, among old parchments, or musty records. They are written, as with a sun beam in the whole volume of human nature, by the hand of divinity itself; and can never be erased or obscured by mortal power.*

These rights are enumerated in the seven articles of the Constitution and in the amendments, most notably the first ten amendments, our Bill of Rights. Among the unique privileges the Constitution defines for Americans are the rights to a representative government, composed of duly elected citizens, with the express purpose and specified powers to secure liberty, and to ensure the safety and welfare of citizens. Rights celebrated by the people include: freedom of religion, speech and press; the right to assemble and petition the government for redress of grievances; the right to bear arms; rights over private property; the right against unreasonable searches and seizures; the right for due process; the right to a speedy and public trial by an impartial jury and the assistance of counsel; and limitations on bail, fines, and cruel and unusual punishment. Further, the Bill of Rights specifies:

> *The enumeration in the Constitution of certain rights shall not be construed to deny or disparage others retained by the people. The powers not delegated to the United States by the Constitution, nor prohibited by it to the States, are reserved to the States respectively, or to the people.*

These colonists, men seeking to forge a better life, many still engaged in the barbarous practice of slavery, took up arms, and risked their lives and treasure to begin unshackling themselves from the depravity and limitations of oppression. While still having far to go, the people had the courage and the fortitude to move in the right direction - toward a condition of liberty and equality under law. Universal values and moral principles were and must always remain the sextant by which the people navigate.

The United States as a nation has stumbled and fallen time and again. People are imperfect, weak and selfish, but they embody the promise of so much more. It took a national upheaval, costing hundreds of thousands of lives, to strike the blight of slavery from this storied land. This turmoil demonstrated that ultimately people of conviction, people of principles, carry the day. For a free nation to survive and prosper those divine principles must endure.

Failure is often a symptom of lack of will.

The ideals, the virtues held in such high regard by our founding fathers, purport a long ancestry. They are found in every major world religious tradition. They were espoused by the Greek philosophers of antiquity beginning with Plato and Aristotle. The works of these philosophers were incorporated into Christian doctrine by the likes of Augustine. The strength and majesty of these arguments correspond to the wisdom of Jesus and are recognized in the teachings of the Buddha, Confucius and Muhammad.

Thomas Jefferson, along with many of his contemporaries, was profoundly influenced by the works of John Locke and the eloquent writings of Cicero concerning human rights and principles of government. The people of this nation, and in turn the men and women serving in America's Army, internalized these values as a means of ensuring peace and prosperity, and as a way of keeping the promise of a vibrant and prosperous future alive for ensuing generations.

Cicero wrote some twenty-five hundred years ago that both justice and law are derived from a higher power and that natural law obliges us to contribute to the general good of the larger society. He stressed that human laws are to provide for "the safety of citizens, the preservation of states, and the tranquility and happiness of human life." He asserts the best means of promoting the virtues which tend toward our own happiness is by living with others in perfect harmony and engaging in charity for mutual benefit.

Chapter 2: Principles Above All Else

America was born and built through the strength of proven values. The United States will prosper or decline in accordance with the health and vitality of those principles amongst the members of society. Soldiers in America's Army, a microcosm of our collective culture, pledge their lives to uphold these values. It's up to Americans to keep them alive through families, through commerce, and through politics. As the revered economist and philosopher John Stuart Mill once observed:

> *War is an ugly thing, but not the ugliest of things; the decayed and degraded state of moral and patriotic feeling which thinks that nothing is worth war is much worse. A man who has nothing for which he is willing to fight; nothing he cares about more than his personal safety; is a miserable creature who has no chance of being free, unless made and kept so by the exertion of better men then himself.*

Values guide; lose your values, lose your way.

Values Forged In Battle

America's Army as an institution must employ determined measures to ensure it can meet its obligations to the American people and sustain the legacy it has forged in battle. In an era of an all-volunteer force, the first task is to attract and recruit men and women who believe in the principles and values upon which the Army is built. The Army, drawing from the population at large, must select and enlist those men and women who will submit to the discipline necessary to sustain a fighting team - a team that adheres to the spirit contained in this creed:

THE SOLDIERS CREED

I am an American Soldier.

I am a Warrior and a member of a team.

I serve the people of the United States and live the Army Values.

I will always place the mission first.

I will never accept defeat.

I will never quit.

I will never leave a fallen comrade.

I am disciplined, mentally and physically tough,

trained and proficient in my Warrior tasks and drills.

I will always maintain my arms, my equipment and myself.

I am an expert and I am a professional.

I stand ready to deploy, engage, and destroy the enemies of

the United States of America in close combat.

I am a guardian of freedom and the American way of life.

I am an American Soldier.

The Army, like all elements of the military, institutes deliberate procedures to further instill core values into soldiers so that the men and women of the Army's ranks will stand together, fight together, and if need be, die together. America's Army needs bright, capable and independently minded people, but ultimately the Army wins or loses on the strength of its teams. Its sharpest, most innovative and creative soldiers must adapt and conform to empower the team. Men and women who stand together are much more capable than individuals standing apart. The Army deliberately and purposefully organizes and deploys to leverage this fact.

Chapter 2: Principles Above All Else

My experience at basic training, you will recall, at Fort Dix, New Jersey, was an adventure. Personally I had two advantages: first, I didn't know what to expect, so I took everything in stride. I was fit and capable enough to master the tasks required. The entire experience was an organized adventure. We started with simple tasks, succeeded with those and moved on to more complex and challenging tasks. With each challenge we learned more about soldiering, about ourselves, and about the capacity of our comrades in arms. The second advantage I sported was that my excursion into the Army was temporary. No matter what happened, whether submerged or nearly drowned in the discipline of marching, or marksmanship, or obstacle courses, come the end of summer, I was heading off to college. I had the best of all possible opportunities.

The Army recruits as enlisted soldiers, and commissions as officers, the most capable young men and women possible. They seek out the brightest intellectually and the most talented physically to form and fashion the strongest and most able fighting teams possible. Everyone, however, comes to the Army as an individual. The Army must remake diverse and independently minded people into driven, disciplined and cohesive teams. The Army does this by pushing people to their limits.

At basic training, and later at my ROTC training camps, and then again at the specialty schools I attended - Airborne, Air Assault, and the Northern Warfare Instructor Qualification Course - teamwork was the mantra and the key. Shared hardship and sacrifice are never more evident than in combat. In training, the Army attempts to simulate, and if possible surpass the conditions soldiers might face in combat, so as to prepare them physically, psychologically, and emotionally. Individuals are pushed to their breaking point so they will come to rely on their fellow soldiers, form bonds and build cohesive teams.

Test your limits; you and your team are more capable than you know.

Army training is performance based - that is, the tasks soldiers undertake in training consist of implementable components. Army tasks are not abstract and theoretical; they are necessary and practical. Soldiers in training must execute specific actions in defined, carefully orchestrated ways. Every task a soldier undertakes has a defined standard and given conditions. Each soldier must meet the standard to succeed at the task. Soldiers are driven to recognize and employ the power of the team.

While always relying on the timeless tenets of successful soldiering, the Army employs an acronym to help new recruits understand and internalize essential soldier values. The acronym is LDRSHIP. These letters, in turn, stand for: Loyalty, Duty, Respect, Selfless Service, Honor, Integrity and Personal Courage. These are the core values needed to sustain a fighting team.

> *Loyalty: Bear true faith and allegiance to the U.S. Constitution, the Army, your unit and other Soldiers.*

> *Duty: Fulfill your obligations.*

> *Respect: Treat people as they should be treated.*

> *Selfless Service: Put the welfare of the nation, the Army, and subordinates before your own.*

> *Honor: Live up to all the Army Values.*

> *Integrity: Do what's right - legally and morally.*

> *Personal Courage: Face fear, danger or adversity (physical or moral).*

Leaders in the Army mindfully and methodically act to develop and reinforce core personal values - the very same values that support and sustain society. Hardship and sacrifice can only be endured if people embody selfless principles. Men and women facing adversity without shared values of virtue and righteousness will succumb to anarchy and strife. Selfish rivalry, discord and dissension are evidence of the lack of both common values and a foundation of sustaining principles. The Army cannot survive and cannot succeed without these values. America's Army is values-based by necessity. The Army is values-driven as an obligation to fulfill its charter and its duty to fight and win our nation's wars.

Chapter 2: Principles Above All Else

In a free America men and women each pursue their own self-interest. They seek fame and fortune, status and influence. The nation was founded to allow men and women to freely pursue happiness. In America's Army men and women subject keen intellects and comfort-seeking bodies to rigorous discipline so as to meet any adversity and stand against any foe, so that America might endure, flourish and prosper. Values are the foundation of this nation and form the nucleus of a soldier team. Every man and women who wears the soldier's uniform must use as their guide a moral compass to do the hard right over the expedient wrong. Only by acting in accordance with values - the principles which sustain us - can we succeed as individuals, as an Army, as a nation.

Carl von Clausewitz may have best summed up the intersection of values at the heart of a soldier when he wrote:

> For a soldier, two qualities are indispensable: first, an intellect that, even in the darkest hour, retains some glimmerings of the inner light which leads to truth; and second, the courage to follow this faint light wherever it may lead.

Values guide us to do what is right. Strive to live up to the highest values.

CHAPTER 3

FOCUS, FOCUS, FOCUS

Life quite naturally presents us with a series of missions: to grow from a child to an adult; to complete school; to find a vocation, a calling, a means of making a living; to establish and maintain a family. Life happens, often without much discernment from, nor reasoning by the hapless actor. We attempt; we succeed or fail; we attempt again. That's just the way life works.

My time with the Army was a series of missions. The early stages of my career were mostly about learning - learning to soldier and learning to lead. The later stages were about building and employing teams to accomplish myriad tasks - some important and influential, some less so.

My very first mission was to complete basic combat training. Those eight weeks immediately after high school were great fun - a real adventure. Basic training set my expectations about the Army - expectations that were, for the most part, fulfilled. The Army offered opportunities to grow, to challenge myself, to do things I would never otherwise have the opportunity to do, and to be part of something that mattered, something noble and noteworthy. I was a soldier in the United States Army.

After completing basic training I enrolled in the University of New Hampshire. My mission became to complete the ROTC officer training program and earn my commission as a second lieutenant. At the same time I undertook two other significant tasks: I served in an Army Reserve unit as a leader in training; and I worked toward completing my bachelor's degree. All three tasks were missions requiring my time, attention, and energy.

Chapter 3: Focus, Focus, Focus

Over the next thirty-plus years, I took on new missions, one after the other. I completed training courses to become qualified in a number of skills and to mature as a leader. I became air assault, airborne, northern warfare instructor, infantry officer, and civil affairs qualified. In the early years I traveled to... I'm hesitant to say "exotic" locales... like Fort Bragg, North Carolina; Fort Drum, New York; Fort Greeley, Alaska; Fort Devens, Massachusetts, Gagetown Training Area, New Brunswick, Canada; and journeyed multiple times to Iceland.

Through most of the 1980s I served with Army Reserve organizations. The primary unit I was assigned to was the 187th Infantry Brigade. The 187th was a separate infantry brigade; that is, it was a unit organized to fight as a brigade, independent of a division structure. The mission assigned to the 187th was the defense of the island nation of Iceland. While the United States was rebuilding its military during the Reagan era, soldiers from the 187th were traveling to Iceland to recon the island and plan and prepare potential battle plans. I remember reading Tom Clancy's novel, *Red Storm Rising*, about a third world war while I was on a training exercise in Iceland. The funny thing is, a significant portion of Clancy's story is set in Iceland. His fiction was our reality.

After the disintegration of the Soviet Union the U.S. Army had scant time to rest on its laurels. The first order of business upon cessation of the Cold War was to harvest a peace dividend. On the heels of Reagan's buildup it was time to break the structure down. The Army, like all human organizations, all life really, faces a never-ending process of transformation. This tearing down, however, was interrupted by a dictator's grab for power in the Middle East. Despite the institution's mission of downsizing, the Army responded, immediately deploying troops into the deserts of Saudi Arabia; a sovereign nation, Kuwait, had to be set free. The Army was on the job. It received orders and automatically focused on a new mission.

Clearly define and understand your mission and
your team's mission.

A Process for That

For every operation of any scale an Army unit undertakes, leaders conduct, as time allows, a detailed planning process that results in the production of an operational plan and execution order. A standard Army order consists of five paragraphs: those paragraphs describe the situation, specify the mission, provide the details of how the mission is to be accomplished, provide the sustainment or resourcing details, and stipulate how mission execution is to be managed or controlled. The very heart of the operations order is the mission statement. The mission statement defines in exacting detail the task to be accomplished and the purpose, the reason for accomplishing that task.

From the most junior private to the organization's commander, every soldier must know and understand the unit's mission. The most important element to be aware of is the reason for accomplishing the task - the "why". With every soldier knowing what is to be done, and more importantly, why it is to be done, each soldier retains the ability to ultimately influence the operational outcome to ensure that the intent is achieved. The very last soldier standing will seek to achieve the mission by acting in a way that conforms to the most important component - why.

Once leaders and soldiers alike understand the mission - the task and purpose - they then devote their time, energy, and talents to planning and preparing for execution. By design, a mission statement causes a unit and that unit's soldiers to focus their attention, their thoughts, and their energy deliberately and directly on the problem at hand. The more attention, energy of thought and energy of action applied toward a given end, the more likely the unit is to succeed.

America's Army explicitly creates, demands and nurtures a mission focus. In the life-and-death business of war fighting, no detail can be left to chance. Everyone's head must be in the game. Everyone must be focused on achieving the appropriate result, and everyone must act for their own good and the good of the team in such a way as to maximize the opportunity for success. Focus, focus, focus is a mental necessity and a physical obligation in combat. Anything less will result in lives lost, resources squandered and mission failure.

The Army achieves mission focus through its disciplined

warrior culture and its myriad processes. The Army has a system, or a method, for conducting virtually every action and activity. The Army's culture and bureaucracy both serve to ensure results. Innovative soldiers make up for the deficiencies most readily apparent in the bureaucracy, but still existing in the culture. When it comes down to it, the strength of America's Army lies within its people getting the job done.

You have heard the adage, "If it ain't broke, don't fix it." Well, the United States Army is a study in contrasts that by design puts that axiom to the test. The Army is constantly changing, constantly evolving, constantly remaking itself - within the constraints opposed and allowed by resources, physical disposition, and mission demands - all ultimately political considerations. Human nature prefers only one thing more than the way things are - that is, the way things were, only better. We always know we've made mistakes; we have the advantage of hindsight to see clearly how we screwed up. If we can adjust our error, rewind and try again, we'll do better and become better. As much as we clamor for change - since change is the enduring condition of life - we hope for some consistency and stability. For men and women accustomed to discipline nothing is more attractive. But that is not how an individual or a team succeeds. To succeed requires being able to adapt and overcome. To effectively employ combat power, to effectively manage change across a dynamic, far-flung enterprise, one seeking a unified objective, requires powerful systems and effective processes. America's Army has both.

Business, like life, is constantly changing - manage change.

A regular criticism of the Army is that it is always preparing to fight the last war. While this is true, the Army methodically collects and uses lessons learned from previous action to better prepare for future operations. Army leaders attempt to think through and anticipate ever-developing circumstances. Like in any other contest, to become the best, to win, the champion at some point reinforces success, "Nothing succeeds like success." The competition, however, is always looking for weaknesses to attack. If the champ can't respond to those threats, he won't remain the champ for long. Our military, and America's Army as the land component, wears the championship belt. It is the Army's task to retain that belt by being agile, flexible and responsive.

The Army, though it can be categorized a number of different ways, is essentially divided into two main components: operational forces and an institutional support base. The operational forces are those units that actually deploy and execute operations across the country and around the world. The institutional component of the Army includes the installations, the depots and arsenals, and school houses and headquarters that recruit, train, organize, maintain, and support the million-plus soldiers and the millions of pieces of equipment, the seemingly endless square miles of training area, and the tens of thousands of buildings and facilities across the world.

The operational army is where the rubber meets the road, where - no kidding - forces are honed to a razor's edge of readiness to mobilize, deploy, and face an enemy. The institutional army is that larger part of the force that makes everything else happen, so that soldiers can deploy to fight and win. The operational army is the element that actually accomplishes the mission. The institutional army is the element that allows the operational army to function. This is an intricate and mutually dependent relationship between the supported and the support. One cannot function without the other. Men and women, the soldiers themselves, routinely transfer between the two elements. But like siblings each element often competes for attention and resources to accomplish a never-ending list of tasks.

If you have served in the Army, or if you have ever been a part of any hierarchical organization, you will understand and appreciate this characterization. When not facing the gravity of an enemy threat, and at times, even when facing a threat, often the greatest enemy is considered the higher headquarters. Leaders at every level of an organization have a defined mission - they are to finely tune and prepare their organization, making it an extremely capable team. They have available limited resources and operate under conditions of constrained time. Left to their own devices those leaders know the condition of their organization, they know what needs to be done and they will get about the business of doing what they determine are the most important tasks. Invariably, however, the higher headquarters will interfere.

The best laid plans never survive first contact with the enemy. Within the Army itself most plans never survive the "good idea fairy" of higher headquarters. Since the Army is an alert, disciplined organization - one that responds to the direction of senior leaders - those senior leaders are often quick to exercise their authority and throw all kinds of havoc into subordinate leaders' plans. Army leaders are so good at reacting that directions from the President or Congress to the Army staff in Washington are regularly implemented at the lowest levels.

Prepare to deal with distractions.

It is a mighty system we have fashioned. It is a proven system of achievement. The Army is grounded in values and hardened by discipline. So, though it seeks to be flexible in action it is rigid in intent. This dualistic nature causes tension between the theory of adaptation and a proven, disciplined legacy of success. Of course each of these is subject to the imposed constraints of resourcing, distribution, and mission - again, ultimately political considerations.

While the Army is composed of grounded, well-intentioned, capable men and women, systems are key to the success of soldiers, teams, and units. Throughout its history America's Army has borrowed freely from the finest fighting forces around the world. It has adopted and then refined processes over many years and at the expense of much time, energy and effort. Army leaders develop, implement and apply processes to organize planning, promote effective decision making, and utilize available resources for maximum impact.

The Army employs effective processes to maximize strengths and mitigate weaknesses. When lives are on the line, there can never be too many resources or too much combat power to ensure success. Fighting forces are, however, always forced to manage limitations. Processes the Army employs seek to deal with limited information, the unknown intentions and expected consequences of an actual or potential adversary's action, the changing conditions of a volatile environment, and the natural weaknesses of human actors.

From one perspective the Army is an anachronism. It is a bifurcated entity that has developed and operates by means of a burgeoning bureaucracy. It manages a global enterprise consisting of nearly one and a half million people, routinely operating in more than 100 countries. At the same time, to win, the Army must be ever-changing, adaptable, and aggressive.

The Army is always attempting to fix or improve the organization. While we live in a modern, increasingly complex, and technologically advanced society, human nature is unchanging. The Army has adopted and adapted means to assure, to the greatest degree possible, that even under the most stressful circumstances Army organizations will persevere and succeed.

Design and employ effective systems for personal and professional success.

The Army, like every professional organization, or organized culture, has developed and operates by means of its own language. Acronyms, and in some cases mere sounds, substitute for words and phrases with specified meanings. As we progress through this chapter we are going to wander into that field of the initiated - those who regularly employ a shorthand or code to more easily relay an idea. While lawyers and doctors are known for deliberately using obtuse, abstract language, the government, most notably the military services, actively develop new terms and phrases to complement the systems and processes they employ.

When I reported to BIAP, the Baghdad International Airport complex, in October of 2005 to help establish the Multi-National Corps - Iraq (MNC-I) counter improvised explosive device task force (C-IED), I was changing worlds. I had been serving as the deputy commander of an Army installation - Fort Dix, New Jersey (now part of Joint Base Dix, McGuire, Lakehurst) - and I was moving into an entirely different field, a different command, and a unique theater of war. I had to quickly educate myself on a new series of terms and acronyms to function as part of a new team. Since we were breaking ground with the improvised explosive device task force, we were even creating our own new terms to add to the Army vocabulary.

In addition to deliberate invention, language commonly develops from normal soldier interaction - soldier speak. Nothing serves as a better example than the word, if we can call it that - *Hooah.* Hooah really amounts to a sound, an utterance, a grunt of sorts. It is most used to affirm or acknowledge, but in effect has meanings as varied as can be relayed by human transmission of sound. By employing various intonations, Hooah can be a confirmation as in "I understand." It can be a celebratory declaration. It can be a request for clarification, or it can just be an expression of emotion ranging from enthusiasm to despair. Hooah is a wonderful example of soldiers creating and adapting something simple to apply across a broad spectrum. The underlying sentiment of the expression, however, is hope. No matter how bad things are, by uttering "Hooah", a soldier expresses hope that things will improve. And so they shall.

America's Army as an institution, when it is not fighting wars, has to engage all that brain power for other purposes. The single most, and best, use of the time available is training and preparation. Soldiers and Army civilians, however, spend a significant portion of their time carrying out prescribed tasks to safeguard soldiers, manage resources, and ensure the functioning of the enterprise.

The Army develops, refines, and maintains an expansive, useful and intimidating array of doctrine. The Army has established a virtual "by the book" way of doing nearly every conceivable task. That doctrine spells out the processes and defines the system upon which the Army is built and sustains itself. The doctrine ranges from law (the titles of the U.S. Code – primarily Title 10 for the military), to executive orders and institutional orders (of the Department of Defense and Department of the Army), to regulations, field manuals, circulars, pamphlets, technical manuals and a variety of other written documentation to cover virtually every task, under every condition, to prescribed standards.

Determine tasks, conditions, and standards for
your organization; then adhere to them.

The biggest challenge, due to the burgeoning bureaucracy's fueling of the mushrooming doctrine, involves the requirements placed on operational and institutional units and soldiers. We have examined all the "must do's" in law and regulation and have actually determined that complying with every demand to the level of every prescribed detail requires more time than is available. The bureaucracy has grown so burdensome that the institution regularly ignores its own self-imposed requirements because ultimately the Army exists not to entertain itself as a "self-licking ice cream cone" but rather as an instrument of the public's will, requiring real-world engagement.

So, the Army has a process, a method, a system for virtually everything. Committing every detail to writing is a convenience that offers new soldiers a means to learn through written doctrine specifically how to accomplish a task or how to engage or leverage the system to achieve a desired outcome. Warfare, however, or even international engagement or humanitarian service, is never as simple, straightforward, or as prescribed as written doctrine. Doctrine cannot keep up with life. This requires thoughtful, adaptable, capable people who can move from the rigidity of doctrine to the fluidity of circumstance, people who can adapt and overcome. Doctrine is the preparatory tool that is the launching pad for the creative endeavor of applying power in a dynamic environment against a thinking adversary.

The two terms we are going to focus on for the remainder of this chapter are those terms referring to the two most critical and most influential processes for tactical success: MDMP and the OPORD. MDMP is the acronym meaning the Military Decision Making Process. OPORD is the short hand for Operations Order. Both of these processes are regularly used to plan, prepare for, and conduct military operations in training, in peacetime, and at war. Adhering to deliberate processes makes for better decision making, more comprehensive and inclusive - that is, more complete - planning, and more vigorous, committed execution. Following ingrained processes, even if truncated due to time constraints, allows for more thorough thinking, which in and of itself will allow for better execution. Effective thinking sets the conditions for and leads to more effective execution.

Disciplined people applying effective processes produce extraordinary results. In the Army this equates to battles won and missions achieved. In everyday life disciplined people applying effective processes amounts to technological breakthroughs and advances, more efficient service delivery, greater customer satisfaction, more tasks accomplished and more problems solved. America's Army succeeds by deliberately and systematically focusing energy - the energy of thought and the energy of action. You can too.

While the systems described here are in fact formal processes preserved in Army doctrine, these methods could prove invaluable to your organization professionally, or you personally. For maximum impact, to succeed like never before, apply the best processes to the circumstances you face. Focus and adapt and you will overcome.

The surest route to success: disciplined people applying effective processes.

The Military Decision Making Process (MDMP)

The Military Decision Making Process is a detailed system for approaching challenges and solving problems. The process guides a practitioner to rationally analyze a situation by thoroughly applying clear, sound judgment, and professional expertise. After painstaking analysis the decision maker(s) or leader(s) develop viable options for a way ahead, resulting in a well thought out, achievable plan. The process is meant to help soldiers think both critically and creatively while planning.

The process seems like common sense decision making, but if there is one thing we know about sense, it is that it isn't that common. You might try using MDMP to approach your next problem at home or at work and see how things turn out.

Army Field Manual 5-0, *The Operations Process* defines the military decision making process as:

> *An iterative planning methodology that integrates the activities of the commander, staff, subordinate headquarters, and other partners to understand the situation and mission; develop and compare courses of action; decide on a course of action that best accomplishes the mission; and produce an operation plan or order for execution.*

The Military Decision Making Process (MDMP) consists of seven steps:

Receipt of Mission.

Mission Analysis.

Course of Action Development.

Course of Action Analysis (War Game).

Course of Action Comparison.

Course of Action Approval.

Orders Production.

Receipt of Mission. The mission is the task to accomplish. In a military environment, everyone has a leader, so a mission is normally assigned. That is, since every unit, every soldier, every commander answers to someone else, the person in the superior position confers a mission to the subordinate individual or organization. This hierarchy holds true from a private in the ranks to the commanding general of a theater of operations. In the United States military the operational commander answers to the Commander In Chief, the President. The President, in turn, is beholden to the people and is accountable to the people's representatives - members of Congress. From top to bottom, everyone has a boss. Missions are determined and assigned based on who has the responsibility (normally defined by law) and the capability to accomplish a task.

Most people don't have the luxury, or bear the burden, of being assigned missions. Not all missions in business and in one's personal life are defined, allocated, and measured. Most often each individual has to determine for themselves what is to be done and why. An advantage within the military's system is that the formalized decision making process compares requirements and capabilities with tasks to be accomplished, and apportions missions accordingly.

Life does not accord tasks quite so neatly. Every individual is both leader and follower to a degree. Men and women, in business and in life, are left to determine how to allocate and invest time, energy and talent. One way or another, everyone has a mission. The questions for you are: Do you approach life deliberately, or not? Do you focus on the most important thing? If not, how has that been working for you?

Mission Analysis. Given a task, the recipient, the commander, the leader, the soldier must determine exactly what that mission means. He or she must cull out specified (tasks prescribed in the order) and implied tasks, decide what resources are required, what other organizations or agencies are involved, and establish a planning, preparation and execution timeline. Understanding the mission, the task to accomplish, the reason for accomplishing the task, the higher headquarters' overall intent and scheme of maneuver and timeline are essential for ensuring all necessary actions are considered, prescribed, planned for, allocated, prepared for and executed to ensure success. The more thought energy and effort devoted to planning and preparation, the easier - and potentially safer -will be execution.

Course of Action Development. Like with any task in life, virtually every mission can be accomplished in multiple ways. Most problems have more than one solution. This is where the decision maker begins to generate options. The planner, or planning team, employs creative thought to conceive of viable alternatives to achieve the mission or solve the problem.

The course of action development is the brainstorming part of the decision making process. Courses of action are constrained only by externally imposed limitations (range of maneuver, time, and so on) and resources available. When considering options and coordinating with associated units and organizations an Army unit may request special or additional resources beyond those already allocated. This negotiation - whether or not the resources are available and will be allotted - factors into the course of action development. Only viable courses of action ultimately are considered, but usually, with the appropriate creative thought, and even considering the imposed constraints, a number of options prove viable.

When you think of the task or tasks you are undertaking in your life, you might allow some time to consider more options. The way to love, or wealth, or success is usually not limited. The avenues for advance are many and varied. Identifying and assessing multiple courses of action will likely result in a better decision and plan of action than if you just move headlong into one perceived option. Many paths lead to victory - choose the best one.

Course of Action Analysis (War Game). With viable alternatives arrayed, the planners work through each option individually, attempting to imagine the course of action playing out. Given the current circumstances, assets available, mission constraints and opposing forces, how would events unfold? Strengths and weaknesses are assessed over time, from the initiation of action to mission completion, to determine how the unit will fair. Planners identify coordination and synchronization requirements and assess overall flexibility of each course of action.

Course of Action Comparison. Here the planners evaluate each potential course of action, first independently to assess strengths and weaknesses, and then against to set mission criteria. Then they compare the courses of action with one another using the mission criteria as a guide. Mission criteria are expectations, constraints, and conditions established by unit leaders and planners to more effectively manage mission execution and conserve unit strength and resources to the greatest extent possible. The criteria might involve time restrictions, casualty estimates, allocation or use of resources like fuel and ammunition, and so on. The disposition and strength of the enemy, the terrain, the weather and myriad other factors all come into play.

The analysis and comparison of the various courses of actions produces a matrix of relative strengths and weaknesses of each potential option. The unit commander, with the aid of the experience, insight and expertise of his or her staff, ultimately must choose a means of execution - a course of action - upon which to build a plan.

Course of Action Approval. As time allows, planners consider every potential detail, every potential constraint, and evaluate these against known asset capabilities. After painstaking research and detailed analysis the commander settles on the best option to achieve the mission. With the course of action decided, planning and preparation begin in earnest.

Orders Production. Using all available information, most of which was consulted or employed to select the course of action, unit leaders construct a detailed plan. Again, as time allows, virtually every potential move and countermove by the enemy, every variable in the weather, every possible miscue, is considered, planned for and coordinated. The order is the comprehensive plan for the unit to achieve the mission.

The decision making process focuses the energy and intellects of leaders and planners. Focus on the task at hand is essential to mission success. The product of MDMP, an order, points the way.

Think through your circumstances; consider all viable options then choose the best one.

The Operations Order (OPORD)

Field Marshall Helmuth von Moltke, the Elder, the Prussian Chief of Staff for thirty years, once observed, "You will usually find that the enemy has three courses open to him, and of these he will adopt a fourth." Because of the unpredictable, chaotic nature of combat, General Dwight D. Eisenhower once remarked, "In preparing for battle I have always found that plans are useless, but planning is indispensable." Napoleon Bonaparte likewise planned meticulously in an attempt to anticipate every conceivable move, "If I always appear prepared, it is because before entering an undertaking, I have meditated long and have foreseen what might occur. It is not genius which reveals to me suddenly and secretly what I should do in circumstances unexpected by others; it is thought and preparation."

The United States Army relies on a formalized five-paragraph field order to ensure no detail is left to chance. When time and circumstances allow leaders conduct a deliberate decision making process and thoroughly prepare a careful plan for execution. In the heat of battle, however, the situation may be obvious, conditions fluid, and the resources and means of control apparent, so soldiers will truncate the luxuries of a detailed plan down to the necessary minimum - what is to be done now to realize the ultimate aim. Nothing focuses thinking like the prospect of bombs and bullets. Here is a brief summary of each of the five components of an operations order:

Situation. The current conditions impacting operations. These range from the terrain, environment and weather, to enemy and friendly forces, to the higher headquarters missions (tasks and intent), to adjacent unit missions (tasks and intent), to various other battlefield considerations and assumptions made to move forward. The situation is the "news" report relaying all relevant facts and assumptions about current circumstances and the way ahead.

Mission. The heart and soul of the operations order. The mission states succinctly, but completely, the task to accomplish and the purpose for achieving that task. This is a short description of the who, what (task), when, where, and why (purpose) of the action to be taken and the reason for taking such action. The mission hones the soldier's focus.

Task and purpose (what to do and why) are the most important aspects of success.

Execution. The details of how the task and purpose are to be achieved. The execution paragraph defines the commander's intent, and outlines in as much detail as possible and reasonable for the situation and time available the concept of the operation and the scheme of maneuver. The execution paragraph is the meat of the plan. It specifies who is to do what, and when, and stipulates the coordination to take place in all phases of execution to ensure the mission success.

Sustainment. Details and describes all the resourcing and logistics processes leveraged to execute the prescribed operation. These details range from material (equipment, ammunition, food and water, and so forth) to personnel services, to the employment and management of health and medical systems. The fate of soldiers and the outcome of battles often rest on the conduct of logistics.

Command and Control. States the location of the commander and specifies the succession of command in effect for the operation. This paragraph details liaison and reporting requirements and enumerates the signals concept and the employment of codes and indicators facilitating mission execution.

The operations order is a standardized format to facilitate thoughtful planning and simple, consistent, thorough communication. To be effective, the plan must be easy to understand. If a plan *can* be misunderstood it *will* be misunderstood, so clarity is essential. Clarity often takes great effort and intense, deliberate consideration to achieve. Working out the details in advance is the surest way to ensure the ability to adapt, overcome and succeed. The more intellect applied to planning and the more sweat roused in preparing, the less blood spilled in execution.

The framework of the military decision making process and the operations order have uses far beyond the battlefield. Each represents a disciplined approach to challenges men and women confront in business and the obstacles people encounter in everyday life. Focus is essential to mission success. A workable, effective decision making process, one that helps you arrive at the best possible decision, and a detailed, but flexible plan, one that allocates limited resources for optimum affect, will serve you well in achieving the series of missions you face.

For you or your team to achieve anything worthwhile you must focus.

CHAPTER 4

THE HEAT OF BATTLE

One thousand, two thousand, three thousand, four thousand. If you are Airborne (an Army parachute infantry soldier) you know this count as the seeming passing of eternity as you plummet to earth just having exited a perfectly functional aircraft. At the count of four you should feel an intense wrenching as, hopefully, your chute deploys and you anxiously look overhead to ensure your risers are not tangled. If all is as it should be you can turn your attention to navigating the descent and preparing to avoid a bone-jarring landing. Then it's on with your mission.

One thousand, two thousand, three thousand. These are the simultaneously instantaneous and seemingly interminable seconds that you count off while holding a live, ignited hand grenade before tossing it into a bunker. If you throw it in without a delay, known as "cooking off", there is a good chance in the three to five seconds the fuse takes to burn that hand grenade could be served up as a gift to the giver.

...Six thousand, seven thousand, eight thousand, nine thousand. Nine seconds is the time it takes to don and clear a protective mask, a task the actor is driven to accelerate in light of potentially deadly and gruesome circumstances.

America's Army is an action-oriented organization. Training is hands on and performance oriented. Every task from dressing (wearing the uniform), to walking (marching), to conducting live fire exercises is measured against conditions and standards. These standards demand and ensure a minimum level of excellence from individuals and from teams.

Soldiers are by design and necessity people of action. Soldiers actively manipulate instruments of power. Soldiering is not something done from an easy chair or a command post. Soldiers are and must be immersed in the fray.

As Bill Mauldin, a two-time Pulitzer Prize-winning editorial cartoonist, best known for his depictions of American combatants in World War II, wrote of soldiers:

> *They wish to hell they were someplace else, and they wish to hell they would get relief. They wish to hell the mud was dry and they wish to hell their coffee was hot. They want to go home. But they stay in their wet holes and fight, and then they climb out and crawl through minefields and fight some more.*

American author and Korean War veteran T.R. Fehrenbach asserted, " ...you may fly over a land forever; you may bomb it, atomize it, pulverize it and wipe it clean of life—but if you desire to defend it, protect it, and keep it for civilization, you must do this on the ground, the way the Roman legions did, by putting your young men into the mud." To secure victory, to secure peace requires boots on the ground - the province of the American soldier.

An army, in order to function and to win, must act. Soldiers either find a way or make one. The means to act, the will to act, and the strength to act are essential for success in military matters - and in life.

To succeed requires deliberate, persistent action.

The Foundation

Among the first things a man or woman learns upon joining the Army is that fitness, physical and psychological, is a requirement. While Clausewitz, the preeminent western military theorist, asserted the first quality of a warrior is courage, Napoleon claimed the first virtue of a soldier is endurance of fatigue. The nature of battle demands a body that can tolerate extreme duress and a discipline of mind that is impervious to the corroding influence of fear. Ordinary men are involved in action, heroes act. War is the realm of physical exertion and suffering, the realm of heroes. The basic building block, the foundation upon which a winning team is forged is conditioned through action.

Ulysses S. Grant observed, "In every battle there comes a time when both sides consider themselves beaten, then he who continues the attack wins." The ability to persevere despite overwhelming obstacles, despite utterly atrocious conditions depends on the foundation of one's convictions. Values must be unequivocal and esteemed above all else. Every fragment of energy must focus on the task at hand, and the individual, the team, or the society that intends to win must be willing to act, and act vigorously.

The Army has adopted conditions and standards for nearly every task. These conditions and standards serve as both guides to facilitate learning necessary skills, and as measures of mastery of military tasks. At the top of the list of prescribed soldier tasks, conditions and standards is physical fitness. A strong foundation sustains a massive and capable structure. Conditioning the body allows for the necessary mental preparation and team building to follow.

I was a typical high schooler - active but not an athlete. I did not participate in high school sports, but I did play pickup games of basketball, football, ultimate Frisbee and trained in martial arts. We didn't have all the electronic devices and video games that are rampant today. We were accustomed to actually going outside and doing things. Prior to reporting to basic training I began to focus on conditioning activities like calisthenics and running to increase my strength and endurance. I did not want to be at a disadvantage having to get into shape at basic training.

During the summer of 1980 the Army was beginning to transition away from a five-event physical conditioning assessment to a three-event physical readiness test. (It's funny how things come full circle; as I retired from the Army in 2011, the Army was implementing a new five-event fitness test to replace the three-event assessment I used for the intervening thirty years.) The 1980 five-event assessment consisted of diverse events such as the run dodge and jump, and the inverted crawl, the horizontal ladder, sit-ups and a distance run. The then-new Army Physical Readiness Test consisted of three events: pushups, sit-ups, and a run. Soldiers could complete the new test virtually anywhere without need of equipment. It served as an accurate assessment of strength and cardiovascular endurance for U.S. Army soldiers worldwide.

In 1980, as they didn't have the details worked out, Army training organizations were testing options - various lengths of time to complete pushups and sit-ups and various run distances. I remember running a one mile event in boots and fatigues on a hot summer day at Fort Dix. I was running neck and neck with another soldier; we were the last event of the afternoon. There were only a handful of runners participating in our heat and the two of us were at the front of the pack. We were so evenly matched and trying so hard, the entire company of soldiers focused on our competition. It was like a track meet. For the life of me, I can't remember who finished first, but I'm thinking I may have edged out that worthy opponent. However, my recollection may just be the optimism of a faded memory.

Every soldier must maintain a minimum level of fitness to remain in the Army. The Army employs height and weight standards and subjects every soldier to two physical fitness tests per year. Failing to meet height and weight standards or not passing a fitness test are grounds for discharge (an option rarely exercised during wartime). Medical consults and remedial training are the typical prescriptions for failure. Any soldier not meeting the standard is given a chance at redemption, and is most often pushed to ensure he or she tightens up and or slims down.

Army leadership established a standard of performance for fitness testing. Soldiers must score a minimum of 60 points on each of the three events. Points are earned by numbers of successful repetitions of pushups and sit-ups and by the running time against a point scale. Soldiers can earn a maximum of 100 points for each event or 300 points overall. The hard chargers and conscientious leaders usually strive to "max" the fitness test to serve as an example for soldiers they lead. Though earning the maximum score on the Army fitness test is nowhere near an elite athlete's standard of performance, it did serve for me as a kind of floor for my conditioning. Anything less than a "max" performance on the PT test I considered a failure - not a morale-busting, depression-inducing failure, but a lapse in my personal discipline nonetheless.

For infantry officers physical and mental discipline are not luxuries; they are a necessities. I worked, what I thought was hard, maintaining my physical conditioning, but it was not until my infantry officer advanced course that I got to see firsthand the level of effort required to be an elite athlete. Among my classmates at the Infantry School (Fort Benning school for boys once again) we had an elite-level triathlete. While we participated in physical training daily, pushing ourselves for an hour or two, he would run ten miles before joining us for our group training sessions. He would swim two miles at lunch, and then ride a bike forty or fifty miles or more in the evening. Where the best among us were running two miles in just under twelve minutes, he was running two miles in just about nine. Being around someone with that level of discipline and focus gave me a whole new appreciation for what it takes to excel at an elite level. While the Army does have its share of high performers, the main rank and file, the majority of soldiers, are average Americans who hold themselves to above-average standards of performance. Each soldier serves as a critical element of a functional, capable, and strong whole - a military team. Ultimately, it is the strength of the team that matters.

Health and fitness matter.

From Sweat to Blood

General Douglas MacArthur once wrote: "The history of failure in war can be summed up in two words: too late. Too late in comprehending the deadly purpose of a potential enemy; too late in realizing the mortal danger; too late in preparedness; too late in uniting all possible forces for resistance; too late in standing with one's friends." To this I would add: too late in acting and acting decisively. Armies succeed through vigorous action. To reinforce the point, Sun Tzu weighs in:

> *When you engage in actual fighting, if victory is long in coming, the men's weapons will grow dull and their ardor dampened. If the campaign is protracted the resources of the state will not be equal to the strain. Thus, though we*

have heard of stupid haste in war, cleverness has never been associated with long delays. There is no instance of a country having benefited from prolonged warfare.

America's Army is an instrument of action. In peace it serves as a deterrent, an insurance policy of sorts. In war, or in time of need, the Army acts. It must exhibit the resolve of character, that moral quality to choose right over wrong, nurtured to maturity in peace. The Army, when all other elements of society flee from adversity, unites and focuses. In this way the Army brings to bear the authority of conviction, the insight of intellect, and the might and power of tools of war. Soldiers act - they fight with weapons and they win with spirit.

Academics, politicians, and pundits often debate existential threats potentially confronting America. As the United States has come to dominate global affairs, external existential threats are more rare. But, for a soldier, every moment in a combat zone poses an existential threat. When committed to war, soldiers are those men and women who have the clearest vision of what is before them. The bravest face glory and danger alike. Their lives are on the line, and yet notwithstanding, they venture forth to do their duty. An existential threat to the United States will only materialize when the nation lacks among its citizens sufficient men and women to act.

During periods of peace the watch words in military organizations are safety and conservation. Nothing is served by wasting limited resources or risking injuring soldiers. The overarching sentiment typically is risk averse. Training is focused on honing battle skills, but preparations are tempered by lack of any pressing peril. Skills developed are tested in complex, multi-faceted training exercises - artificial constructs to simulate conditions of war. Success is achieved by exceeding standards, minimizing distractions (usually people problems), and accomplishing myriad bureaucratic and organizational tasks. Mentoring junior leaders, selecting and developing talent, and building effective teams are the order of the day. In the end, however, during peacetime the only means to put one's self and the organization to the test is through artificial exercises and an incessant routine of inspections. For a soldier, war is the ultimate test. As Thucydides once posited, "To do their duty is their only holiday, and they deem the quiet of inaction to be as disagreeable as the most tiresome business." The Army acts or prepares for action - it has no other purpose.

Ask anyone who has served as a soldier about their experience (or, I presume, if you wore the uniform you will bear this out) and they will invariably come back to two main themes: the people they encountered and the things they did. In most cases, both were extraordinary.

As I look back over thirty-plus years I recall meeting remarkable people and teaming with them to do remarkable things. We laughed together; we trained together; we struggled together. We crawled through mud with machine gun rounds whistling overhead. We jumped out of airplanes and climbed up rope ladders into hovering helicopters. We traversed frozen glaciers and navigated raging rivers in the wilderness. We traveled to remarkable places, saw extraordinary sights, and did exciting things. Being a soldier is an adventure, an adventure of the highest order. Despite all the hardships, all the sacrifice, all the discomfort and pain, no matter what else happens in life, soldiers know they did something, something memorable, something worthwhile.

Working together people can do what seems impossible.

The Army trains hard to prepare for every operation, but the Army trains hardest to prepare for war. Every pint of sweat offered in training saves blood on the battlefield. Realistic training is essential to prepare soldiers for the conditions of a battlefield. A combat environment is so intense soldiers must rely on reflexive actions instilled in training to move them forward - actions they commit to muscle memory through drill and repetition. Soldiers are trained to act.

In addition to being the means to victory, the means to applying the national will, action serves as a release valve for fear. By moving, by engaging mind and body, soldiers overcome the shadow adversary, the internal obstacle, the daunting specter of fear. Action is the bridge one must negotiate to move from intention to realization, but action is also the means to overcome the recalcitrant effects of dread and apprehension. Fear will paralyze a man. Fear keeps millions of people from moving forward in life every moment of every day. The Army, however, cannot afford to allow soldiers to fall prey to fear. So America's Army, by design, acts.

The United States has summoned soldiers to the colors at least once in every generation since the founding of this nation. Young men and women have repeatedly answered the call. They have filled the ranks, donned the uniform, endured the conditioning, and sequestered their egos to serve as one among many. They serve to persevere and prevail. American soldiers fought then, and still fight today, to establish and preserve this nation and the ideals upon which it is founded. American soldiers have fought to liberate societies and stem the tide of evil's advance. American soldiers sacrifice, and because they are disposed to act - they face the specter of death. That America's Army is oriented to act, despite what may stand in its way, makes all the difference.

Fear limits you only when you allow it to.

Principles of War

Let every nation know, whether it wishes us well or ill, that we shall pay any price, bear any burden, meet any hardship, support any friend, oppose any foe, in order to assure the survival and the success of liberty.

John F. Kennedy proclaimed these words, confident in his conviction, because he had men and women willing and able to take the action the words imply. The United States Army allows that confidence. Kennedy's statement would suffice as a job description for a U.S. Army soldier, for soldiers pay the price, bear the burden, meet the hardship, support the friends, and oppose the foes to assure the survival and success of liberty.

Karl Kraus once observed, "War is, at first, the hope that one will be better off; next, the expectation that the other fellow will be worse off; then, the satisfaction that he isn't any better off; and, finally, the surprise at everyone's being worse off." War is hell, but throughout history war has held a romantic allure for many who consider it from a distance. The reality is, however, until men lose the desire to oppress, to dominate, and to wield supreme power, war and the instruments of war will be with us. America's Army serves to limit or eliminate such threats.

At first glance war seems an exceedingly complex and sophisticated undertaking. Upon closer examination, however, one discovers that war is a scaled-up version of any two opposing forces encountered in life. The same principles apply in a struggle between two opponents as in a battle for supremacy in a business market. The complexity and sophistication arise in war due to the numbers and the capabilities of participants. The principles applied in war are the same that apply in all conflict.

How well the parties to a conflict apply the various principles of war determines the outcome. That they must apply the principles of war at all, however, demonstrates one of two things: either the actors have failed to invoke and apply more noble principles of conduct; or an opposing force is seeks to impose its will. As Sun Tzu said, "The supreme excellence is not to win a hundred victories in a hundred battles. The supreme excellence is to subdue the armies of your enemies without even having to fight them." In the U.S. Army's case, the decision to fight is not for soldiers to make - politicians make those decisions. It is the Army's job to act, to carry out and succeed at the prescribed task.

The principles of war individuals employ in interpersonal conflict, and that America's Army employs in combat are: Objective, Offensive, Mass, Economy of Force, Maneuver, Unity of Command, Security, Surprise, and Simplicity.

Objective. Direct every effort toward a clearly defined, decisive, and achievable objective.

> *Don't fight a battle if you don't gain anything by winning.*
>
> --General George Patton

Offensive. Seize, retain, and exploit the initiative to retain freedom of action and achieve decisive results.

> *Not only strike while the iron is hot, but make it hot by striking.*
>
> --Oliver Cromwell

Mass. Synchronizing and concentrating the essential elements of power at the decisive time and place.

> *The principles of war could, for brevity, be condensed into a single word: concentration.*
>
> --B. H. LIDDELL HART

Economy of Force. Employ all available power in the most effective, judicious way possible.

> *Never wrestle with pigs - you get dirty and they enjoy it.*
>
> --GENERAL CREIGHTON ABRAMS

Maneuver. Apply power flexibly; move to gain positional advantage and exploit success.

> *Nothing is more difficult than the art of maneuver. What is difficult about maneuver is to make the devious route the most direct and turn misfortune to advantage.*
>
> --SUN TZU

Unity of Command. Mass power toward a common objective and a unified purpose under one responsible authority.

> *Nothing is more important in war than unity in command.*
>
> --NAPOLEON BONAPARTE

Security. Reduce vulnerabilities; protect and preserve power by never permitting an unexpected disadvantage.

> *Not by standing still, but by growing, moving, being energized, do we become secure.*
>
> --WYNN DAVIS

Surprise. Strike decisively in a time, place, or manner for which the opponent is unprepared.

> *Surprise is the master-key of war.*
>
> --B. H. LIDDELL HART

Simplicity. Employ clear, uncomplicated plans and concise orders; minimize misunderstanding and confusion.

> *An order that can be misunderstood will be misunderstood.*
>
> --FIELD MARSHAL HELMUTH VON MOLTKE, THE ELDER

Thinking of these principles in the framework of success presented here in *Why America's Army Succeeds*, you might group these principles as follows: Economy of Force, Security, and Simplicity are means of conserving what you need and what you value; Objective, Mass, and Unity of Command are elements of focus; and Offensive, Maneuver, and Surprise are tenets of action. While not necessarily a clean fit, the principles of war lead us back to the means to succeed in life. One must advance (action oriented), concentrating on worthwhile goals (mission focused), for the right reasons (values based).

Focus your and your team's energy on doing the right thing for the right reasons.

Risk and Reward

I had already been wearing the uniform for ten years when Saddam Hussein's forces seized Kuwait in 1990. Assigned to a training unit at the time, I requested to serve, essentially adding my name to a long list of volunteers for Desert Shield / Desert Storm. Ultimately the assembled operational forces were adequate for the job, and casualties were low enough, so that I was never called. I spent some time in the Balkans in 1996, but that was a peace-enforcement mission. The biggest risks there were avoiding mine fields. Everyone was careful to stay on well-traveled routes.

Special Operations forces assisted the Northern Alliance in routing the Taliban in Afghanistan in 2001-2002. While I joined the Army to do the hard jobs and shoulder the burden, I never endured the test of combat (actually engaging an enemy). There was one time though...

Chapter 4: The Heat of Battle

Assigned to the Multi-National Corps headquarters in Iraq (my Iraq tour stretched from 2005 to 2006), I was part of a small team working in the operations directorate establishing a counter improvised explosive device (C-IED) task force. The task force was the brain child of our team leader, a former explosive ordnance disposal (EOD) commander - the EOD guys are the ones who handle explosives for a living - now serving on the staff. The C-IED task force concept was to unify EOD, military police, engineers, intelligence, and operational units to protect against these potentially devastating explosive devices and ultimately to get "left of boom" and attack the IED network (money, supplies, and bomb makers) itself.

My work space was on the second floor of the Al Faw Palace at Camp Victory on the Baghdad International Airport Complex. Closing in on the end of my workday, it was about 9:30 pm; I was preparing to head back to my hooch (living quarters; a small room in a conex a half mile from the palace). I was on an interior wall, so I could not see outside from my desk, but in an instant the entire headquarters lit up with excitement. Now we were used to an occasional fire-fight on the perimeter, or even a mortar attack or some rockets, but what we saw outside was remarkable.

The entire perimeter was lit up by rifle fire. Tracer rounds were streaking across the sky in every direction. It was like a fireworks display, but we knew these weren't fireworks. We wondered: Are we being attacked? Were we being overrun?

As a lieutenant colonel staff officer my personal weapon was a 9mm Beretta pistol. I had two magazines of ammunition - not exactly an arsenal. The Baghdad International Airport Complex housed thousands of American and coalition troops and they were all armed. It was dark. There was no way of knowing who was who. If the base was under attack, in addition to an infiltration by actual insurgents, we risked a great deal of fratricide with a bunch of support troops running around shooting things up.

Being an infantry guy though, I knew I had to act. I was strapping on my gear, getting ready to defend the walls if necessary. I'd fight my way, with my trusty pistol, to a rifle as best I could and take on the enemy. Before I had an opportunity to head for the gate, however, we heard an announcement on loudspeakers. The complex was not under attack. The Iraqi national soccer team had just beaten the Syrians. The display we were seeing was not the result of insurgents storming the perimeter - it was the Middle East tradition of celebratory fire.

Though I was relieved I wouldn't have to venture out into what could have proved to be a very messy situation, we still could see the rounds flying, and hear bullets pinging as they hit the ground. So instead of venturing out, I waited. After about thirty minutes the celebrating began to abate. I then strapped on my gear for the half mile trek back to my room hoping to avoid an errant strike. As I made my way across the compound I saw some of our supporting contractors adroitly ducked under cover. What goes up must come down - and it was raining lead.

We learned the next day some thirty to forty local civilians had been injured by stray bullets. Luckily, no coalition troops had fallen victim to the celebration. The Iraqi troops, who were the main source of the celebratory fire, discharged over one million rounds of ammunition that evening - a loss we had to resupply. The soccer victory was sweet for the Iraqis, but the celebration was expensive. That is the closest I came to actual combat in my thirty-plus year career with America's Army - I filled different roles.

Success demands you take risks.

I was serving as a National Defense Fellow in the United States Senate during the run up to the Iraq War in 2003. I was sitting against the wall behind the senators on the dais in the Armed Services hearing as General Shinseki, then Army Chief of Staff, was being pressed for his estimate as to how many troops it would take to secure Iraq after successfully deposing Saddam Hussein. After attempting to avoid the question a number of times he answered that he expected it would take on the order of several hundred thousand soldiers (a force much larger than the administration was committing to the effort). I learned then, and during my seven years watching and working with Congress since, that decisive, values-based, focused action, the distinguishing feature of leadership, is a rarity in politics.

Seven of my last ten years serving on active duty I was assigned to Department of the Army. We wrestled with issues of resource allocation and policy. Working predominantly in strategic communications, I focused my efforts on educating and informing members of Congress about our activities and needs, maintaining public support, and facilitating our recruiting effort. A strong economy and a shooting war are not necessarily the best circumstances for recruiting soldiers.

Volunteering to serve in the military during peacetime is a different animal than volunteering during a time of war. Virtually everyone who enlisted or accepted a commission since September 2001 knew that they may have to put their lives on the line. Only exceptional people are willing to act when exposed to such risk. It is a remarkable tribute to the people of the United States that men and women still step forward, still answer the call, still willingly risk everything for something they cannot see, or hear, or touch. They risk their lives for intangible values and enduring principles - something they can only feel - the prospects of liberty and the bounty freedom offers.

Success is moving in the right direction. You succeed only when you move in the right direction - act in certain ways for the right reasons. America's Army succeeds when it is employed for the right reasons and focused on clear, worthwhile goals. These principles (values based, mission focused, action oriented), these tenets, these guidelines apply to the circumstances you face in your personal life as well as to the situations and challenges you face in your career and business. The principles of success are the same for combat as for business and life. Base your conduct (words and deeds, thoughts and actions - your life) on noble values - principles worthy of your commitment. Focus on laudable goals - goals that advance life, not destroy or inhibit it. And act - vigorously, enthusiastically, and spontaneously, for that is the mission you have been given.

Achieve your mission - live your life fully. The last measure of devotion is demanded of every soldier. Life demands the same from you.

Act decisively - take the risk, and seize the reward.

To succeed in business and in life, you must act!

PART 2

IMPACT OF THE INDIVIDUAL

CHAPTER 5

INSPIRING MOMENTOUS ACTION

"I can't hear you, for what you do overwhelms everything you say." Actions speak louder than words. Nowhere are actions more important, more crucial or more critical than when lives are on the line. The realm of military leadership is a time and a place where lives hang in the balance. What leaders do, matters. Leaders choose the objective and set the course. Good leaders guide and encourage along the way. Great leaders lead the charge.

Winston Churchill, reflecting on combatants' sacrifices of World War II, declared, "Never have so many owed so much to so few." A finer point can be made directing that statement toward great leaders. A few people - leaders - influence the masses. A few people - leaders - guide the many. A few people - leaders - inspire and show the way. It is to these few that the many owe their triumph as well as their tragedy, their opportunity and prosperity or their lack and their want. The motives, the focus and the actions of a few sweep the lives of many to soaring heights or shadowy depths. What individuals do, matters; what leaders do, matters most.

In a nation such as the United States of America, every individual intentionally matters. America is governed by means of a representative democracy - a republic. Individuals offer lasting contributions toward every collective undertaking and make significant impacts on and off any contested field. Individuals determine who goes where, to do what, and why. Individuals set America's Army in motion – they unleash the fury and endure the fallout. For an Army unit deploying anywhere around the world every detail, even those left to chance, are the burden of someone's responsibility. The person who sees (who has the grand vision), the person who influences (who has the power), the person who decides (who has the position), leads - by design or by default. The decisions, the actions of key individuals, the influence of leaders cannot be overstated.

We all follow, we all lead; like it or not.

The 237-plus year history of America's Army reflects the contributions of countless leaders, men and women who bore the responsibility of leadership in times of trial. This section presents select examples of individuals who took on tough tasks, individuals who guided, directed, and cajoled their teams to extraordinary achievements, individuals who led soldiers to success. Consider the examples of these leaders and then lead well.

Impact of the Individual

The Army, by necessity and by design, operates in an uncomfortable space, a space many people readily judge and condemn; however, it is a space relatively few are willing to venture into. It is a space of danger and risk, hardship and sacrifice, uncertainty and ambiguity. Combat zones and battlefields are not sterile environments offering black and white distinctions. Good and evil, right and wrong are often not clearly defined. Life and death choices are to be made with limited information. Operating in this sphere requires special attributes and unique talents - these are talents most people possess, but talents most people are unwilling to use. Surviving the crucible of combat requires courage, preparation, and discipline. Succeeding requires vision, tenacity and wisdom. Great Army leaders succeed.

Despite how a mission is framed (securing the peace, protecting the populace, destroying the enemy), soldiers presume the charge is worth the risk and the potential cost. Soldiers swear an oath to support and defend the Constitution of the United States. They trust, explicitly, that if they are ordered into action their leaders and the American people have thoroughly weighed all options and have fatefully determined that the circumstances demand risking the lives of those sworn to serve. With this confidence America's Army sets out to achieve its task. Whatever the expected outcome, whatever the anticipated results, the Army must succeed. It is the responsibility of leaders to ensure the Army does succeed - does accomplish its appointed mission.

As an instrument of power America's Army is employed to change things - current or future conditions, current or future circumstances. The Army is a harbinger of change. The Army is only used - dispatched, deployed - to change outcomes, to influence or modify results. Despite the size and reach of the Army and the awesome force it controls and exploits, and from an outsider's view its status as a seemingly anonymous and nondescript entity, the Army is a system made up of flesh and blood. The Army consists of emotional, feeling, and physically bounded human beings. The mysterious power the Army wields is the collective strength of men and women focused toward the same ends, acting to achieve the same results. Individuals provide the strength, and individuals - leaders - guide and direct the power.

Just as action springs from the seed of a solitary thought, a single individual controls the fate of a unit, the fortune of an Army, and the destiny of a nation. As your thoughts and your actions not only influence your own success, but the success of every element of which you are a component part, the success you enjoy or the failure you endure contribute to the experiences of your family, your community, your nation and the world. Your impact - the impact of you, a lone individual - is far reaching and long lasting. In the same way, every member of a soldier team relies on every other member, every individual affects the whole, and ultimately, every soldier team depends on the character and competence of its leader.

While every individual influences the team, the team leader influences most.

The success of America's Army achieving its missions in peace and at war has hinged, and continues to hinge, on the decisions - the thoughts and actions - the motives, the focus, and the conduct of men and women - leaders. The Army succeeds when leaders guide, direct, and act for the right reasons, to achieve appropriate objectives, with the discipline, vigor and intensity needed to accomplish the task. Leaders embody the motives by which units advance. They determine the direction and set the focus. They inspire the action - the exploits, the diplomacy, the heroics - which decide the outcome.

Leaders are key and essential to every collective undertaking. As mentioned previously, the Army has a process for practically everything. One of the important processes the Army utilizes to monitor the status of units is a readiness reporting system. Of the myriad distinct items on a unit readiness report, one of the most important is select gear identified as key and essential equipment. These items are required to be on hand and operational for a unit to be considered able to accomplish its mission. An example of such a piece of equipment for an engineering organization might be a bulldozer. In this case, the engineers could not accomplish the task for which the unit was designed without a bulldozer. Even more important than equipment, leaders are key and essential to every unit's ability to accomplish its mission.

Leaders by their conviction, their focus, and their discipline are the sparks that fire a powerful engine of change - America's Army. Thomas Fuller might just as well have been referring to Army leaders when he said, "A strong will, a settled purpose, an invincible determination, can accomplish almost anything; and in this lies the distinction between great men and little men." The legacy of America's Army hosts a pantheon of great men. Winning and losing are the products of action. Leaders are men and women of action. While failure may be the result of circumstance, success is the invention of leadership.

America's Army is an instrument of power. It is a force employed to execute the will of the people through the direction of the people's elected representatives. The Army plans to achieve its mission, prepares to achieve its mission, and acts to achieve its mission. The Army intends to succeed, and applies itself - to the point of exhaustion or destruction - to the single-minded purpose of accomplishing its given mission. So what is, in fact, meant by success?

Americans have a mindset about success when it comes to the employment of its army. Winning - victory, uncompromising triumph - is the notion Americans most often entertain when sending soldiers off to war. This is an attitude groomed partly from necessity, to sustain both the morale of the troops and the populace, and partly from the scourge of hubris - arrogance of power untempered by compassion. Though the basest fraction of human nature craves utter dominance (an opponent's unconditional surrender and absolute submission), people routinely discover the use of force rarely produces the pre-imagined results. Franklin Roosevelt wrote,

> *I have seen war... I have seen blood running from the wounded. I have seen men coughing out their gassed lungs. I have seen the dead in the mud. I have seen cities destroyed... I have seen children starving. I have seen the agony of mothers and wives. I hate war.*

While the employment of instruments of war and the use of violence are last resorts, the process by which success is achieved is universal. The means to success: values based (acting for the right reasons), mission focused (doing the right things), and action oriented (moving courageously and vigorously) works for individuals, works for leaders, works for organizations, and works for the nation. America's Army succeeds when it intends to further worthwhile ends (values based), by focusing its energy, intellect, and resources on specific objectives (mission focused), and acts vigorously and decisively to accomplish its mission (action oriented).

I do not intend to imply that the means to success are easy. Achieving worthwhile goals, important tasks, and necessary missions are rarely easy. That is why America's Army is the organization that is dispatched to take on and complete the most challenging assignments. Leading effectively under the most extreme conditions is the most difficult job of them all - the leader brings the disparate pieces together at the decisive moment in the critical place. Success is a daunting task for a leader.

Nothing worth having comes easy.

Whether you are leading one (yourself) or leading a family, a business team, a community or large organization, you are confronting the most profound challenge of life. By choosing to lead, you are assuming responsibility for success, and succeeding, like leading effectively, requires overcoming the greatest obstacle known to humankind: the self. To lead and to succeed you must prevail over fear, frailty, ignorance and doubt. You must embrace the potential you possess. You must choose the direction and set the pace. You must become a soldier on course to achieve your life's mission.

The history of America's Army, the experience of American soldiers, the nobility of great leaders offer telling illustrations of success. Combat, by its very nature, exposes in real time and in uncompromising detail the essence of the individual. The intensity of a combat environment and the gravity of the risk forces individuals to confront the self and the reservations of ego. To succeed, a soldier, and to a greater degree a leader, subjugates ego - displaces self as the center of the universe; endures hardship - foregoes comfort and security; and acts decisively - despite pain and loss, to achieve a worthwhile goal. In war the stakes are too high to do anything else.

America's Army has succeeded because of great soldiers, because of great leaders. America's Army has forged a means to succeed, a means applicable to any endeavor in life.

Leadership

Even in an age of surgical precision, the use of force normally, and most frequently results in destruction. One crass, but telling portrayal of the Army is an organization to kill people and destroy things. While technically this may be what the Army does to accomplish its mission, Andrew Jackson once offered a judgment about the employment of force, "Peace, above all things, is to be desired, but blood must sometimes be spilled to obtain it on equitable and lasting terms." Jackson likewise asserted, "Every good citizen makes his country's honor his own and cherishes it not only as precious but as sacred. He is willing to risk his life in its defense and is conscious that he gains protection while he gives it." America's Army is an instrument of the people's will. The Army exists now and must endure until people around the world are enlightened enough to make war and the machines of war obsolete. Until then, Army leaders prepare.

U.S. Army doctrine defines a number of factors, attributes and principles for leaders to embody and exhibit. Army Field

Chapter 5: Inspiring Momentous Action

Manual 6-22 (formerly Army Field Manual 22-100) defines an Army leader as:

> *Anyone who by virtue of assumed role or assigned responsibility inspires and influences people to accomplish organizational goals. Army leaders motivate people both inside and outside the chain of command to pursue actions, focus thinking, and shape decisions for the greater good of the organization.*

Field Manual 6-22 further defines leadership:

> **Leadership** *is the process of influencing people by providing purpose, direction, and motivation while operating to accomplish the mission and improving the organization.*

America's Army employs a Be-Know-Do construct as a way of highlighting and focusing leaders and potential leaders on the key factors of leadership. What leaders Do springs from what they Know and who they are (Be). Core values and beliefs form the leader's foundation, and knowledge and experience gird the individual, while action emerges in the circumstance. Army leaders prepare throughout their military careers, within the framework of Be-Know-Do, to be able to act at a moment's notice and lead regardless of the challenge.

To achieve unity of effort military organizations long ago evolved a hierarchical structure. Soldiers earn and are appointed to certain ranks. The various ranks, from private to general, have prescribed duties and responsibilities. Every unit has a focal point of authority and responsibility. The ultimate authority and responsibility for a military unit resides in its commander.

> **Command** *is the authority that a commander in the military service lawfully exercises over subordinates by virtue of rank or assignment. Command includes the leadership, authority, responsibility, and accountability for effectively using available resources and planning the employment of, organizing, directing, coordinating, and controlling military forces to accomplish assigned missions. It includes responsibility for unit readiness, health, welfare, morale, and discipline of assigned personnel (FMI 5-0.1).*

The commander is the senior leader of an Army organization. He or she is formally charged with leading and bears both the authority and the responsibility of that charge.

To help develop and educate Army leaders, Army doctrine affords a leadership requirements model. The model attempts to encapsulate the character traits, the capacities, and the competencies leaders need to succeed. The model presents attributes for leaders to possess and behaviors for leaders to exhibit. This model is an ideal toward which Army leaders strive in their personal and professional development. Each factor is worth considering.

Attributes Defining an Army Leader
(what an Army leader is):

A Leader of Character (core internal factors essential to a leader) - a soldier who adheres to the Army Values (loyalty, duty, respect, selfless service, honor, integrity, personal courage) demonstrates empathy for fellow soldiers, subordinates and superiors alike (sees things from others' perspectives and cares about people), and embodies the Warrior Ethos (mission first; failure is not an option; sustain the team).

A Leader with Presence (appearance, demeanor, words, and actions defining others' perceptions) - a soldier with military bearing (professional image and commanding authority), who is physically fit (healthy and emotionally and physically strong; capable of enduring extreme stress), confident (composed, calm, steady and self-assured), and resilient (recovers quickly while maintaining mission and organizational focus).

A Leader with Intellectual Capacity (the mental resources and conceptual abilities impacting effectiveness) - a soldier with agility (flexible, quick, anticipates and adapts, breaks out of habitual thought patterns to improvise), judgment (assesses shrewdly, forms sound opinions and makes sensible decisions based on limited information), who is innovative (creative, novel and original, introducing new ideas as needed), possesses interpersonal tact (conscious of others' character and motives, understands others and interacts effectively), and demonstrates all appropriate domain knowledge (possesses necessary facts, beliefs, technical, tactical and situational knowledge and cultural and geopolitical understanding).

Core Army Leader Competencies
(what an Army leader does):

Leads - leads others (motivates, inspires, and influences others to take initiative and work toward a common purpose; completes critical tasks and achieves organizational objectives; establishes and imparts a clear intent and creates and promulgates a clear vision; maintains and enforces high standards; and uses appropriate techniques to energize and guide while balancing the needs and welfare of team members with mission requirements); extends influence beyond the chain of command (employs indirect means of diplomacy, negotiation, coordination, partnering and conflict resolution to advance organizational goals; understands complete sphere of influence; builds trust, consensus and alliances by and between partners and all interested parties; shapes perspective of others toward organization); leads by example (serves as a model for behavior (through words and deeds); displays character; exemplifies the Warrior Ethos; demonstrates commitment to the Nation, the Army, the unit, soldiers, and partners; leads with confidence in adverse circumstances; demonstrates technical and tactical mastery; models conceptual skills; seeks and is open to diverse points of view); communicates (clearly expresses ideas and actively listens to others; determines information sharing strategies and employs engaging communication techniques; ensures shared understanding; and is sensitive to cultural factors).

Develops - creates a positive environment (cares for people and their wellbeing; sets and maintains positive expectations and attitudes for healthy relationships and an effective work environment; fosters teamwork, cohesion, cooperation and loyalty; creates a learning environment; encourages subordinates to exercise initiative and take ownership; is fair and inclusive; encourages communication; anticipates needs and accepts reasonable setbacks); prepares self (understand strengths and limitations; maintain physical and mental wellbeing; practices and rehearses;

is self-aware and recognizes impact on others; cultivates all facets of knowledge and intellectual capability; maintains relevant cultural and geopolitical awareness); develops others (encourages and supports growth of individuals and teams; assesses developmental needs; fosters development through challenges and enrichment; counsels, coaches and mentors; facilitates ongoing and institutional development; and builds team skills and processes).

Achieves - gets results (provides guidance and manages resources to ethically accomplish organizational objectives by supervising, managing, monitoring and controlling work; prioritizes, organizes and coordinates team taskings; identifies and accounts for individual and group capabilities and commitments; designates, clarifies, and deconflicts roles; identifies, secures, and allocates resources; removes impediments; recognizes, rewards, and constantly strives to improve performance; provides consistent feedback; executes in accordance with the plan; and compensates for external influences as appropriate).

Leaders direct, guide, and lead to ensure soldiers have the opportunity to accomplish the multitude of distinct tasks that amount to mission success. The success of Army teams depends on the commitment, the discipline, and the fortitude of a wide array of diverse individuals - men and women who support and encourage one another to overcome nearly insurmountable obstacles. Soldiers strive valiantly to succeed even in the face of impossible odds. Patrick Henry once stressed, "Adversity toughens manhood, and the characteristic of the good or the great man, is not that he has been exempted from the evils of life, but that he has surmounted them." Great leaders surmount adversity and make mission success possible.

Leadership, in a word, is inspiration. Nowhere is inspiration, or lack thereof, more apparent and significant, and more urgent and crucial than on a battlefield. The single defining characteristic of a leader, any leader, good or otherwise, is inspiration. A leader inspires people. A leader stirs people. A leader, through word and deed, causes people to move, to act, to create or destroy. A leader ignites desire, whether to realize pleasure or avoid pain, and gets people to do things they otherwise would not do, for good or ill.

Chapter 5: Inspiring Momentous Action

To inspire action, a leader provides either one or both of the indispensable and invaluable assets required to achieve any purpose: vision and motivation. Leaders spend their time, energy, and talents creating and sharing relatable visions of worthwhile objectives. A worthwhile vision benefits those who seek to create it, to achieve it, to realize it. In the same way, leaders provide the energy, the drive, and the discipline to move the team forward toward the goal. Teams fail when leaders fail to inspire.

To lead is to inspire; to provide vision and or motivation.

As for me, I've always considered two traits as essential for inspirational leadership. I say all the factors, attributes and principles come down to: "C2". If you have ever been a soldier, you are probably familiar with this acronym. C2 has long referred to "command and control." Command and control, however, are not the essential elements of leadership I mean when referring to C2. Inspirational leadership is a product of caring and competence. It is about a leader knowing what he or she is doing - being tactically and technically competent at the task at hand - and genuinely caring about people. If a leader is not competent he will not likely achieve his objective. If he or she is competent but doesn't care about people he or she may achieve the objective, but that leader will not be a success. Leadership is about connecting people and succeeding as a team.

Successful leaders are competent and caring; they care about their people and about the mission.

Leading When It Matters

An American president once declared, "The character that takes command in moments of crucial choices has already been determined by...the little choices of years past - by all those times when the voice of conscience was at war with the voice of temptation, whispering the lie that 'it really doesn't matter.'" Army leaders are warriors. They are fierce, aggressive, and tenacious. Army leaders are diplomats. They are intelligent, caring, and seek the common good. Army leaders are heroes. They are courageous, committed, and vigorous actors. Army leaders prepare to lead when it matters.

Being a great leader is a lonely calling. Knowing the right thing to do is hard enough; doing it is sometimes next to impossible. But that is what great leaders do - make the impossible possible. In considering success Joseph Newton expressed it this way, "Every man has a train of thought on which he travels when he is alone. The dignity and nobility of his life, as well as his happiness, depend upon the direction in which that train is going, the baggage it carries and the scenery through which it travels." For a soldier, for a leader, that train of thought involves life-and-death consequences that reach far beyond the individual. The success of the team, and perhaps the Army, and perhaps the nation depend on the train of thought of the leader. Achievement depends on choices leaders make.

You too are a leader. You are challenged to manage power and you must face fear. You must make hard choices. Be vigilant administering the assets you possess. By abdicating responsibility, people surrender power. Don't knowingly or unwittingly forfeit your personal power. Advocating a path of ease and comfort over a course of challenge and achievement, causes people to forego their natural capacity to grow. It is by trial and tribulation that men strengthen themselves and exceptional societies evolve. Leaders bear the burden of personal responsibility. Running from adversity only fashions regrets, never victory. Lead when it matters.

There has never been a time when leadership hasn't mattered. Leadership matters most when the people are most lost and confused. The way out of the tumult is by relying on the proven tenets of success: focus on what is important - what is needed, and act decisively and vigorously based on enduring principles. Power rests with you if you will but shoulder the burden and wield it. Your contribution, your leadership, to your family, your team, your nation matters.

Leadership matters - your leadership.

Chapter 5: Inspiring Momentous Action

One might draw a comparison of an ordinary life to a soldier's expedition. The challenges of life, though potentially not as intense or as all-consuming as combat, are assuredly as pressing - life and death hang in the balance. Soldiers, by necessity, sacrifice, endure, and strive - they willingly endure hardship for a cause greater than self. Values, focus, and action determine the course a soldier traverses. These are the same features that mark every life. The Army, because of the nature of its business, attempts to standardize a system for success despite any adversity. Individuals the world over can do the same. Unfortunately, most people are reluctant to try.

It has been said, "The real tragedy is the tragedy of the man who never in his life braces himself for his one supreme effort, who never stretches to his full capacity, never stands up to his full stature." Soldiers endeavor to push themselves and test themselves. Leaders among men excel in an uncommon hour. The great American soldiers you are to learn about now accepted the challenge of leadership, prepared themselves, and acted when it mattered. They fulfilled Longfellow's edict:

Lives of great men all remind us,

We can make our lives sublime,

And, departing, leave behind us

Footprints on the sands of time.

Inspire momentous action with your life.

You possess the potential of an outstanding leader;
you are one heroic act away from greatness.

CHAPTER 6

GEORGE WASHINGTON
FOUNDING FATHER OF AMERICAN LEADERSHIP

*If Historiographers should be hardy enough to fill the page
of History with the advantages that have been gained
with unequal numbers (on the part of America) in the
cause of this contest, and attempt to relate the distress-
ing circumstances under which they have been obtained,
it is more than probable that Posterity will bestow on
their labors the epithet and marks of fiction; for it will
not be believed that such a force as Great Britain has
employed for eight years in Country could be baffled ...
by numbers infinitely less, composed of Men oftentimes
half starved; always in Rags, without pay, and experi-
encing, at times, every species of distress which human
nature is capable of undergoing.*

Penned shortly after America's victory over the British, these
words reveal that even George Washington was astounded that
something so improbable had become reality – that a bunch of
half-starved citizen soldiers cobbled from thirteen disparate
colonies had triumphed over battle-hardened veterans of the
world's mightiest empire. That Washington managed to lead
such an army to victory, without sacrificing the principles for
which he and the new nation stood, is almost miraculous – a
testament to his visionary leadership.

Given the magnitude of his achievements, it's not surprising
that early biographers treated Washington as a demigod, em-

bellishing his accomplishments with fantastic accounts of his virtue, bravery and military genius. The famous "cherry tree" story is one of many legends that began surrounding the sainted "Father of His Country" shortly after his death. In the modern era, however, revisionists have tried to debunk both the man and some of his finer qualities. To pierce Washington's "aura of divinity," they have suggested that Washington was largely motivated by self-interest – for example, a desire to expand his land holdings into the Ohio Valley – and that his leadership skills were honed as a plantation taskmaster.

The first view denudes Washington of his humanity and diminishes his importance as leader of the Continental Army. It implies that he was an unwitting instrument of Providence – a dumb character in a divine play who performed his assigned role according to the preordained storyline. Here, Washington is not "the indispensable man" of the Revolution, but a talented actor – someone who just happened to win the roles of Commander-in-Chief and President.

The revisionist view overstates Washington's human failings, treating each as a "gotcha moment" worthy of a *60 Minutes* exposé. From this vantage point, American victory in the Revolution was not preordained, but flowed from a remarkable confluence of personalities, events and coincidences. Although this view also diminishes the importance of Washington's leadership, it approaches the "miracle" of the American victory from the opposite direction, implying that success was a lucky break – one of the luckiest in human history.

Washington was neither a demigod nor a lucky incompetent. He was a *very* self-aware individual who devoted much of his life to overcoming his flaws. More than any other Founder, he knew that every utterance he made and every action he performed would be recorded for posterity – that he was *role-model-in-chief* for both the military and the new republic.

He did everything he could to make himself worthy of such a role.

Washington may not have been a born leader, but he deliberately crafted himself into one. He used even his flaws – vanity, ambition, a fierce temper and an obsession with his personal reputation – as raw materials from which he later constructed a wise and visionary leader. By continuously recognizing and learning from mistakes (often hard and bloody mistakes), he strove to remake himself into a more noble, more enlightened man.

As a boy, Washington hand-copied the *Rules of Civility & Decent Behavior*, a Jesuit guide to gentlemanly conduct. The book guided his conduct for the rest of his life. Though some of the book's admonitions seem trite ("Put not off your Cloths in the presence of Others, nor go out your Chamber half Dressed") or even oddball ("Spit not in the Fire, nor Stoop low before it neither Put your Hands into the Flames to warm them, nor Set your Feet upon the Fire especially if there be meat before it"), other precepts stressed what we now call *social skills*:

> *Every Action done in Company, ought to be with Some Sign of Respect, to those that are Present.*

> *Being to advise or reprehend any one, consider whether it ought to be in public or in Private; presently, or at Some other time in what terms to do it and in reproving Show no Sign of Cholar but do it with all Sweetness and Mildness.*

> *Be not hasty to believe flying Reports to the Disparagement of any.*

Washington chose as his own role models some of the most virtuous men of the classical past, including the Roman statesman Cato. He was especially fond of a play about Cincinnatus, the Roman farmer who left his plow to lead an army that saved Rome. Following the victory, Cincinnatus returned to his farm, refusing the role of dictator offered by the Senate.

From his boyhood, Washington yearned for military glory, though he never received a formal military (or university) education. This shortcoming may have contributed to two of the biggest fiascos of the French and Indian War (1754-1763). In fact, Washington may have single-handedly *started* the war by mistakenly attacking a French diplomatic mission in June of 1754. Immediately afterward, he oversaw construction of the hastily built defenses that he named "Fort Necessity." Because Washington had only cleared the trees and brush sixty yards around Fort Necessity, the entire French and Indian force closed to the edge of the perimeter, took refuge behind trees and stumps, and began to pour murderous fire down upon the beleaguered defenders. The result was a slow-paced slaughter lasting for nine hours. In addition to suffering 300 dead and wounded, Washington was forced to sign a surrender document in which he admitted assassinating the French "diplomat."

In June 1755, while slogging through the Alleghenies with an army commanded by General Edward Braddock, Washington recommended that a lightly equipped "flying column" be detached from the main column to Fort Duquesne. The next day, disaster struck when the French and Indians stumbled on Braddock's vanguard at the edge of a clearing. In the ensuing battle, hundreds of British and American soldiers fell to enemy *and* friendly fire, including General Braddock.

With Braddock and his aides-de-camp dead or wounded, Washington charged into the midst of the slaughter to rally the remaining British. "Riding back and forth amidst the chaos, two horses were shot out beneath him and four musket balls pierced his coat, but he miraculously escaped without a scratch." Despite Washington's unquestioned bravery, the outcome was a massacre, with the British suffering 900 dead and wounded out of a force of 1,300.

It would be an understatement to say that, after witnessing the horrific consequences of impetuous and arrogant leadership, Washington strove to never repeat these mistakes, but there were also positive lessons gleaned from the experiences, including the importance of leading by example. This prompted him to ride into the middle of cannon and musket fire time after time during the Revolutionary War, despite pleas from his aides-de-camp not to risk his life. Aside from one sojourn to Mount Vernon, Washington also stayed with the troops in the field throughout the entire war.

The *kind* of man that Washington eventually became is known today, in military and management circles, as "the visionary leader." This rare individual possesses abilities and personal qualities that set him apart from the vast majority. Among other traits, the visionary leader:

♦ has a clear, encompassing and fear-reaching vision regarding his goals *and* the organization needed to accomplish the goals;

◆ is skillful in designing an organizational culture that makes it possible to attain these goals and ideals;

◆ has the ability to inspire others to follow him to attain that vision;

◆ instills in others the beliefs and values of the vision, so that they become empowered to move beyond the leader's expectations;

◆ balances seemingly contradictory aims, including: strategy and tactics; big picture ideas and details; theory and practice; and lofty goals with practical actions; and

◆ inspires and motivates others to devote themselves to a cause bigger than themselves – a cause for which they will die, if necessary.

Only a handful of leaders have risen to such prominence throughout history, including religious figures such as Jesus, the Buddha and Muhammad, as well as generals such as Napoleon, Robert E. Lee and, of course, George Washington.

Such vision does not, however, mean that the leader is blind to reality – to the practical steps needed to transform abstract principles into flesh and blood.

When Washington took command of the Continental Army in September 1775, he was under no delusions about what it would take to defeat the British. For example: while many of the Founding Fathers (and many average Americans) believed in the myth of the Minuteman – that patriotic militiamen were innately superior to British regulars and hired mercenaries – Washington knew that an army of short-term volunteers, no matter how dedicated to the cause, could not defeat the enemy. "To expect then the same service from Raw, and undisciplined Recruits as from Veteran Soldiers is to expect what never did, and perhaps never will happen."

Upon arriving in Boston, Washington immediately set about disciplining his crews of fair-weather freedom fighters into a first-rate European army. Given his service during the French and Indian War, the model he chose to emulate was the British army.

Contrary to the common belief that Washington's "strategy" was to outlast the British in a prolonged war of attrition, he was trying to do no such thing. From the start, he sought opportunities to engage the enemy. It was only after the disastrous Battle of Long Island in 1776 and his ill-advised attempt to hold Upper Manhattan that he became more selective about when and where to fight.

There is no better evidence of Washington's determination to take the fight to the enemy, and the growth of his strategic vision, than the Battle of Trenton.

By December 1776, the patriotic fervor that had excited the fledgling nation the previous summer was gone. Morale was plummeting in the wake of humiliating defeats in New York, which had nearly driven the Continental Army from the Northeast, and threatened to split the thirteen states in two. Washington urged Congress to promote long-term enlistments, but they did nothing to keep his army from evaporating.

Washington now determined on a bold stroke. He would re-cross the Delaware by night and attack the Hessians at Trenton. He chose the most opportune time – the day after Christmas – judging wisely that after the festivities of the holiday the soldiers would be ill prepared for defense.... At the twilight hour, as the earliest stars began twinkling from a clear sky on that cold Christmas night, the little army of twenty-four hundred men began their struggle with the ice floes and the rapid current. Encumbered with their cannon and baggage they occupied many hours in crossing. By midnight the sky was overcast with clouds and the snow was falling, and the remaining hours were intensely dark. But the men labored on with brave hearts and at four o'clock, without the loss of a man, the army was safely landed on the Jersey shore. This was at Mackonkey's Ferry, nine miles above Trenton, and the march down the river was one of extreme suffering, for the snow had turned to rain and hail, and the roads were in a dreadful condition. In two divisions, commanded by Sullivan and Greene, the army reached the little capital by converging roads almost at the same moment, and began a simultaneous attack. The enemy was wholly unprepared. Rall was roused from his bed to take command, but he soon fell mortally wounded. The battle was sharp and decisive, and was all over in three quarters of an hour. The American victory was complete. Less than two hundred Hessians made their escape; a hundred or more were killed and wounded, while about nine hundred and fifty were made prisoners. Six cannons, twelve hundred muskets, and other stores were also taken. The American loss was two killed, two frozen to death, and a few dozen wounded.

A week later, Washington scored another decisive victory – this time at Princeton.

In less than two weeks, Washington won two victories, took a large number of prisoners, greatly increased the size of his army and – most importantly – won a great propaganda victory that fueled enlistments and re-enlistments. Before Trenton, "many of the soldiers were ready to desert the cause as their enlistments were up. Washington urgently appealed to the men to step forward and stay with him in this noble cause. Hesitantly at first, but then almost completely, the soldiers stepped forward because of their trust in and regard for Washington. In that moment, he saved the army and the revolutionary cause." These actions were hardly those of a general hoping to gradually wear down the British, but of someone who knew that decisive victories were needed in order to keep his army – and the Revolution – from disintegrating.

In December 1777, Washington faced circumstances just as dire as those preceding Trenton when he led his poorly fed, ill-equipped soldiers into winter camp at Valley Forge. Though Horatio Gates and Benedict Arnold had won a stunning victory at Saratoga in September, Washington had lost the capital of Philadelphia. The French had yet to enter the war on the American side, and soon a smallpox epidemic began decimating the weary, weakened troops.

Even as food and clothing were being secured and adequate shelters built, Washington and his officers drilled the men into shape — those who had not deserted – with the help of . Day after day, the men were trained in military tactics and instilled with discipline. The commander also inspired his men by having them read the Revolutionary pamphlets of Thomas Paine, who had written, "The harder the conflict, the more glorious the triumph."

Chapter 6: George Washington

By spring, Washington felt his troops could fight the British on equal terms and was desperate for a chance to prove it. He got his wish in June of 1778 at Monmouth, New Jersey. On a steaming afternoon, Washington's newly-trained army fought a large force of British Redcoats. While officially a draw, the Battle of Monmouth was a moral victory for the Continental Army. "For the first time, American soldiers and British soldiers fought to a standstill professionally.... From that point on, Washington always felt confident and his soldiers felt confident that they could stand up to the British in the open, in the field of battle, and win."

In just over two years, Washington designed an organization and organizational culture that made it possible to attain his goals, inspired others to follow him in attaining the vision, and instilled that vision to such a degree that his men were prepared to carry on without him, if need be.

Ironically, the greatest test of Washington's military leadership took place not on the battlefield, but well after the British defeat at Yorktown. In March 1783, a conspiracy was hatched by a group of congressmen and some of Washington's most trusted officers, including Henry Knox and Horatio Gates. Initially, the plan was to threaten a military coup in order to assure passage of important revenue-raising legislation, but a split developed among the officer corps, with Gates leading a faction that was prepared to seize control of the government. The crisis reached a boiling point on March 11, when rebellious officers scheduled a meeting to coordinate the strategy. Washington countermanded the order, and scheduled a meeting for March 16.

In the hours before the assembly, Washington struggled to write a speech that would dissuade his disaffected brethren from pursuing this course – a course that had crushed so many republics before, and would cause so many later revolutionaries to abandon their promises of liberty and equality in favor of despotism and dictatorship. The dream of American democracy was something very personal to Washington. He made that clear in his address, telling his officers that he would view a betrayal of the Revolution's ideals as a personal betrayal.

But as I was among the first who embarked in the Cause of our common Country. As I have never left your side one moment, but when called from you on public duty. As I have been the constant companion and witness of your Distress, and not among the last to feel, and acknowledge your Merits. As I have ever considered my own Military reputation as inseparably connected with that of the army. As my Heart has ever expanded with Joy, when I have heard its praises, and my indignation has arisen, when the mouth of detraction has been opened against it; it can scarcely be supposed at this late stage of the War, that I am indifferent to its interests. ... And let me conjure you, in the name of our Common Country, as you value your own sacred honor, as you respect the rights of humanity, and as you regard the Military and National Character of America, to express Your utmost horror and detestation of the Man who wishes, under any specious pretences, to overturn the liberties of our Country, and who wickedly attempts to open the flood Gates of Civil discord, and deluge our rising Empire in Blood.

In all likelihood, Washington had won over his officers before he began the speech. In a theatrical gesture that has since become legendary, he set his notes before him and then paused, reaching into his pocket to produce a pair of glasses. "Gentlemen, you will permit me to put on my spectacles," he declared rhetorically, "for I have not only grown gray but almost blind in service to my country." Within moments, there wasn't a dry eye in the house.

Like his hero Cincinnatus, George Washington refused the mantle of a Caesar when it was proffered, choosing to cast aside self-interest and that of his unpaid and under-appreciated officers. "Upon learning that Washington intended to reject the mantle of emperor, no less an authority than George III allegedly observed, "If he does that, he will be the greatest man in the world."

Washington may not have been a military genius. Of eight major engagements that he led, he won three, lost four, and one was inconclusive. At the time, victory was far from certain, bold actions were required, and Washington was under no illusion that time was on America's side:

> *While this version of the Revolutionary War possesses all the seductive charm of a great adventure story with a happy ending, at least for the American side, it is not one that Washington himself would have recognized or endorsed.... In fact, to the extent that waging war was about raising money and men, time was on the British side, because the London government had developed, during the eighteenth century, the most powerful and efficient machine for waging war in the world, fully capable of projecting and sustaining its power almost indefinitely.*

Washington's genius lay in recognizing this, as well as recognizing talent in every rank. He surrounded himself with the most capable men and, more important, established an organization through personal example that kept the army intact and kept his vision intact. Holding that army and the new nation together for eight long years, under the worst of circumstances, was his signature feat – and one that should not be underestimated.

What's even more remarkable is that, in many respects, Washington's service to his country had only just begun.

Remain grounded in values; discipline yourself and your team; offer an inspiring vision.

CHAPTER 7

MERIWETHER LEWIS
LEADING THE CORPS OF DISCOVERY

Meriwether Lewis' world was constantly in flux. Born in 1774, just two short years before the signing of the Declaration of Independence, Lewis never knew a time before the formation of the United States of America. He was groomed and educated during a period in which the United States was changing almost daily. Following George Washington's call for volunteers to put down the Whiskey Rebellion of 1794, Lewis joined the Virginia Militia. He accompanied Washington, marching with 13,000 other men, to Western Pennsylvania to put down the rebellion.

As far as rebellions went, the uprising was relatively tame. The rebels had already retreated to their homes by the time Washington's band of militiamen arrived, but it was an important turning point for Lewis who had been, until then, mostly a young man of letters.

Coming of Age in a New Republic

Imagine growing up in a new nation, one where laws were constantly being tested, men were frequently being raised into and dropped from high offices, and citizens were stretching and pulling against the boundaries imposed upon them. Of course, for a young boy, the freedom of exploration in a new world open to possibilities means significantly more than the political discourse in a city hundreds of miles away. It's incredible to contemplate what anyone, especially Meriwether Lewis, would have witnessed in such a time.

Chapter 7: Meriwether Lewis

Meriwether Lewis had long been drawn to the outdoors. As a young child, he frequently snuck away in the dead of the night with his trusty dog to hunt, often in the heart of winter. The years he spent in the Goosepond Community of Georgia shaped him into a young man of conviction and intellect. His mother, ever present and always practical, taught him how to recognize herbs and plants that could be used for food and medicine.

A life spent scrounging for fowl with his dog may have prepared Meriwether Lewis for the outdoors, but it certainly didn't prepare him for the culture shock of his move back to Virginia at the age of 13. Lewis came from a military family, and therefore one of privilege – enough privilege that his guardianship was transferred to his father's brother Nicholas Lewis. Under the wings of Matthew Maury and Parsons William Douglas (who had tutored Thomas Jefferson, James Monroe, and James Madison), Lewis came of age and took over management of his late father's estate – Locust Hill.

One can imagine that as a young man, coming of age in the shadow of a new nation's great leaders, Lewis must have been given every opportunity to challenge himself.

More importantly, it was at a young age that Lewis actively accepted the mantle of responsibility by taking control of his father's estates. In the few short years he spent at Locust Hill in Albemarle County, Virginia, Lewis increased its size and spent many hours walking its lands and observing the local flora and fauna.

By the age of 20, Lewis had graduated from Liberty Hall (today's Washington and Lee University) and had met Thomas Jefferson. If it was a strange path that led Lewis to become an explorer and discoverer, it was those years in Albemarle County that started his journey.

Volunteering to Serve His Country

The shape of his character was evident at an early age. Meriwether Lewis did not ask for permission to lead his dog into the woods in the middle of the night; he did not hesitate to provide what sustenance he could for his family, or to dive headlong into his books. He had a curious mind that thirsted for knowledge, but he knew how to harness that desire to learn and use it as a catalyst to promote change in his own life, and in the lives of others.

By answering Washington's call for militiamen in 1794, he took the next step in the development of a strong character. After the rebellion was put down, Lewis decided to stay under the command of General Daniel Morgan in Pittsburgh, patrolling and ensuring peace in the area.

In 1795 Lewis accepted a commission in the United States Army. He developed a deep respect for his first commander, General "Mad" Anthony Wayne, and upon joining the Chosen Rifle Company, he met and befriended William Clark. This time period, between the end of the American Revolution and before the early wars of the 19th century, was by no means quiet. As the United States expanded its territory and negotiated treaties with Indian tribes on its western borders, Lewis moved frequently and rose in the ranks quickly – he was promoted to captain on December 5th, 1800.

It was a combination of Lewis's steadfast service and his time spent at Locust Hill that gave him the opportunity to lead Jefferson's proposed expedition to the west coast. In 1801 Jefferson appointed Lewis as his aide, allowing him to serve in the role of assistant and private secretary. For some time, eager to explore the newly acquired Louisiana Territory, Jefferson discussed with Lewis at length the prospect of an expedition. Lewis, who had spent his childhood combing the woods of Georgia and observing the plants and animals of his estates at Locust Hill, was excited to be a part of the journey and promptly volunteered.

It was only a matter of time before Lewis had convinced William Clark to join him, and together they started planning the trek.

The Corps of Discovery

The expedition of Lewis and Clark has become American folklore – a story every schoolchild learns and a history that can be seen throughout the Pacific Northwest, especially in Oregon and Washington where the expedition culminated.

Open an atlas and you will find countless reminders of the contributions of Meriwether Lewis – cities, counties, rivers, and mountains along the way named for him and his reliable co-captain. It's easy to forget that these men were young, and in many ways inexperienced. At only 30 years of age (William Clark was 34), Lewis had already become a man of the world many times over – growing his father's estates as a teenager, quelling a rebellion in his early twenties and serving as personal aide to a president. His attention to detail, ability to speak clearly and directly, and his willingness to consider all sides of a given argument made him an ideal leader for such an expedition. His men eagerly followed him. Only one man died during the two-year journey to the Pacific Ocean and back, and that death was a result of appendicitis.

How does one measure the importance of a single man, a leader of a group of nearly thirty, who traversed the wilds of an entire continent in search of economic and scientific discovery? It is impossible to know, beyond the journal entries kept by both Lewis and Clark during their journey, what happened during those two years, but its impact is still felt today by millions of residents who call the Pacific Northwest and the northern areas of the Louisiana Territory home.

While it was circumstance that put Lewis in charge of Jefferson's Corps of Discovery, there could have been no better man for the job given the challenges that were presented and the skills required to overcome those challenges.

Meriwether Lewis' first thought in a crisis was not of survival or self-preservation, but the protection of those around him. He sought to resolve every crisis with minimal bloodshed. For more than a century after his journey, men would travel into the west and come face to face with tribes like the Teton Sioux, and conflicts would arise. Despite the months spent in the territory of the Sioux, Lewis managed to avoid physical conflict. He did not make mistakes – he offered clear and concise orders that were followed to the letter, not just because he was accustomed to being in command, but because he knew that without such orders, men on such a long journey would lose discipline and suffer.

What made Meriwether Lewis such an exceptional leader was not the fact that he had trained for so many hours in the craft of exploration, or that he had been in the U.S. Army for nearly a decade. It was his innate ability to see his men as not just subordinates, but as family members. He cared deeply about every man.

It took a degree of courage to set out on any journey of which the end result was completely unknown. The trip from the western edges of known American territory to the Pacific Ocean was just such a journey. The challenge set before Meriwether Lewis was to venture into the unknown, and successfully protect and lead a group of explorers for more than two years, through two winters, and in the middle of often hostile Indian territories. He met the challenge undaunted.

A cool and collected man, Lewis' leadership style was classic in its approach. He maintained a strong moral code, valuing his position as leader and always acting as he expected his men to act. From poling a canoe down the Columbia River to cooking for his men, he gladly did his share of the work and made sure his men knew that whatever hardships they faced, he would face alongside them.

More than anyone else on the expedition, Lewis valued the goal of the mission. Tasked by President Jefferson with two assignments (to explore the Louisiana Purchase and the Northwest for scientific discovery, and to uncover the Northwest Passage, a water route to the west coast), Lewis was steadfast in recording nearly everything he saw. Using the talents he had developed with his dog as a young child in Georgia, and as the teenage master of Locust Hill, Lewis took the scientific role of his journey very seriously.

He pushed his men hard to reach the next rise, but he always had a clear sense of the needs of his men. He knew when to take a break and when to be inspirational. At the same time, he knew when to push harder and to instill a little toughness to get past the next obstacle at hand. He always maintained a bit of distance between himself and his men, but knew when to bridge the gap and become a kindred soul in the hardships they all faced. As a result, the members of the Corps of Discovery completed their journey and made tremendous contributions to science and the expansion of the country.

Leading in the Field

Telling the story of Meriwether Lewis is often done in two parts: his journey with William Clark to the west coast, and the years of training and preparation that made him the perfect fit for such a journey.

In those early years, as a young man in Georgia and then Albemarle County, Virginia, Lewis was frequently looked to as a leader, but rarely placed in such a role. In the Corps of Discovery, he had the tools in place, but the success of the journey depended upon his ability to know the goal of the mission and remain action oriented at all times.

Chapter 7: Meriwether Lewis

Before setting foot outside known American territories, Meriwether Lewis took the role of the party's naturalist, as well as its diplomatic lead, due to his years of experience in politics as the personal aide to Thomas Jefferson.

His role as the leader of the expedition was amorphous - he would be responsible for recording and sending back samples of flora and fauna discovered on the trip, but he would also be responsible for communicating with Indian tribes along the way and establishing American sovereignty in those lands. This started as early as St. Louis, where Lewis and Governor Stoddard announced to assembled Indian representatives that Jefferson was the new "Head Chief" of the United States and that he was now their leader.

Early in the journey, his leadership skills were put to the test. In February 1804, while in St. Louis for the official transfer of the Louisiana Territory into U.S. control, three men under his command at Camp Dubois (where the Corps was preparing for their journey in May) were insubordinate - they visited a grog shop after their sergeant specifically ordered them not to. When Lewis returned to Camp Dubois, he had all three men confined for 10 days. He reminded those men and everyone else in the party that when he was not present, his sergeant's orders were the same as his own. His abilities to delegate, and to discipline those who did not follow orders in a reasonable manner, made him an effective and respected leader.

Another element of Lewis's leadership style that undoubtedly contributed to the success of the expedition was his willingness to listen both to his men, and to the Indians encountered on their journey. Lewis was a well-educated man who had studied geography and surveying extensively prior to setting out with the Corps of Discovery. As a result, he was well prepared to combine the maps they had with native knowledge of the lands, and his training in geographical properties, to choose the correct route. It may seem obvious to us now that the Continental Divide was west and that certain rivers lead that way and others don't, but this was land on which no American or European (save a handful of intrepid trappers) had ever set foot.

Lewis was blazing new trails, and many leaders in his position, with as much knowledge as he had, would have forged ahead according to their own observations. Lewis was not such a man. He carefully considered all possible options and actively sought out the opinions of the enlisted men. These men were equally well trained in the outdoors - a reason why so many had been chosen for the expedition - and had many insights to offer about the best course of action. Multiple journal entries note Lewis and Clark stopping and inquiring of the men the best course of action. In one particularly famous instance, Lewis and Clark held a vote at Camp Clatsop to determine whether they would stay for the winter. Every person in the camp, including Shoshone guide Sacagawea, and Clark's slave, were allowed to vote. At a time when the opinions of women and slaves were considered dispensable, Lewis wanted to hear every voice that was affected by the choices he made.

Not without Challenges

The journey of Lewis and Clark is often illustrated as two men in furs standing on the precipice of the Continental Divide, looking out over the undiscovered lands of the Pacific Northwest.

That the party successfully reached the west coast with only one fatality, and that they were able to collect countless scientific samples and survey numerous geographical elements, serve as a testament to the focus and attention given to the mission by Meriwether Lewis. He was a man capable of understanding that the mission was only as important as the men carrying it out, and yet he never let hardships or rumblings of discontent derail their push forward.

In fact, during the journey Lewis was frequently injured as he took on duties for himself that could otherwise have been delegated. In one instance, he fell twenty feet from a rock out-cropping and just barely caught himself with his knife, jamming it into a crevice to stop his fall. In another instance, Lewis was overcome by the poison of an ore he had tasted and was forced to purge himself. In a rather infamous incident, Lewis was shot in the thigh by Pierre Cruzatte, thinking he was aiming at an elk. Lewis was gracious, though a little terse, and allowed the man to go free, understanding that pettiness would not be good for the morale of his men.

In yet another occurrence, Lewis and Clark split up to explore two regions near the Marias River. Lewis took four men with him to explore the path of the river. While sleeping, they were attacked by Blackfoot Indians. Almost killed in their sleep, the five fled immediately, covering nearly 100 miles in a single day to outpace their would-be attackers. It was yet another example of Lewis remaining calm under extreme pressure to ensure his men were delivered safely from danger. Where others would have panicked, Meriwether Lewis took firm command and ensured survival.

The Legacy of Meriwether Lewis

Meriwether Lewis was a man of conviction who took his mission very seriously. His decisions were almost always driven by the goals specified by Thomas Jefferson - Lewis's mission. He never compromised his values to attain those goals. He drove his men hard and expected exceptional things from each of them. In return, they performed and gave him their utmost respect.

From the first hostile encounter with the Teton Sioux, to the vicious crossing of the Continental Divide, to the damp, bitter winter in Fort Clatsop, the Corps of Discovery was frequently challenged by hardships that would have driven many others back, or perhaps ended their lives. Meriwether Lewis was a staunch leader, with such a clear vision and such a strong foundation of knowledge that nothing deterred him. He knew when to advance, and he knew when to withdraw. He knew never to let pride get the better of him.

When the explorers' practiced method of meeting a new Indian tribe failed with the Teton Sioux in present-day North Dakota, multiple arguments broke out. The combined efforts of Black Buffalo, the Teton Chief, and Lewis kept men from taking up arms against each other. Eventually, however, the Corps was forced to leave. Lewis understood that to achieve his mission, it was necessary to protect his men and avoid an open fight.

When examining the legacy of Meriwether Lewis, it is hard to imagine such a man feeling anything but pride in his accomplishments, yet Lewis never considered his job complete. Unable to close diplomatic relations with every tribe he met, and never finding a water route to the west coast (which we now know doesn't exist), he felt that he had failed Jefferson.

His men, and his partner William Clark, knew better; modern-day students of history know better. Meriwether Lewis' expedition was a tremendous success, and not just because the Corps reached the west coast and returned largely unscathed. It was a success because a single man, with a powerful understanding of the human spirit and the value of that land he was actively discovering, led the longest expedition in U.S. history to that date.

When he returned to St. Louis in 1806, Lewis sent a series of letters to Thomas Jefferson describing the route he had taken to reach the west coast and summarizing the discoveries he and Clark had made. The information in those letters was sufficient enough that Jefferson deemed it worthwhile to pursue American interests beyond the Louisiana Territory. It was the efforts of Lewis and Clark that made it possible for the Oregon Territory to come under U.S. control. Without his strong leadership and the success of his expedition, it is very likely that the land now comprising Washington, Oregon, Idaho and Montana would have been claimed by another nation.

Ironically, Lewis's contribution to the growth of the United States and his understanding of the land that it thereafter controlled was soon dismissed. It was nearly 100 years before Lewis was publicly recognized and credited for what he, William Clark, and their band of determined men achieved. Today, Lewis is a figure of folklore in Oregon, Washington and Idaho. Lewis' adventure is studied by school children very early on. His name adorns buildings, county seats, cities and businesses in the region, and his legacy lives on in the accomplishments he achieved during those two years as leader of the Corps of Discovery.

Meriwether Lewis based his actions on sound principles, focused his energy and efforts on the task before him, and acted vigorously until the mission was complete. He ventured into the unknown, shouldering the mantle of responsibility. He inspired his soldiers, he shared their hardships, and he was an exceptional leader of men.

Know yourself and the members of your team (capabilities and limitations); adapt; see the task through despite the challenges.

CHAPTER 8

JOSHUA LAWRENCE CHAMBERLAIN
A QUIET HERO

The Civil War in America, in addition to ripping the nation apart at its very core, provided a massive stage upon which drama after drama played out every day. The inestimable horrors of war created a level playing field where things such as social strata, geographical origin, age or upbringing mattered little. Upon this stage some men proved to be cowards, while others grabbed as much glory as they could with as little effort as possible. Still others rose up through the ranks to become committed, unselfish, fair, and impartial leaders who instilled only the highest degree of character in those whom they led. General Joshua Chamberlain numbered among the latter.

This quiet college professor, who preferred music, poetry, higher learning, and church activities, would have been expected to be among the least of those thought to posses battlefield courage and leadership ability; yet, this young man displayed not only incredible aptitude for leadership, but also an undying commitment to a cause for which he was willing to risk his life. And risk it he did, time and time again.

Born in Brewer, Maine, on September 8, 1828, Joshua Lawrence Chamberlain was the eldest of five children. His parents, Joshua and Sarah Dupee Chamberlain, were attentive and loving, yet held their children to a strict moral code of conduct and mindset. Because of sharing the name of Joshua with his father, Chamberlain was known as "Lawrence" to all his immediate family members.

Chamberlain came from a long line of military leaders on both his mother's and his father's side of the family. He was named for Captain James Lawrence, the American naval captain of the frigate *Chesapeake*. In 1813, in a raging battle with the H.M.S. *Shannon*, Captain Lawrence, after being mortally wounded, cried out, "Don't give up the ship!" In later years, Joshua Chamberlain would do his namesake proud.

The eldest son, living on a 100-acre Maine farm, could be expected to contribute more than his fair share of hard work. It was true with Chamberlain. In addition to the various farm chores, he worked in a brickyard and a ropewalk where hemp was made into such things as fishing line and ships' cables. All of the Chamberlain boys learned how to hunt; however, Joshua preferred to observe rather than kill wildlife.

Joshua Chamberlain developed a love for music and singing through school and local church services. Eventually, he purchased and taught himself how to play the bass viol.

For a time, Chamberlain attended a military school since his father had his heart set on his eldest son one day attending West Point. There Chamberlain learned the basics of military drill and also was tutored in French and Latin. It was at military school that he discovered his love for the study of languages.

West Point may have been the elder Chamberlain's choice, but not his wife's. Sarah had always known that her son would become a minister. After joining and attending the Congregational Church in Brewer, Joshua Chamberlain himself chose the route his mother had laid out.

His choice for higher learning was Bowdoin College in Brunswick, Maine; however, entrance to the college required a working knowledge of Greek. Undeterred, Chamberlain spent the better part of each day for six full months mastering this difficult language. The result was his acceptance into the college in 1848. This same sense of undaunted determination would shine in his later Civil War exploits.

While attending Bowdoin, he frequented First Parish Church, where he fell in love with the minister's adopted daughter, Fanny (Francis Caroline Adams).

Also a member of the First Parish Church congregation was the soon-to-be celebrated author, Harriet Beecher Stowe. Her book, *Uncle Tom's Cabin*, published in 1852, changed the hearts of many with regard to the issue of slavery in the nation.

Chapter 8: Joshua L. Chamberlain

Although Joshua Chamberlain was smitten by the lovely Fanny Adams, any thoughts of marriage would have to wait. Following his graduation from Bowdoin, he enrolled at Bangor Theological Seminary to train for the ministry. Before leaving Brunswick, he proposed to Fanny, saying, "I know in whom all my highest hopes and dearest joys are centered. I know in whom my whole heart can rest – so sweetly and so securely."

Upon entering Seminary in 1852, in addition to the normal courses in which he was enrolled, Chamberlain embarked on yet more language studies. He mastered Arabic, Hebrew, and Syriac. Chamberlain further filled his days instructing courses, leading the church choir and teaching Sunday school. He sometimes assisted his father, who was a surveyor and appraiser of timber. When they worked with French Canadians, Chamberlain served as his father's interpreter.

Two significant events occurred following his graduation. He was invited to become a professor at his alma mater, Bowdoin College, for the academic year 1855-56, and in December of the same year, he and Fanny were married.

Life settled into a comfortable routine for Chamberlain. He and Fanny purchased a home and four children were born to them – only two of whom survived. The comfortable routine of family and career was soon to be interrupted when national events in 1861 spelled war.

Chamberlain was much more outspoken about the national situation than other faculty members at Bowdoin, which didn't make him the most popular man on campus. He was adamantly opposed to slavery, both in the moral and religious sense, but he also denounced secession as a nullifying of the South's loyalty to the government they had pledged to sustain. He began to talk openly of joining the Union forces to put down the rebellion.

Not wanting to lose their beloved professor, Bowdoin College offered Chamberlain a two-year leave to study and travel in Europe. Though tempted, he turned down the offer.

Here he was, a man who loved and respected life; who had a safe home, a loving wife and two small children; who had a secure position at Bowdoin; and who had no qualifying experience in military matters (save a year or so in military academy as a young boy). However, none of the negatives seemed to matter.

In the summer of 1862, Joshua Chamberlain traveled to Augusta to pay a visit to Maine's governor, Israel Washburn, to offer his services. The governor, who was under pressure due to President Lincoln's call for troops, was delighted. The governor and his adjutant general needed not only enlisted men, but qualified officers, as well. Chamberlain was offered a colonelcy and command of a regiment.

In spite of intense opposition from his colleagues at Bowdoin – which included protest letters mailed to the governor stating that Chamberlain was unqualified – the governor's need was too urgent to pay them any mind. August 6, 1862, marked the day that Professor Chamberlain became Lieutenant Colonel Chamberlain of the 20th Maine Volunteer Infantry Regiment.

The War Years - Sloppy Appearance; Sloppy Formation

The 900-plus men in the 20th Maine were from the backwoods. They possessed strength, determination, independent-thinking minds, and a good deal of healthy curiosity. Soldiers, they were not. They knew nothing of rank-and-file marching or military courtesy. Each man served as a volunteer and they ranged in age from 18 to 45.

After traveling by train and then by the steamer *Merrimac* to Alexandria, Virginia, they *marched* into the nation's capital. Their sloppy appearance, and even more sloppy formation, elicited hoots of derision from those who watched them pass by.

By September 12, 1862, the 20th Maine - decked out in new uniforms, carrying new rifles, and walking in new leather shoes - headed toward Antietam just as that conflict was winding down. At a ford in the Potomac, the Union army had plunged in to pursue fleeing Confederates. Due to massive firing coming from the bluffs on the Confederate side, the men in blue were ordered back. The 20th had received orders to cross the river as well, but never had those orders rescinded. No sooner had they reached the far bank when the bugles sounded retreat.

With his men on foot hurrying to escape the onslaught, Chamberlain was on horseback in the middle of the river calming, steadying, and encouraging his men through the deepest parts. He watched as several drowned attempting to ford. Before the retreat was complete, Chamberlain's horse was shot from under him. He returned to the Maryland shore as wet as his men. In this first battle, he had already won the respect and admiration of his men.

Following Antietam, General McClelland began the first of his many delays and long periods of inactivity. Chamberlain used this time to get his troops into shape. He and his leader, General Adelbert Ames, set to work with company drill, battalion maneuvers, loading and firing rifles, marching, and military courtesy. Before it was over, the men were ready to kill Ames (a West Point graduate) – a sentiment most soldiers feel toward a hard-nosed drill master.

As the troops drilled, Chamberlain set about learning the art of war. He wrote to Fanny to send him military books from his own library. Every night found him at Ames's tent, or Ames at Chamberlain's tent as the rookie learned from the West Point man everything he could in a short amount of time. Realizing that his ignorance could cost the lives of his men, he dove into his military studies as doggedly as when he taught himself the Greek language years earlier.

Joshua Chamberlain adapted quickly to the soldier's life. He told Fanny in a letter that he was in the saddle sometimes 12 to 15 hours a day, but he said, "I enjoy these rides much." While other officers resided in houses commandeered for that purpose, Chamberlain chose to sleep on the ground with his men, and did so throughout the war.

Unlike his years as a professor, this green officer felt he was finally being appreciated for who he was. Here, no one was ridiculing him for his choice to serve his country; no one was questioning his wisdom or ideas with regard to educational reform. He had an important mission and new purpose. In his current circumstance there was no time for limited thinking.

Battle of Fredericksburg

The next action for the 20th Maine was at the Battle of Fredericksburg. This clash came to be known as the most one-sided battle of the war, because the Union casualties numbered nearly twice that of the Confederates. The Confederate defenders were ensconced on the heights above the city behind a rock wall.

Much has been written of the bungled attack plans throughout the Battle of Fredericksburg. Not one Union soldier was able to reach the Confederate trenches without being mowed down. It was a bloody massacre. Chamberlain and his 20th endured minor losses in the battle, however. They become trapped in a frozen killing-field west of town. Chamberlain and his men were pinned down. They were forced to use corpses as shields. Unable to advance or withdraw, through the cold night hours they built a defensive breastwork by stacking dead bodies - a gruesome affair.

The following spring a smallpox outbreak plagued the Union army. Chamberlain's 20th was ordered into quarantine and found themselves guarding a telegraph line that led to General Hooker's headquarters. Anxious to contribute, Chamberlain found a way to return to the fray. Rejoining the Fifth Corps, he was involved in an exchange with General J. E. B. Stuart during which another horse was shot from beneath him. Chamberlain's troops, once again in retreat, were forced to cross a pontoon bridge in the driving rain. Chamberlain long remained on that bridge – which threatened to be washed away by high water – steadying the men with his calm demeanor and encouraging words. Championed by the infantry soldiers and his officers, he was promoted to Colonel.

Battle of Gettysburg

By the summer of 1863, the bulk of the forces on the Eastern front were gathering for a showdown. General Lee, greatly encouraged by the victory at Fredericksburg, was now ready for another invasion of the north. The Union forces raced to stop him. Two powerful armies faced off near a small town in Pennsylvania known as Gettysburg.

Throughout several hot days of late June, the 20th Maine marched toward Gettysburg. Covering as much as 23 miles a day, the men maintained a good pace. Chamberlain had a habit of frequently resting his men, for which he was sometimes criticized; however, they always arrived in time and ready to fight.

In the early fighting, the Confederates quickly took a hill known as Round Top and were advancing to take a second hill nearby, Little Round Top. The 650-foot-high hill secured the left end of the Union Line. If the Confederates were to take it and plant artillery there, they would have a place from which to attack the Union rear lines and force their retreat from all of Cemetery Ridge.

At one point, one of General Meade's engineers was sent to check on Little Round Top and discovered it undefended. The race was on to gather troops to take it. Colonel Strong Vincent, a 26-year old from Pennsylvania who commanded the 3rd Brigade of the 1st Division, V Corps, responded to the cry for help.

Quickly, Vincent led 1,350 men of his brigade to Little Round Top, a number which included Chamberlain and his 20th Maine. His last words to the remaining contingent of the 20th Maine were: "This is the left end of the Union line. You understand? You are to hold this ground at all costs!"

The Confederates, led by General Oates, wanted to take the position as desperately as the Union forces wanted to defend it. It has been said in later years that the whole of the Civil War rested on a few hours of fighting for Little Round Top.

Wave after wave of attack advanced against Chamberlain and his men and they continually forced the enemy back. As his forces were thinning out, Chamberlain pulled everyone into the fight - even his cooks and the walking wounded. Soon, one-third of his men were either dead or too severely injured to fight. By now, ammunition was running perilously low. What to do?

Chamberlain knew that to remain on the defensive was suicidal. They would soon be rushed, and killed or taken captive. If they were too weak to repel, then the only answer was to attack. Repositioning his men, he ordered them to fix bayonets and charge. Suddenly, each man was rekindled with hope and courage. As one fighting unit they rushed down the hill toward the opposing forces flushing snipers from their hiding places. The confederates were overcome by the audacity of the charge. Bewildered and confused, many surrendered on the spot. While a second Confederate line attempted to hold off the attack, Walter Morrill's B Company (a group that Chamberlain had ordered to guard his flank) opened fire from behind a wall. General Oates' men were now surrounded. They subsequently panicked and retreated. Chamberlain and his men had clearly saved the hill.

Of the 20th Maine, 358 riflemen survived the fray, 90 were wounded and 40 killed. Chamberlain's command succeeded in capturing almost 400 Confederate soldiers. Chamberlain himself received a wound in the foot, which may have been from flying shrapnel. Sadly, the young officer who rallied the initial defense of Little Round Top, Colonel Strong Vincent, died in that battle. Chamberlain was lauded and honored by a number of his superiors for his service and bravery.

Many Union officers, Chamberlain included, fiercely believed that the retreating General Lee should have been pursued relentlessly; however, as had happened previously, those in charge, for various reasons, failed to act. Even though the Battle of Gettysburg will forever be viewed as the turning point of the struggle, the war itself dragged on for another two years.

Battle of Petersburg

In a number of ensuing battles Chamberlain and his men fought valiantly until they ended up at the Battle of Petersburg, in Virginia. The Confederates were neatly holed up in the city. Their position offered amazing protection and more than ample fortifications.

Chamberlain and his brigade had advanced ahead of the Union troops to capture a crest near the city in an exposed position. Soon he received a verbal message indicating that General Meade had ordered an attack across a large barren area that would leave Chamberlain's brigade totally unprotected, inviting sure death. Because the order was verbal, Chamberlain sent back a detailed message clarifying his position and that of his men – questioning the validity of the order. His communication was overruled, and as a result, the 20th Maine stepped off into the Confederate killing field. Once more, Chamberlain's horse was shot from under him and he continued the charge. In the melee that ensued, the colors fell; Chamberlain picked them up and used them to wave his men on.

But Chamberlain's luck was running out. Still holding the banner, he was struck in the right hip by a Minié ball (called "minnie" bullets by the fighting men). The ball slammed through his body and came out the left hip joint.

When the stretcher bearers came to get him, he was so sure of death he insisted upon being left so others could live. His words were ignored. He was subsequently carried three miles to a field hospital in the rear. There, the surgeons discovered the extent of the wound, which was so extensive they were ready to give up. It was Chamberlain who insisted they operate.

In a miracle of medical science these skilled surgeons, working under the crudest of conditions, reconnected the severed parts. Because his death was so certain, several officers came to visit him and thank him.

On June 20, General Grant issued a "deathbed" promotion of Chamberlain to brigadier general. This was the only battlefield promotion ever extended by Grant.

However, in spite of his obituary having been written and published, Chamberlain's grit and determination pulled him through. Not only did he survive the great loss of blood, the three-mile trek to the field hospital, and the surgery, but he also then survived being carried sixteen miles by eight litter-bearers to City Point. From there he was placed aboard a hospital transport and taken to the Naval Academy Hospital at Annapolis.

Early in his recuperation days, with Fanny by his side, he teetered on the brink of death. As the days passed he turned a corner and from that point the healing sped up exponentially. By September, he was anxious to get back to the war. By now the glory of war had long since lost its splendor, but Chamberlain never lost his conviction that the cause for which he fought was just and right.

Still unable to walk any distance or even ride a horse, he returned to his post. In a very short time, the stress of duty and exposure to ice, sleet, and cold caused a physical setback. He was then sent to a hospital in Philadelphia. While convalescing, he received many offers of civil positions, but he was not done fighting. After a month, he slipped quietly out of the hospital and returned to the front.

By November of 1864, Sherman had completed his trek through the Shenandoah Valley and captured Atlanta. The tide was turning, and was now greater than ever.

Battle of White Oak Road

Chamberlain's next clash with the enemy was the Battle of White Oak Road in Virginia, where Grant's plan was to cut off supply lines to the withering Confederate armies. As his men were on the attack, Chamberlain on his war horse, Charlemagne, was out ahead of the charge. As Chamberlain reigned in his horse to slow it, the horse reared just as a bullet ripped through its neck muscle. The bullet proceeded to hit Chamberlain near his heart, tearing his sleeve and bruising his arm. It surely would have killed him had it not been slowed by his leather case of field orders and a brass-encased mirror in his breast pocket.

Stunned and unconscious for a few moments, he soon recovered enough to ride away and rally his men into battle. Riding among them he begged, encouraged and sometimes threatened those who were fleeing. Quickly, he regrouped his men and had them charging once again. Charlemagne then collapsed from loss of blood and was sent to the rear, out of harm's way. A fresh mount was found for Chamberlain, who continued to lead his men. Those who witnessed the scene said he looked like death on a pale horse.

In the end, Chamberlain had pitted his regiment of barely 1,700 against 6,000 of General Anderson's Confederate troops, inflicting casualties of over 400 and capturing more than 200. This action cleared the way for Grant's grand attack on White Oak Road.

Confederates Surrender

By April 2, Richmond and Petersburg were in Union hands. On April 7, 1865, the armies of both sides were amassed for what many believed would be the last major conflict. As Chamberlain moved toward the right flank of the formation, a lone horseman carrying a white flag rode directly toward him. The man, dressed in grey, stated to Chamberlain that Lee desired a cessation of fighting until surrender could be discussed with Grant.

Chamberlain could scarcely believe what he had just heard. After four long years of killing, it was finally over.

Out of all the officers of the Union forces, General Joshua Lawrence Chamberlain was selected for the honor of receiving the Confederate infantry surrender. The few days between the surrender conference and the formal infantry surrender seemed almost surreal in their quiet. No guns, no artillery, no fighting, no killing; only stillness.

On April 12, as Chamberlain officiated astride a recovered Charlemagne, he allowed no band playing, no cheering, no gun salutes – only respect for their vanquished foe. The Confederate soldiers and officers never forgot that gesture. As one by one they retired their arms, ammunition, uniforms, and flags, they were shown honor and respect by Chamberlain and his men.

Chapter 8: Joshua L. Chamberlain

Following the war, Chamberlain entered politics and served as the governor of Maine for four years. Later he served as president of Bowdoin College, where he instigated the reforms that he had dreamed of before the war. He actively wrote about his war experiences, in addition to accepting public speaking invitations around the country.

The veteran was privileged to attend the fiftieth anniversary of the Battle of Gettysburg where he was joined by many of the elderly survivors of that momentous battle. Together they reminisced about how Chamberlain's decision to mount a counterattack from Little Round Top most certainly saved the day, and possibly the course of the war.

Chamberlain died in 1914 at the age of 85. His dear Fanny preceded him in death by only a few years. A minister and college professor had proved himself a man among men - a leader of American soldiers.

Leadership requires conviction; courage demands a willingness to assume risk; honorable men are empathetic.

CHAPTER 9

ALVIN C. YORK
CONSCIENTIOUS OBJECTOR TO MEDAL OF HONOR

What makes a man stand up when those on his right and left have been mowed down? What makes a man advance into a wall of lead when it would be easier to stay put, or safer yet, to seek shelter? What makes a man act when, by taking initiative, he risks forfeiting his very life?

The conviction of a noble cause, faith of character, and an urgency to save lives drove Alvin Cullum York to stand up and advance into a gauntlet of death. York earned the Medal of Honor for his heroic actions on the 8th of October, 1918. One man made a courageous contribution to the allied victory in the Meuse-Argonne offensive that, in concert with countless other selfless acts of sacrifice and bravery, ultimately led to the cessation of the Great War.

Alvin York did not set out to become a hero in the War to End All Wars. He was a soldier, extra called upon to do his duty. He would fulfill that duty as best he could.

Raised in the Tennessee back country, Alvin grew up hunting and fishing and working the farm. At an early age he became an expert shot with handguns and rifles. He later remarked how easy his army marksmanship training had been.

Alvin, in his early 20s, was thrust into the role of family bread-winner and caretaker when his father died. To earn money, York drove steel on the railroads, and cut and hauled trees. He was a hard worker, skilled with tools, and devoted to the welfare of his mother and eight younger siblings. He did suffer one youthful indiscretion, however; he was a violent alcoholic. As a young man, he liked to stay out late, drink moonshine and gamble away his wages. York was arrested a number of times for bar fights. His mother continually prayed for him and pleaded with him to change his ways, but the temptation to drink was, for a time, too overpowering.

Finally, York began to realize all the pain he was causing and all the good things he was missing because of his immaturity and rashness. One evening York returned home late after a night of drinking and gambling to find his mother in a state of despair. He promised her then and there he would quit drinking and smoking, gambling and brawling. York proved true to his word. Soon thereafter, York underwent a conversion experience at a revival meeting on January 1, 1915, that set him on a new course. Always a student of scripture, he took up his studies with a new fervor, ultimately becoming an elder in his church.

The Yorks belonged to a pacifist Protestant denomination that shunned secular politics: the Church of Christ in Christian Union. Though it had no specific doctrine of pacifism, the congregation opposed all forms of violence. As the war raged in Europe, concern grew that America might be pulled into the fray. She was, and Alvin York's convictions and faith would be tested.

In June of 1917 all American men between the ages of 21 and 31 were required to register for the draft. York registered as the law demanded, but dreaded the prospect of having to go and kill. He claimed an exemption from draft on the grounds that he, as he wrote, "Don't want to fight." His initial clam to be a conscientious objector was denied. He appealed the denial, but that appeal also failed. York was drafted into the Army and soon reported to Camp Gordon, Georgia, where he was assigned to the 328th Infantry Regiment of the 82nd Infantry Division.

While the Army had provisions for conscientious objectors to serve in non-combatant roles, York struggled with his pacifist convictions. While training, he engaged in long heartfelt discussions with key officers in his unit, other committed Christians. They eventually changed his thinking. York reconsidered the morality of war and finally determined that God meant for him to fight, and would keep him safe. He became convinced of the rightness of the cause.

The 82nd Division completed training in April of 1918 and set sail for Europe. After a few days' layover in England, the division landed in France in May. York saw his first action in late June, manning trenches and patrolling no man's land in the Montsec Sector of the Allied lines. The soldiers of the 328th were anxious at first - those pesky bullets humming around - but soon realized that worrying served no purpose, as "you never hear the one that gets you."

The Meuse-Argonne offensive, part of the Allies' Grand Offensive on the Western Front, began September 26th, 1918. This was the biggest, and the deadliest, operation of World War I for the American Expeditionary Force. The advance along the entire front eventually resulted in the armistice signed on November 11th. York's 82nd Division, having arrived in France in May and seen some action, moved into position to contribute to the final push.

During the early going of the offensive the Allies and Germans engaged in a give-and-take campaign. Forces would advance and fall back, up and down the line. Every inch of ground was contested, and the cost to both sides mounted. On October 2nd, elements of the 77th "Liberty" Division from New York advanced into the dense Argonne Forest. The 308th Infantry Regiment attacked, believing a French unit was covering its left flank and American units were covering its right. The French advance stalled and soon the 308th, along with one company from the 307th Infantry Regiment and two machinegun companies from the 306th, were cut off and surrounded by German forces. This isolated battalion of fewer than 600 men, running low on food, water, and ammunition, fought on. They became known as the Lost Battalion. York's outfit advanced knowing the Allies were attempting to relieve these beleaguered men.

Artillery, gas, snipers, and machinegun fire, though far from welcome, had become somewhat routine for the soldiers of the 82nd Division. Alvin York saw men, "just blown up by the big German shells." Airplanes buzzed overhead most of the time, swarming like hornets, seeking someone to sting. The forest looked like a disaster zone. Once mature, lush growth now looked like the aftermath of a tornado.

The morning of October 7th was drizzly and damp. With shells bursting all around, men of the 328th Infantry Regiment lay in quickly dug, shallow holes or in roadside depressions waiting to go into action. Orders came for York's unit to take hills 223 and 240 on the morning of October 8th. The task that day, the 7th of October, was to survive.

Throughout that long night the big guns flashed like the thunder and lightning of a violent storm back in Tennessee - though this storm showed no signs of abating. All the Americans could do was wait, and watch, and pray. The 328th's sister unit across the road absorbed more than their fair share of direct hits. York lost friends that night - good men. The primary activity that evening was evacuating the wounded and collecting the dead. The wet, the cold, the dead and the dying reminded York of the Bible story of Armageddon.

The 328th's mission was to advance across the valley to the ridges on the other side, seize two hills, then press on to the Decauville Railroad. For the faithful, Psalm 23:4 said it best, "Yea, though I **walk through the valley of the shadow of death**, I will fear no evil: for thou art with me." The mission "zero hour" (launch time) was set for 6 o'clock, just before first light.

York's unit expected an Allied onslaught to strike the German line at 0600 hours, but none came. Instead, German artillery fired a heavy barrage of explosive shells intermixed with gas at the 82nd Division forces. The Americans put on their masks and pressed forward through the barrage. The 328th's action in the war to this point had been defensive; now it was time to press the attack. The 328th, however, soon found themselves in the midst of a German killing field. Machineguns were firing on York's unit from the front, the left and the right. American soldiers were being mowed down like hay in a field.

The American losses were heavy. About halfway across the valley the advance faltered. With withering machinegun fire coming from three sides, the German defensive line was just too strong. The remaining elements of the 328th dug in. The defending forces had the Americans just where they wanted them. The brush on the hillside obscured the machinegun nests entrenched along the commanding ridges. The Americans had no idea what they were shooting at, while the Germans were making quick work of the assaulting troops - and still the Americans had no supporting artillery.

Huddled down in the valley, the Americans determined that a frontal assault against the machineguns would be suicide. They resolved to infiltrate around behind the defenders and strike them from the rear. The Americans had to circle around the ridges some 300 yards to their front. York was part of a 17-man team (a sergeant, three corporals, of which York was one, and 13 troops), remnants of four squads, sent around the enemy's left flank with the intent of silencing those machineguns. Sergeant Early, the senior-most man, led the reinforced squad on the assault. The team moved quickly and quietly, making good time. The brush, along with the hilly terrain concealing the German machineguns, allowed the American infiltrators some additional cover.

When the American squad was in place behind the German position, Sergeant Early gathered his leaders to set a plan of attack. They settled on hitting the machinegun nests directly from the rear. This left the right and left flanks exposed, but offered the Americans the best chance at surprise. The team set up in a skirmish line and dropped over the crest of the hill.

The first two Germans the Americans ran into were wearing Red Cross armbands. When they saw the Americans the two bolted like scared rabbits. Trying to catch the Germans before they could warn the others, the American team called for the two to surrender. One soldier even fired on them, but missed, and they got away. York's team continued to advance toward the sound of the machineguns that were holding up the Allies' advance. The Americans could not see the Germans, nor could the Germans see this daring band of Americans.

Moving with haste, York's team jumped across a small stream of water and ran headlong into a group of 15 to 20 Germans. Upon seeing the Americans, the Germans believed they had been surrounded by a superior force and surrendered. The Americans had stumbled upon a German headquarters, flush with orderlies, stretcher bearers, and runners, along with a major and two other German officers. Having captured the headquarters, York's team turned toward the real threat - those deadly machineguns.

In policing up the headquarters, the element of surprise was lost. A number of German gunners turned their weapons away from the front and instead attempted to neutralize the threat in their rear area. The German machine gunners sighted in on the Americans and opened fire. Of the 17 Americans, the Germans killed six and wounded three. Sergeant Early and the two other corporals were gunned down, leaving York in charge.

While some of York's team were not in the line of fire, York was out in the open. The German machineguns were spitting fire. The undergrowth all around York was being cut down. The seven men remaining in the American squad were focused on two things: securing the prisoners and dodging the hail of bullets. York now acted on his own.

York was flat on the ground. The firing around him was deafening. He was caught in a death match; it was going to be either York or the Germans. York was determined to give them his best.

York later recalled his shooting as being like a turkey shoot back in Tennessee. For the German gunners to fire effectively on him, they had to expose themselves. As he saw a head pop up from behind cover, he would fire a shot and knock it down. The Germans were so close York could not miss. Every shot counted, and every shot hit its mark.

There were some thirty German machinegun nests on the ridges surrounding York's position. He fired fast and furiously. Initially, he fired from a prone position on the ground, but as he got a rhythm going, he stood up and fired from an off-hand position. This was York's preferred shooting stance. He could maneuver his weapon freely and reach his ammunition more easily. The barrel of his rifle was getting hot and his ammunition was running low, but he kept on shooting just the same, and Germans kept falling.

Just then, a half-dozen Germans jumped up out of a trench and charged with fixed bayonets. Needing only to cover twenty-five yards, the Germans seemed to have the advantage. With only a few rounds left in his rifle, York flipped out his .45 pistol. Instead of aiming for the lead man, York started at the back. He took out the sixth man, then the fifth man, and so on. The idea was, just like with turkeys, if you take out the first, the rest will scatter, or in this case fall to the ground and squeeze off a round. York wanted to keep them running, until he got each one.

With this threat neutralized, York resumed firing his rifle and turned back to those machineguns. York's confidence was growing as each German fell. Not wanting to kill any more than he had to, York yelled for the Germans to surrender. Whether it was the din of the battle or his English, none of the Germans gave up, so York kept knocking them down. That German major the Americans were holding nearby finally stepped forward.

The German major's English was as good as York's. He told York that if York would stop shooting the Germans, the major himself would get them to surrender. York agreed. The major blew on a whistle and the Germans began to abandon their positions. They gathered around and threw down their weapons. All but one German came off the hill; that one tossed a hand grenade, but York silenced him, too.

Now with nearly 90 prisoners, York and his remaining seven men had to return to friendly lines. York quickly organized the Germans into two ranks. He called his squad forward out of the brush and positioned them strategically along the column. He had the German soldiers carry the wounded Americans - he wasn't going to leave any Americans behind to die. York took up a position just behind the German major and another officer at the front of the column, and with his gun in their backs he had them hike along.

As York's squad with its 90 prisoners was moving from the German rear area they surprised the very front line of the German defenses and picked up another forty or so prisoners. With a total of 132 German prisoners, York was growing concerned about the danger of American artillery observing such a force on the move and opening up. The column did take some heavy shell fire, but York hustled them along to safety.

Regimental and division leadership were astounded upon seeing the company of prisoners York and his small team managed to bring in. Best of all, the machinegun nests all along that valley were neutralized and the offensive could continue. Word was spreading along the front that even the Lost Battalion had been found.

After a brief respite and a warm meal, York and his men returned to their outfits. They pushed on to the Decauville Railroad.

The 328th Infantry and Sergeant York stayed in the fight until the 1st of November. They remained on the front lines and bore the brunt of the battle through those tortuous woods. York wrote in his diary that both the woods and the soldiers "were messed up right smart."

Having made it through such harrowing action in the valley of death on October 8th, York remembered that was not the closest he came to getting killed during the war. The nearest he came to dying, he believes, was a few days later on the 12th of October.

The 328th was surprised by a heavy barrage of German artillery fire. York and his men were caught out in the open. With nowhere to hide, immediately the troops began to dig in. If a soldier cannot maneuver out of a kill zone, the best protection from falling artillery is a hole in the ground.

After being at the front for a while, soldiers can tell both where artillery shells will land and how big they are. These shells were close enough that dirt was flying nearby. The closer the shells got, the faster the troops dug. One shell burst right in front of York's position. Dirt went flying; York and his men went flying. Luckily, however, no one was hurt, though it was a very close call.

On November 1st York and his men were given a reprieve from fighting as the 328th came off the line. They went to a German rest camp to recuperate. The unit had been so badly decimated that it hardly seemed the same unit.

As a result of his action on the 8th of October, his exploits since then, and his demonstrated leadership potential, Corporal York was promoted to Sergeant. Sergeant York believed it was divine providence that kept him safe that fateful day and up until the end of the war. Bullets whizzed overhead, they pummeled the ground all around him, but he never got a scratch; "A higher power guided and watched over me and told me what to do."

On November 11th, 1918, the Armistice was signed ending the War to End All Wars. York was ready for it to be over. There had been enough fighting and killing. The Americans had done what they had set out to do.

Sergeant Alvin C. York was one of the most highly decorated and celebrated American soldiers of the First World War. Following the war, York was received by President Wilson, Secretary of War Baker, and other prominent Americans. He was honored by the Tennessee Society in New York City and by notable groups around his home state of Tennessee. The story of the extraordinary deeds of this plainspoken, unsophisticated, and uneducated American soldier revolved around the theme of a patriotic sharpshooter and a mountaineer of deep faith, who "seemed to do everything correctly by intuition."

York refused to profit from his notoriety and fame. He did accept a gift of a farm by the Nashville Rotary, but went on to struggle as a farmer. He worked tirelessly for causes he believed in, both charitable and civic. He supported economic development of the rural areas of Tennessee and promoted programs to educate the mountain boys and girls of the state through a foundation he established.

York attempted to re-enlist in the Army during World War II, but at 54 years of age, and in less than perfect health, he was instead appointed an honorary colonel in the Signal Corps. He toured the country (usually at his own expense) raising money for the war effort through bond drives.

Alvin York died in 1964 at the age of 76. General Matthew Ridgway remarked that York "created in the minds of farm boys and clerks ... the conviction that an aggressive soldier, well trained and well armed, can fight his way out of any situation." York was a man of high moral standards, who focused on the mission at hand, and who didn't shy away from doing what needed to be done. Sergeant Alvin York was a man who made an impact. He is a true American hero.

Rely on your moral compass (enduring values); focus in the moment on the task at hand; act for the greater good.

CHAPTER 10

GEORGE C. MARSHALL
ORGANIZER OF VICTORY

On a sunny summer day in Uniontown, Pennsylvania, sometime around the year 1890, two young and industrious boys, Andy and George, started a ferry service in order to convey the girls of the town across a small and winding creek. George took the tickets, while Andy acted as the "pole man" performing the physical labor to propel their small boat from one side to the other. On their maiden voyage, they successfully transported all the girls from a bank of dry ground to the not-so-distant shore on the other side. The rosy-cheeked boys, full of pride from their triumphant crossing, quickly made preparations for the return passage since the only purpose of the ferry was to courageously carry the girls to the far side of the babbling stream and back again. Unfortunately for George, this is where the trouble began.

The girls, displeased with the process of repeatedly handing over their tickets for review and punching, flatly refused to cooperate, rudely upsetting George's well-laid plans to carry out a proper ferry service. With his cap on backwards and a punching machine in his hand, George felt disgraced as the girls jeered and mocked him. The ultimate indignity came when Andy, engineer and business partner, joined in on the razzing that the would-be conductor shamefully bore. Acting on the inspiration that only humiliation can provide, George rashly pulled the cork from the floor of the boat, creating a geyser of water that simultaneously drenched the girls and sank the boat to the bottom of the tiny brook. The "obstreperous" girls, as George referred to them, waded across the stream angrily, threatening to tell their fathers.

When recalling this incident late in his life, General George Catlett Marshall stated, "I never forgot that because I had to do something and I had to think quickly, and what I did set me up again as the temporary master of the situation."

Throughout his life, General Marshall continually acted as the master of his situation with the same quick thinking and sharpness of mind that he displayed as a young boy in Uniontown, Pennsylvania. He matured in knowledge and stature and in favor with those around him, eventually relying on the personal character traits of hard work, self-discipline, honesty, respect for others, open mindedness, humility, and loyalty to govern his success both as a man and career soldier in the Unites States Army. His long and remarkable career, underscored by the values that governed him, put this son of a coal merchant in the company of Presidents Franklin Delano Roosevelt and Harry S. Truman, British Prime Minister Winston Churchill, French Prime Minister Charles de Gaulle, and other world leaders such as Chiang Kai-shek and Joseph Stalin.

Because of his humble, unassuming personality, his name is less familiar today than those of the flamboyant and highly-publicized battlefield generals of World War II. These men included Dwight David Eisenhower, the Supreme Allied Commander of the D-Day invasion of Normandy and eventual President of the United States; General Douglas MacArthur, hero of the Philippines and iconic champion striding ashore at Manila Bay with a long-stemmed pipe clenched tightly in his teeth; and the aggressive tank commander General George S. Patton, whose exploits will punctuate history for all time. These men all had one thing in common: they answered to their superior officer, General George C. Marshall.

For most men, serving as Chief of Staff of the Army throughout all of World War II would be the capstone on an extensive and noteworthy career, but General Marshall, a man driven by the mission at hand and the call of his country, continued to serve. President Truman sent him to China as a special emissary in 1945, and upon his return home in 1947, the United States Senate unanimously approved his appointment as Secretary of

State. Free from official government duties in 1949, he served as President of the American Red Cross and chaired the American Battlefield Monuments Commission. President Truman came calling once more in 1950, appointing Marshall as Secretary of Defense, a position he held until September 1951.

In 1943, and again in 1947, *Time Magazine* named him "Man of the Year;" he is the only individual to earn the honor more than once who never held a position as head of state. *Time's* recognition of Marshall paled in comparison to his selection as the 1953 recipient of the Nobel Peace Prize for developing a plan to rebuild the countries and economies of Europe after World War II. The official title of this plan (European Recovery Program) will forever remain obscured in the shadows of history in favor of its universally referred-to name, the Marshall Plan.

Between his days as a cork-pulling ferry conductor and his status as a Nobel laureate, George Marshall spent decades refining himself as a man of values, action, and honor. His military career spanned more than forty years, after which he added another half a dozen in civil service assignments. In total, he dedicated nearly two-thirds of his life to the United States of America.

He graduated from the Virginia Military Institute as First Captain of Cadets and joined the Army as Second Lieutenant Marshall in 1902. He married Lily Coles just before leaving on assignment to the Philippines. The most influential military leader in his early career was General John J. Pershing, whose legendary career rose to stratospheric levels when, in 1918, he achieved the rank of General of the Armies. Only Pershing and George Washington have ever held such a rank. Marshall joined the American Expeditionary Force in 1917 to fight the Germans in the Great War.

Marshall functioned as the Chief of Operations of the 1st Division under Pershing's overall command during the arduous St. Mihiel Offensive. He was also the chief planner of the Meuse-Argonne campaign in 1918, wherein he spearheaded the build-up and tactics used by the infantry to defeat an experienced and aggressive German army. It was here that his style and quality of leadership began to achieve notoriety among his peers. George Marshall was beginning to make a name for himself as a man of action who knew what a fighting force needed and how to make it happen. After the war, Pershing specifically requested him as his personal aide, a relationship that reflected positively on each man's career.

Marshall served capably in World War I, showing the strength of his intellect and the depth of his character on the battlefield, all the while defining himself as a leader. When the war ended in 1918, his temporary promotion to Colonel reverted back to Captain, until he reached the rank of Major —— where he languished for ten long years. Many officers experienced a lack of purpose during this period when career advancement opportunities stagnated. Marshall, however, being a man driven by the significance of his mission and the greater importance of preparing the Army for the next war, continued to thrive as an individual and leader.

Among the opportunities Marshall grasped during the inert years after 1918 were his appointments as an instructor at the Army War College in Washington D.C. and at Fort Benning, Georgia (1927-1932), where he shaped the tactical thinking of hundreds of up-and-coming leaders, including George Patton. He also met his second wife, Katherine Brown, while at Fort Benning. Lily Coles, his wife of 25 years, had died of complications after surgery. As a Colonel he commanded the 19 Civilian Conservation Corps camps in South Carolina, and then in 1936, as a Brigadier General, he supervised another 35 camps as commander of the Vancouver Barracks in the Pacific Northwest. His style brought order to the camps, and the experience provided him insight into leading large, newly formed groups of American men. Indeed, his prowess in creating strong and effective organizational structure had become a talent that soon would slingshot his career to the highest levels of military hierarchy. He practiced and theorized on strategies that he believed would dominate the next war, wherever it might be. He did not believe the trench warfare that marked World War I in France would dominate future battles, so he shifted his thinking. Marshall created new strategies and ceaselessly trained his students and subordinates to adapt to constantly flowing and shifting battlefields. He further instructed them to use new technologies such as tanks, airpower, and modern communications devices.

By 1938, Marshall returned to Washington as the Deputy Chief of Staff of the Army serving under General Malin Craig. It was in this position that he first met FDR and began cultivating a relationship with him built on the pillars of candor, loyalty, and mutual respect. Later, after Marshall replaced Craig as Chief of Staff, Roosevelt, in his usual personable manner, called him «George.» The Chief of Staff instantly informed the President that he should refer to him as "General Marshall." This somewhat humorous story clearly illustrates Marshall's personality of keeping social distance from his associates, a trait many referred to as stoicism.

Roosevelt elevated "General Marshall" to Chief of Staff of the Army (four stars) on September 1, 1939, the very same day Germany invaded Poland halfway around the globe, marking the first military conflict of World War II. America's isolationist mindset, strongly reflected by Congress, amplified the daunting task of rapidly building a fighting force that would dominate on a global scale. During the war, Marshall defined his purpose with great eloquence, "We are determined that before the sun sets on this terrible struggle our flag will be recognized throughout the world as a symbol of freedom on the one hand and of overwhelming force on the other." No longer a tactician, Marshall's outlook clearly indicated his conversion to a strategist and progressive thinker with a worldview.

The United States Army consisted of approximately 200,000 men and officers when Marshall became chief of staff, and by the end of the War he had skillfully increased that number by a multiple of forty to a total of 8.2 million combat-ready troops. He incessantly inspected outfits, challenging and chiding their commanders to improve. General John P. Smith received a letter from Marshall calling him to action:

> *...now I am rather fixed in the belief that some of the [corps] headquarters are not functioning at the speed demanded by the emergency. There is too much of the time-clock procedure.... The last has been a frequent criticism of your headquarters from any number of directions. I am inclined to think that several of your staff are not sufficiently aggressive, energetic, and far-seeing.*

While a member of the Joint Board, the precursor of the Joint Chiefs of Staff, as well as the Combined Chiefs, Marshall fought intensely for a long-range strategy of handling a global war containing major fronts in two hemispheres. He showed tremendous forethought for strategic planning and even greater insight with regards to global military actions when in 1939, a full two years before the United States entered the war, he advocated an overall policy to defeat Germany first. According to Marshall's way of thinking, the "Germany First" strategy would concentrate the preponderance of Allied military might to defeat Hitler in Europe, while simultaneously fighting a holding action against Japan in the Pacific, thereby diverting the bulk of the nation's limited resources to the Atlantic or European campaign.

American and British planners worked for months creating detailed plans predicated upon the Germany First concept; however, FDR provided an unclear response without giving his authorization. Secretary of War Henry Stimson demurred on the plan's implementation until Marshall argued that since the President hadn't disapproved of the plan, Army and Navy commanders were free to move forward. After that, the Germany First strategy, codenamed RAINBOW 5, became the official Allied approach to World War II, and under Marshall's competent and, at times, bullheaded leadership, the buildup and deployment of America's armed forces came to reflect its stratagem. Marshall frequently disagreed with Admiral Ernest King of the Navy, refusing to send Army units to the Pacific. King, in frustration, decided to launch Pacific operations, such as an invasion of Guadalcanal, using only units from the Navy and the Marines. Because of focused commitment to his mission, General Marshall did more to shape Allied forces during the war than did any other individual.

Notwithstanding his steadfast hold on strategy, Marshall made a name for himself as one who ignored old rivalries or one-upmanship, considering them schoolyard folly. He took the lead in abandoning Army-Navy squabbles by working closely with Admirals King and Stark. He also nurtured one of the most important and successful relationships of the War when he befriended British Field Marshal Sir John Dill, who served in Washington as Chief of the British Joint Staff Mission.

Marshall continued to resist any departure from the Germany First plan throughout 1941 and 1942. Britain's Prime Minister, Winston Churchill, argued passionately for a Mediterranean campaign in North Africa and Italy; this was a digression Marshall could not abide, so he devised plans for an invasion of

France to begin in 1943. He wanted to take early action, striking a deathblow to the heart of Nazi power and ending the war in Europe as rapidly as possible. Both Roosevelt and Churchill realized the impracticality of taking this bold action too soon and overruled any such invasion, choosing instead to increase operations in North Africa and eventually Italy, at least somewhat. The rejection, however, was not a total loss. The need for a cross-channel invasion was obvious to everyone, and Marshall's efforts won a formal recognition that the time had come to act.

Operation OVERLORD, as the invasion of France was codenamed, would include forces from many nations, thereby requiring unprecedented levels of coordination and communications between the fighting forces of various countries, as well as between various branches of service such as the Army and the Navy. The best way to address the myriad conflicts expected to arise was to appoint one man to take overall command of all military forces involved, a Supreme Allied Commander. Henry Stimson told FDR that Marshall was the man for the job:

...I believe that the time has come when we must put our most commanding soldier in charge of this critical operation at this critical time...General Marshall already has a towering eminence of reputation as a tried soldier and as a broad-minded and skillful administrator...I believe that he is the man who most surely can now by his character and skill furnish the military leadership which is necessary.

Roosevelt did not want to deny Marshall the job he most coveted and had earned, neither did he like the idea of losing his best general to a far-off assignment, so he uncharacteristically confounded himself with indecision. While at the Tehran Conference in Iran in the fall of 1943, the President asked Marshall who, in his opinion, should lead the Normandy invasion: Marshall himself, or Eisenhower? Marshall's response exemplifies the humility of self and loyalty to a cause that mattered so much to him. He informed his boss of his willingness to serve wherever the President would have him go. Roosevelt took the opening that his Army Chief of Staff so selflessly provided and named General Eisenhower to the coveted position. He told Marshall, "I didn't feel I could sleep at ease if you were out of Washington."

General Eisenhower looked up to Marshall while working on his staff in Washington at the start of the war. He once confided to an aide, "I wouldn't trade one Marshall for fifty MacArthurs. My God! That would be a lousy deal. What would I do with fifty MacArthurs?" No man did more to advance the career of Dwight Eisenhower than George C. Marshall. Eisenhower commanded OVERLORD to resounding success and continued across Europe until Nazi Germany capitulated; all under the dependable guidance and steadfast loyalty of General Marshall. Displaying his appreciation for Ike's efforts, Marshall arranged for the General's son, John Eisenhower, to visit him in London after his graduation from West Point, a gracious and loyal gesture. Eisenhower himself treasured several of the lessons of leadership Marshall taught him and considered him to be the best leader under whom he had ever served. Nevertheless, in 1952, when Senator Joseph McCarthy despicably accused Marshall of anti-Americanism, Eisenhower, on the presidential campaign trail, removed a statement defending the General from a speech to avoid controversy. Marshall remained silent on this betrayal.

Congress promoted George C. Marshall to the rank of General of the Army in December of 1944, the first of only five men in United States military history to become a five-star general. Soon afterward he retired to a life of privacy and relaxation, or so he thought, for in that very same month, President Truman sent him to China as special emissary with the hope that he could utilize his exceptional talents of persuasion and reason to broker a coalition government with Chiang Kai-shek, the British, and the Russians.

He remained in China for thirteen months working diligently, but unsuccessfully, to broker peace in the burgeoning world power. Immediately upon his return home in January 1947, the United States Senate confirmed his nomination by Truman as Secretary of State. Most world leaders respectfully continued to refer to him as "General" Marshall as he tirelessly worked to politically and economically heal a wounded world. On June 5, 1947, while speaking at a commencement ceremony at Harvard University, he unveiled his plan to reconstruct the war-ravaged countries of Europe, a plan that when enacted became the crowning achievement of an already extraordinary career.

The Marshall Plan allowed the United States to provide financial assistance to European nations in order for them to rebuild after the devastation of war. Underlying these stated goals and practices, the political agenda of the Marshall Plan was to stem the tide of Russian communism from flowing across the weak and susceptible countries of Europe. President Truman's pledge of military support to Greece and Turkey to aid in the resistance of communism formed a philosophy known as the Truman Doctrine. Marshall ironically, as a career military man, favored an economic solution. So successful was his plan that a poll of historians and political scientists conducted by the Brookings Institution in 2000 listed it as the greatest achievement of the federal government during the last half of the twentieth century.

In addition to being the catalyst for the creation of NATO — another bellwether during Marshall's tenure with State — the humanitarian impact of the Marshall Plan is simply so colossal that it is impossible to measure in terms of dollars invested, lives saved, businesses spawned, or even nations stabilized. Since the plan's implementation and Europe's emergence from beneath the rubble of World War II, the interaction of countries within the framework of both a continental and global community has never been the same. As the efforts of the Marshall Plan began to take hold, and with its benefits becoming more apparent, the Nobel Prize Committee honored its author with the Nobel Peace Prize in 1953. In the larger scope of history, the plan's significance is such that Marshall's name is more closely associated with it than with his unsurpassed military accomplishments.

Having successfully navigated the waters of international affairs, Marshall left the State Department in 1949 and retired once again. President Truman, like Roosevelt, was unwilling to let his best man go and appointed him to be Secretary of Defense in 1950, a position in which he served for only one year. It was not an idle year; however, as the fledgling Korean War demanded his considerable talents to rebuild the country's armed forces, plan long-term strategies, and unite foreign powers for the common good.

By the end of his career in 1951, the General had devoted nearly fifty years of his life to the country he so loved. Always driven by a sense of duty and committed to the values of freedom and opportunity he so dearly respected, General Marshall acted as a leader with honor, dignity, and stringent fidelity to his country. Winston Churchill, a man with whom Marshall repeatedly disagreed, characterized him thusly:

During my long and close association with successive American administrations, there are few men whose qualities of mind and character have impressed me so deeply as those of General Marshall. He is a great American, but he is far more than that. In war he was as wise and understanding in counsel as he was resolute in action. In peace he was the architect who planned the restoration of our battered European economy and, at the same time, labored tirelessly to establish a system of Western defense. He has always fought victoriously against defeatism, discouragement, and disillusion. Succeeding generations must not be allowed to forget his achievements and his example.

President Truman similarly honored his accomplishments: "I don't think in this age in which I have lived, that there has been a man who has been a greater administrator; a man with a knowledge of military affairs equal to General Marshall."

On October 16, 1959, General of the Army George C. Marshall passed away at Walter Reed Hospital in Virginia. His burial at Arlington National Cemetery justly surrounds him with many of the soldiers he honorably led throughout his remarkable life.

You are responsible for yourself; focus on the big picture, while understanding what resources are available and what can be done; live so that others might prosper and you will lead a full life.

CHAPTER 11

GENERAL DAVID H. PETRAEUS
RENAISSANCE MAN

In a case of happenstance that appears significant only in hindsight, David H. Petraeus grew up near the United States Military Academy (USMA) at West Point—so close, in fact, that he would sneak onto the campus to play during the summer. Yet his family had no military tradition—his father was a Dutch seaman who immigrated to America at the beginning of World War II. Petraeus attended West Point mostly because in 1970, it was one of the few universities interested in recruiting a soccer player like him for a full scholarship. Even at the time he accepted the appointment, he did so fully aware that he could transfer prior to his junior year with no military obligation.

But it was during his second year at the USMA that he recognized how well the Army fit with his high standards for personal achievement, and his competitive nature. At one point he contemplated competing for one of eight slots in medical school offered to the USMA graduates every year, not out of any interest in medicine but simply because it was an honor offered to the best.

Petraeus' leadership characteristics had started to emerge long before the USMA or the Army, though. The son of an Army officer who lived nearby and knew him as a boy described him as "the 'alpha dog,' the kid who led the pack of neighborhood boys." Those same characteristics had prompted the community of retired military personnel living near the Academy to shepherd a teenage Petraeus toward attendance there.

It was a wise move. Shortly before the 2003 invasion of Iraq, retired General Barry R. McCaffrey described Petraeus—then commanding the 101st Airborne Division, one of the lead units in the invasion—as "probably the most talented person I have ever met in the Army." This was high praise indeed coming from the man who had himself led the 24th Infantry Division in General Norman Schwarzkopf's famed "left hook" offensive against the Iraqi Army during Operation Desert Storm, and later headed the Office of National Drug Control Policy. And indeed, on the path from newly commissioned lieutenant of infantry to major general commanding one of the Army's most storied divisions, Petraeus had proved himself over and over again.

Yet to deem Petraeus a "born leader" would be a mistake, or at the very least would miss the larger picture. One issue he faced was the fact that many of his accomplishments had been achieved while assigned to staff positions rather than command of combat units. While other notable Army officers, including no less a personage than General Colin Powell, had experienced similar career paths, it was a potential handicap when leading combat troops.

By March 2003, when formations of the U.S. Army and Marine Corps waited on the Kuwait-Iraq border for orders to advance, the United States had already been at war for a year and a half. Moreover, conflicts in Somalia, Bosnia-Herzegovina, and the first Persian Gulf War had made many senior soldiers combat veterans, wearing a coveted "combat patch" (known more formally as the Shoulder Sleeve Insignia-Former Wartime Service) on their right shoulders. (The insignia of a soldier's current unit of service is worn on the left.) Some had also earned the Combat Infantryman Badge, awarded to infantry and special operations soldiers for participation in combat against enemy forces.

At that time, David Petraeus had neither. The timing of various postings along his career path had kept him from combat deployments, and author and journalist Rick Atkinson, who was embedded with the division headquarters of the 101st during the Iraq invasion, "suspected that he was keen to earn the credential of the blooded vet."

Petraeus had first come to the 101st Airborne in September 1991 as a lieutenant colonel and battalion commander, just months after the unit had returned from Desert Storm. Though he had literally been planning for the day he would take command of a unit for sixteen years, saving up ideas and notes in a folder labeled "First Day of Command," in many respects he was not a natural at the job.

His language was more akin to the "Boy Scouts," as David Cloud and Greg Jaffe describe it in *The Fourth Star*, than to the rough and profane lingo of the infantry. He had earned a Ph.D., which to the "grunts" he commanded was automatically suspect. While his haircut was well within Army grooming standards, the infantry soldiers of his battalion wore "high and tight" haircuts (shaved all the way up the sides and back of the head) as a point of pride to set themselves apart from other soldiers. When Petraeus' officers mentioned that soldiers had commented on their commander's lack of a high and tight, he responded that he had never worn his hair that way because his wife didn't care for it so short. Yet realizing that this was a crucial part of his command image, not only did he arrive the next day wearing a high and tight, he went a step further and mandated it for his soldiers.

Despite such moments of awkwardness resulting from his personality, however, Petraeus had from the beginning taken steps to build the *esprit de corps* of his men. Creating a special physical fitness test for his unit that went far beyond the Army standards, he announced that all soldiers who could pass it would bear the title "Iron Rakkasans" (the term "Rakkasan" for members of the 187th Parachute Infantry Regiment dated to World War II, when it was bestowed by Japanese soldiers whom the unit fought) and have their names engraved on a plaque displayed at the battalion headquarters. Other steps were less popular; he also required his soldiers to button the top button on their battle dress utilities. The men complained that this made them look "stupid," but that was exactly Petraeus' intention—it served to unify them. As Cloud and Jaffe further relate in *The Fourth Star*, Petraeus explained that "it made others joke about us, which pulled us together."

The Impact of Individuals

The movement of the 101st Airborne Division from its home station at Fort Campbell, Kentucky, to Kuwait in early 2003 was a massive logistical challenge—one that entailed, as Atkinson describes it, moving "5,000 vehicles, 1,500 shipping containers, 17,000 soldiers, and a couple hundred helicopters" halfway around the world in just over a month. Overcoming that challenge repeatedly demanded direct action by key individuals, the sort of action that when applied at precisely the right time and place magnifies the impact of one person.

The first step in the movement was from Fort Campbell to the port at Jacksonville, Florida, where the division's equipment would be loaded onto five ships. Accomplishing this would take 1,400 rail cars, which rail company CSX had promised would come as four 34-car trains per day, but as the deployment started, on average only three trains a day were arriving. Petraeus personally called the president of CSX—at 11:00 one night—to explain that, as Petraeus later told Atkinson, "he was contributing to the diminished combat effectiveness of my division." The 101st got its rail cars.

When unionized stevedores at the Jacksonville port slowed the embarkation process with mandatory two-hour lunch breaks and a leisurely work pace, the division fired them, and its own soldiers in combination with the non-union supervisors loaded the ships. Brigadier General Edward Sinclair, the assistant division commander of support for the 101st, was "personally guid[ing] vehicles into the hold at 3 a.m."

It took the intervention of key leaders to overcome bureaucratic nonsense as well. Logistics personnel at Fort Campbell had been unwilling to release 40,000 desert camouflage uniforms to the division, but a call from Petraeus to the vice chief of staff (the second-highest-ranking officer in the Army) had broken that logjam. In Jacksonville the division hit another wall of red tape, the delay in the deployment order from the Pentagon meant there was no legal authorization to pay for transporting the division to Kuwait. Petraeus cut through this obstacle by devising a "training exercise" that "just happened" to require moving 112 of the division's helicopters to Jacksonville.

Petraeus would later bring the same kind of personal impact to the U.S. counterinsurgency operations in Iraq and Afghanistan, generating very visible results. After taking command in Iraq, for example, he created the Force Security Engagement Cell (FSEC) to pursue reconciliation with those elements of the insurgency who were willing to renounce violence and could be brought into the political process. His choice for commander of the FSEC was British General Graeme Lamb, selected not for political reasons but because he was the best man for the job—as Petraeus put it, the British had long experience dealing with reconcilable insurgents from their operations in Northern Ireland.

It was the efforts of the FSEC that led to the "Sunni Awakening," the alignment of Sunni tribal sheikhs against Al Qaeda in Iraq (AQI) and the employment of their tribal members in the "Sons of Iraq" militias that took the lead in expelling AQI from Sunni-dominated provinces such as Anbar. Along with the U.S. troop surge and the use of new counterinsurgency tactics under General Petraeus, the Sunni Awakening was a key factor in the turning tide in Iraq beginning in 2007.

The Importance of Discipline

People who achieve critical results tend to stand out from the pack. Although ability is certainly important, one of the most important factors is discipline. The ability to persist at a difficult task, to learn a complex skill, or to adhere to a previously devised plan even in the face of adversity can easily outweigh greater talent in a less-disciplined individual.

Although Petraeus' abilities have never been doubted, his discipline is unquestionable as well. Attending the U.S. Army's Ranger School—generally considered the Army's most physically and mentally challenging course—as a lieutenant, he garnered all three of the prizes awarded to the top students in each class. Even as a senior officer in his forties and fifties he could outrun most of his young subordinates, and shortly before the 2003 Iraq invasion ran the Army Ten-Miler road race in less than 64 minutes. But it is an event from Petraeus' tenure as a battalion commander in the 187th Parachute Infantry Regiment of the 101st Airborne that perhaps speaks most to his level of personal discipline.

While observing a live-fire exercise being conducted by a unit from his battalion, he was shot in the chest by a negligent discharge from one of the soldier's weapons. He was taken by MEDEVAC (medical evacuation) helicopter to the base hospital to be stabilized, then on to Vanderbilt University Medical Center, where his surgeon was Dr. Bill Frist—who would later be the U.S. Senate majority leader. After a five-hour surgery, Frist told Petraeus' wife that her husband's recovery would require ten weeks.

Petraeus was having none of it. Within days he was insisting on a transfer back to the Fort Campbell post hospital, which he received, and once there it was not long before he began agitating to be sent home, concerned about missing his battalion's upcoming field exercise. To convince his doctor, he had him remove his IV tubes, got out of bed, and pumped out fifty push-ups on the floor of his hospital room. He was discharged a few days later, albeit subject to a promise that he would not over-exert himself. Petraeus' interpretation of "no overexertion" was to head to the gym, where he rode an exercise bike, jogged, and eventually began running 440-meter sprints until he caused his injured lung to bleed.

Mission Focus

In February 2007, Petraeus arrived in Baghdad to take command of U.S. forces in Iraq from General George Casey. The "surge" of 20,000 additional troops had recently been approved by President George W. Bush, and Petraeus planned to use those troops in a very different manner from what had been done before. The existing strategy had been to patrol from the massive forward operating bases (FOBs), but doing so both isolated U.S. troops from the populace and as a practical matter limited their influence to little more than what they could see as they patrolled.

The new strategy—described in the revamped counterinsurgency field manual that Petraeus had recently helped author—would send American soldiers to live and work in small combat outposts scattered around the cities. While this would mean more austere living conditions and more exposure to hostile action, it was in Petraeus' opinion what was needed to achieve results. He was not afraid to make an unpopular decision and take on additional risk in order to do so, nor to break with the conventional wisdom of existing tactics.

In his command philosophy, Petraeus often departed from a focus on what were traditionally considered "military" issues. His daily command briefings covered subjects like Iraqi electricity output (something dear to the hearts of the populace, who had to contend with frequent outages), water purification, infrastructure repair and reconstruction, Iraqi politics, and economic development. He recognized the need to address the issues that would truly affect normalization in Iraq and achieve a reduction in violence, since the U.S. military did not possess the troop strength to achieve these ends through force alone.

Petraeus also made a point during his tour as commander of U.S. forces in Iraq to talk to the men and women at the "tip of the spear," the ones who were patrolling and dealing with the Iraqi people and local leaders on a daily basis. He traveled out to frontline units at least twice a week, where he made a point to "kick out their bosses, close the door, and ask the young officers what they thought was really happening in their sector. What had they learned? What mistakes had they made? What did they need to win?" He understood that in any organization, more information should flow up than flows down, that the people with the expertise and the most valuable knowledge are the ones who are hands-on.

The focus was not on appearances and process for the sake of process; it was on effective and efficient processes. When Petraeus took over as commander of the International Security Assistance Force (ISAF) in Afghanistan, there were those who were concerned that the "soft power" approach he had used in Iraq, with its focus on improving civil conditions, might be less effective there. Yet his emphasis in Afghanistan—an environment fundamentally different in many ways from Iraq—was on building precision-killing assets. He integrated "intelligence, U.S. law enforcement, and special operations hunter-killer teams" to kill insurgents while minimizing the risk of collateral damage among the civilian populace.

Ironically enough, this tour in Afghanistan was technically a demotion for Petraeus. Although he had long held the rank of full (four-star) general and continued to do so, after departing his command in Iraq he had taken the position of Central Command (CENTCOM) commander, the immediate superior of both the Multi-National Forces-Iraq (MNF-I) and ISAF commanders. Obviously, taking the position following the departure of General Stanley McChrystal was never a question of position or ego for Petraeus—it was a question of what the organization and the mission needed.

Organizational Transformation

David Petraeus came of age in an Army that was suffering in the throes of its post-Vietnam crisis. Morale, discipline, drug use—the young officers taking their first leadership roles in the early and mid-1970s faced challenges far beyond simply facing an enemy in the Asian jungles or across the North German Plain. But he—along with other leaders like General John Abizaid—had the vision to recognize that the Army must transform to deal with a changing world.

After Vietnam, the Army had focused on its main Cold War mission: turning back a Soviet invasion of Western Europe. But as the Berlin Wall fell and the Warsaw Pact and then the Soviet Union itself collapsed, that particular mission, which for so long had focused the educating, training, and equipping of the U.S. Army, faded away. It was happy coincidence that Saddam Hussein timed his invasion of Kuwait in 1990 to offer a massive conventional battle of just the sort that the American military had long prepared to fight.

After Desert Shield/Desert Storm, conventional threats gave way to a very different operational landscape. The demands of Bosnia-Herzegovina, Haiti (where Petraeus spent three months in 1995 assisting the UN military mission and developing concepts of civil-military operations), the Kurdish regions of northern Iraq, and Somalia presented challenges that were outside the scope of most military thinking. (The U.S. military was not even certain what to call operations of this type, through the 1990s starting with "peace operations" and later moving to the inelegant "military operations other than war," or MOOTW in the inevitable acronym.)

Operations in Iraq and Afghanistan forced—quite painfully—a focus on counterinsurgency tactics and the skill sets needed to reconstruct a war-torn country. The ongoing tension has been between the need to have an Army capable of large-scale conventional operations as well as these low-tech, long-duration missions, which require substantially different mindsets, skills, and equipment. David Petraeus stepped up to become one of the men leading this transformation, recognizing that any organization must adapt to the realities it faces to remain relevant and effective.

In 2008, he chaired a promotion board responsible for selecting the next crop of new, one-star generals. Included in the list of forty freshly minted brigadiers were Sean MacFarland, who had been one of the American commanders who built alliances with Sunni sheikhs in Iraq, and H. R. McMaster, who had been outspoken and controversial in advocating for new tactics to defeat Iraqi insurgents. In this Petraeus demonstrated his dedication to choosing rising leaders based on proven ability, independent and critical thinking, and a willingness to speak out in support of unconventional ideas.

Retiring on August 31, 2011, after 37 years of Army service, Petraeus voiced a reminder to all those listening. "We have re-learned since 9/11 the timeless lesson that we don't always get to fight the wars for which we're most prepared or most inclined," he noted, adding a warning that the United States must "maintain the full-spectrum capability" developed—sometimes with difficulty—over the past ten years. As the changes he experienced in the U.S. Army over nearly four decades demonstrate, organizations must have the flexibility to adapt to the unexpected—sometimes with little notice—and leaders must be willing to articulate a vision for change, provide the resources to enable it, and motivate those they lead to participate.

Openness to Ideas

The U.S. Army is many things, but on one level it is a massive bureaucracy. It also remains, unlike much of the civilian sector and the modern business world, rigidly hierarchical. It is not, in short, an environment that is automatically conducive to radically different thinking, new ideas, or change.

Petraeus was willing to look to any source of ideas or information, judging that source on its merits rather than any preconceived notions. As a young lieutenant serving with the 173rd Infantry Brigade (Airborne) in Vicenza, Italy, in the mid-1970s, he had learned about legendary French paratrooper and officer Marcel Bigeard during a training exercise with a French army unit. Bigeard had fought in the French counterinsurgencies in both Indochina and Algeria, had developed the tactics employed in the latter conflict, and had begun the process of rebuilding the French Army after the disastrous outcome of the war in Indochina.

The selection of a French officer as a role model struck many of the soldiers around Petraeus as odd, however, and it was yet another obstacle he had to overcome once assigned as a battalion commander in the 101st Airborne. He kept an autographed picture of Bigeard—a gift from his father-in-law—on the wall in his office, but few of his peers or subordinates had any idea who the man in the photo was.

Nevertheless, Petraeus was not dissuaded. He accepted valuable ideas and concepts from wherever he found them, and even as a general rewriting the Army's counterinsurgency manual he would still refer to Bigeard and the French general's tactics as they applied to the conflicts facing the U.S. military.

Throughout his career—which has now taken him to the directorship of the Central Intelligence Agency—General David Petraeus repeatedly showed that disciplined, capable, thoughtful individuals in key roles and with the insight to act at places and times of particular criticality can influence the path of an organization—even an organization as large as a 17,000-man infantry division or the United States Army. His success points to the importance of focus on the true mission rather than superficialities, of motivating the organization's members to perform and excel, of setting high standards, and of being willing to move beyond conventional wisdom or comfortable thinking.

He had advanced and championed ideas about the nature of the Army's mission and the employment of military power that were initially considered quite unorthodox, doing so well before they gained widespread acceptance and an air of respectability. By the time Robert Gates had taken the reins as Secretary of Defense, he was reinforcing the very notions that Petraeus had long embraced. "The U.S. military's ability to kick down the door must be matched by our ability to clean up the mess and even rebuild the house afterward," Gates asserted in a speech.

General Petraeus married a high level of energy, discipline, and dedication to ample intelligence and talent to achieve results. Yet his energy, discipline, and dedication quite likely played at least as large a role in his success as his native ability—and those are assets accessible to everyone; an individual need only be willing to act.

Never settle for mediocrity; discipline prepares for excellence; flexibility and creativity are seeds of success.

PART 3

THE POWER OF A TEAM

CHAPTER 12

AMERICA'S TEAM

We tend to see life and the world from a single perspective, "my" perspective — me in relation to everything else. We perceive history as a grand epic shaped by the actions of extraordinary men and women. We stand in awe of visionary, dynamic and disciplined leaders and applaud their stupendous accomplishments. America's Army offers countless examples of such leaders, of self-sacrifice, heroics, and singular achievement. As we ourselves are individuals we tend to believe success is the result of individual labor, solitary action. While it is true that individuals give life to and nurture creative ideas, and individuals first aspire and then inspire, the measure of a person's greatness is that man's or that woman's impact on other people, on mankind. Every life is a singular journey, but each life draws from, gives to, and holds meaning in relation to every other. The insight of a unique perspective, the genius of a creative idea, and the enthusiasm of an inspiring leader all pale in comparison to the power of a team.

Soldiering is a team sport. Soldiers fight, strive, sacrifice and endure as members of a team. They suffer hardship, overcome adversity, and engage enemies in a coordinated and synchronized fashion — not always well, not always triumphantly, but always together. American soldiers are warriors that represent the tip of the spear — an American spear. The Army, through the actions of its soldiers may win battles, but ultimately it is the commitment of a nation of similarly committed people that wins the war. In a democracy (like that of the United States), however much citizens would like to, they can never divorce themselves from the front. Even if they dismiss the deployment of troops and the carnage of combat, citizens still share responsibility for America's Army. All Americans are part of America's Army team.

America has long been portrayed as the land of the rugged individualist. Americans, if truth be told, enjoy the moniker as it conveys a sense of strength and self-direction, independence and ability. But while Americans might revel in the romantic notion of living as rugged individuals, the reality is far different. America's success has been the product of diverse, energetic, progressive teams — individuals coming together for collective purposes, to advance mutually beneficial ends.

While it takes tough, optimistic, focused individuals to achieve progress, improvements themselves are not the consequence of isolated actions. Every single act generates a stream of effects that influence the lives of countless other people. How well people collaborate and synchronize activities to press toward a worthwhile goal makes all the difference. This is the dynamic of teamwork the Army strives to foster: tough, optimistic, focused individuals applying energy and intellect collectively to achieve meaningful results.

Advancement, growth, and development are the product of cooperatives, groups, societies. An idea or impetus for change originates with an individual, and may be fostered by an individual, but the impact of that idea, the energy of that creation is a social product. Individual actions influence, energize and generate communal effects. These effects are felt by the community and are embraced by the community.

The power of individuals flows through and animates groups. Human beings are social creatures. Life is a shared adventure. Men and women laugh and cry, struggle and triumph, live and die, together. Bringing people together and focusing them on a common purpose generates power — power that can be used to create or to destroy. Men and women working together are the power of America's Army. Similarly, cooperation and collaboration are the greatness of American business, American industry, the entire nation.

The founding fathers were rightfully suspicious of a large standing army. An army represents power, and the allure of power is a force too great for most mere mortals to resist. Maintaining a large standing army within the infant republic would have been both expensive for and threatening to the very people who sustained it. The American experiment was meant to be a trial of self-government. Responsibility and authority were to be, and had to be, relatively distributed so that all citizens had a stake in the system and all citizens maintained access to opportunity. Of course, this is an ideal depiction, as in the early years of the republic a number of groups were disenfranchised by design. The magic about aspiring to ideals, however, is that if the ideals are kept alive and nurtured, eventually people recognize the wisdom inherent in those ideals and muster the courage to move toward them. In America this proved to be a noble, albeit troubling and painful process.

After having violently resolved its gravest liability, namely the hypocrisy of slavery in a nation dedicated to liberty, the twentieth century proved to be the era of America's coming of age. America transformed out of tragic necessity and in response to unprecedented opportunity. America's Army likewise transformed.

In the Great War, the Great Depression, World War II and the Cold War, America faced monumental threats. The challenges these threats presented (wars, economic calamity, struggles for supremacy on a global scale) required that the United States muster and focus the power of her people like never before. America's Army was the instrument of that power. The Army was the manifestation of the ultimate team. Americans united to defeat aggression, beat back tyranny, and overcome threats to liberty. The Army was a primary tool (one of few) used to reshape the world.

People united generate extraordinary power and are capable of astounding accomplishments. Working together, people can produce immense, complex, and glorious creations. The potential power of a team, small or large, is awesome. Men and women relying on one another are able to effectively mitigate individual weaknesses, leverage talents and strengths, and sustain motivation and focus. America's Army deliberately seeks and intends to be such a dynamic team. America's Army, rightly used, rightly disciplined, rightly led, is a powerful force for good. No man is an island unto himself. No man exists, endures, or flourishes alone. America's Army leverages the power of teams so that society might flourish, so that humanity might advance, so that liberty might endure.

Business and life are team sports.

Break Down Individuals, Build Up Teams

To most civilians the idea of joining the Army is daunting. The obvious and immediate consequences of enlisting are a change of venue and adjustments to lifestyle. Enlisting means going to new places, meeting new people, and taking on new challenges — likely pushing beyond one's comfort zone. A primary objection to joining the Army is the requirement to forfeit individual freedoms and forego personal pleasures. Soldiers do surrender a degree of freedom. They give up autonomy to pursue a different kind of opportunity — to become effective members of a team. To build a winning team requires that individuals curb their ego gratification needs and instead focus on the good of the group and the mission at hand. While there are valid, legitimate, and justifiable reasons for not joining the Army, most people rationalize what comes down to excuses so as to avoid having to subject themselves to discipline, discomfort, and ultimately, risk.

Opportunity costs abound for any choice in life; joining the Army is no exception. Soldiers give up, for a time, other career options, certain styles of dress, and unconstrained modes of behavior, and submit to the needs and requirements the Army prescribes. I started with the Army in 1980. Those old enough will remember that long hair was a big deal back in the ‹70s, and still nursing the wounds of the Vietnam era, uniforms on campus were not exactly popular. The hairstyle trend was only just starting to move back to closely cropped hair in the mid ‹80s. I felt self-conscious showing up to college with very little hair, and I was anxious about standing out (and not in a good way) when I wore the uniform. But I matured and I adjusted. Hair styles eventually moved back in the Army's direction and Americans let go of the pain of the past.

People come up with hundreds of reasons not to join the Army. They usually point to the opportunity costs (education, career, financial, and so on) and other tradeoffs as explanations. They fear the discipline, they regret the notion of conforming, and they want to be in control — flexible, carefree and autonomous individuals. The little-known, oft-rejected secret, however, is that success in life requires the very same skills and experiences the Army has institutionalized: discipline, teamwork, enduring hardship, and taking risk.

Success requires discipline, tenacity and the willingness to take risks.

Eventually, every thriving individual discovers that to succeed requires suppressing ego needs, being attentive to the needs of others, and trading off a multitude of opportunities to focus intellect, talent and energy on select worthwhile objectives — objectives with social impact. Success in most endeavors requires a polished appearance, personal discipline, and the need to conform and comply with the demands of social life and contemporary business. These are not just the demands of military life.

To succeed in business and in life, ambitious people must learn and apply, in their personal and professional lives, the skills and lessons many shy away from when considering the Army. Serving in the Army is different; make no mistake about it. The prospect of being a soldier can be unsettling. Army life is both a challenge and an ongoing chore for those with little self-control, who lack ambition, who are unwilling to stretch beyond their comfort zone and who are reluctant to face fear, but life in general is unsettling for those people. The teamwork required in the Army, and the discipline, the dedication, and the commitment are the skills all people must acquire if they are to succeed in life. America's Army is a calling for people who want to take on a challenge, are willing to discipline themselves, and are capable of facing fear to grow, adapt, and learn.

To function as a member of a team a soldier has to be willing to forfeit individual privileges and individual liberties. Every member of an effective Army unit is assigned tasks to accomplish and has roles to fulfill. Only by working together diligently do individuals succeed as a team. The environment soldiers must operate in and the adversities soldiers must face demand the Army deliberately build strong, cohesive teams. Men and women from diverse backgrounds, people of difference races and religions, and hailing from varied geographic regions, let go of their past identities and attachments. They do this not to conform mindlessly, but to consciously and deliberately become part of a powerful team. Regardless of former differences soldiers strive shoulder to shoulder, they suffer and they endure together. The gravity of soldiers at war was once summed up by Alexander the Great, "Upon the conduct of each the fate of all depends." Teams work best when soldiers, after enduring hardships and meeting challenges together, come to believe supremely in each other. Upon forging this ultimate bond of trust the team is made — their unity is unbreakable; a potent force is born.

Trust is the ultimate bond.

The Army actively works, from the first day initiating new recruits, on breaking down self-centered identities and in place of those identities building up teams. I experienced this in basic training, during my officer training, in operational units, and at all levels of commands repeatedly over the course of my career. Success or failure in big things and in small, in war and in peace, depends on the capacity of the team.

Soldiers deserve the most knowledgeable, the most competent and confident, and the most noble and selfless leaders possible. The Army seeks to select and groom the best men and women to fulfill this duty. Leaders are not appointed for self-aggrandizement, but rather always for the exclusive purpose, privilege, and challenge of building and leading effective, powerful teams. Individuals are the spark that fires the engine and that guides the undertaking, but it is the collective strength of the team that generates the power to make winning possible. Great leaders deserve credit for their vision, their passion, their discipline, and their drive, but they only succeed because they are perched upon the shoulders of giants: men and women who form the team, who bear the burden, who face the foes, who get the job done.

America's Army today is an all-volunteer force. While this makes for knowledgeable, professional teams, it presents some inherent risks. America's Army has an ever-declining proportion of Americans serving. The Army is and should represent America. Currently (since 1973), U.S. Army soldiers are a self-selecting group. A consequence of this circumstance is that American soldiers are less likely to reflect the diversity, the values, and the culture of society at large. Three risks are most evident and worrisome in maintaining an all-volunteer force:

1. The military increasingly becomes isolated and detached from Americans. No longer do the majority of men and women who most enjoy the fruits of liberty contribute to preserving that liberty. Only certain types of people, those predisposed to the values and discipline of service, even consider joining the military. Looking at enlistment statistics, one could argue military service has become a family business. While the Guard and Reserve continue to remain integrated with society, the chasm between the professional military and citizenry grows larger. An all-volunteer military risks establishing and maintaining a warrior class. Expressed here are the sentiments of three very different men. Keep these in mind when considering the virtue America risks losing:

    Our honor lies in doing our duty toward our people and our homeland, as well as in the consciousness of our mutual obligation to keep faith with one another, so we can depend on each other. --Hasso Von Manteuffel

    The right is more precious than peace, and we shall fight for the things which we have always carried nearest our hearts. --Woodrow Wilson

    Do your duty in all things. You cannot do more, you should never wish to do less. --Robert E. Lee

2. The expense. A professional military is expensive. The Services attempt to retain experience and expertise, which increases the count of senior people and the cost. At the same time, the populace, loath to endure hardship, shells out ever larger sums of money to pay others to take the risks and make the sacrifice. This becomes an easy, but no less costly

trade-off, when government money is borrowed or manu-
factured by a printing press.

3. Political convenience. A professional military, detached
    from the population, represents a convenient tool for mili-
    tary adventurism. Politicians of all persuasions seek to wield
    and exercise power. Since only a very small minority of the
    population, a self-selected group of professionals, stand
    to bear the burden, the military becomes the tool of first
    choice to advance nearly every special interest.

America's Army is and must remain a powerful team dedicated to doing what is right — not what is convenient, not what is
expedient, not what earns vote. America's Army is of the people,
by the people, for the people. All Americans are called to contribute to its legacy. Theodore Roosevelt spoke these words to
acclaim the valiant individual; I have modified them to speak of
a soldier team:

> *The credit belongs to the men and women who are actu-
> ally in the arena; whose faces are marred by dust and
> sweat and blood; who strive valiantly; who err and come
> up short again and again; who know the great enthu-
> siasms, the great devotions, and spend themselves in a
> worthy cause; who at the best know in the end the tri-
> umph of high achievement; and who at the worst, if they
> should fail, at least fail while daring greatly.*

We succeed or fail together - all of us.

Focused Power

Dwight D. Eisenhower, Supreme Allied Commander of forces in
Europe for the D-Day invasion and later president of the United
States, examined his own conscience, and looked out over a land
flush with opportunity. Recognizing the responsibility inherent
in prosperity he implored all Americans:

> *May we pursue right - without self-righteousness. May
> we know unity - without conformity. May we grow in*

strength - without pride of self. May we, in our dealings with all people of the earth, ever speak the truth and serve justice. May the light of freedom, coming to all darkened lands, flame brightly - until at last the darkness is no more.

The United States Army has participated in a dozen major wars and countless expeditions and operations of all types (exploration, peacekeeping, humanitarian, law enforcement, counter-terrorist, etcetera) around the globe since its founding in 1775. Essentially, though not evenly distributed, America fights a significant war each generation. Millions of men and women have served — have answered the call to the colors, have worn the uniform. The United States has sustained nearly 1.4 million dead and over 1.5 million wounded as a result of these conflicts. America's service men and women have borne a heavy burden. The scars of war, physical and psychological, endure for the combatants' lifetimes and weigh on society for generations.

We repeatedly sacrifice our youth and our innocence for an idea. We focus the energy of the Army and the lives of young men and women on accomplishing a task. We hope and pray that the idea that drives that commitment to a task measures up to the standard of an ideal — a value worth fighting for, a principle worth killing for, an objective worth dying for.

If you ever get the chance, I would ask that you visit and tour a military cemetery, memorial or battlefield monument. They are located all over the United States and in a number of places around the world. The American Battle Monuments Commission manages 24 overseas military cemeteries and 25 memorials, monuments, and markers, commemorating the service, achievements, and sacrifices of members of U.S. armed forces for actions in World War I and World War II. The Normandy American Cemetery, overlooking the broad expanse designated as Omaha Beach for the D-Day landings in France in June 1944, serves as the final resting place for 9,387 U.S. service men and women.

The carefully aligned white crosses, the green grass, and the sparkling water offer a poignant reminder of what those brave men and women were seeking, were striving for, were fighting for. They fought to make men free, so that peace might take root and prosperity flourish. A 22-foot bronze statue known as «The

Spirit of American Youth Rising from the Waves» ascends as a tribute to the souls lost. On the colonnade is chiseled: «This embattled shore, portal of freedom, is forever hallowed by the ideals, the valor, and the sacrifices of our fellow countrymen.» Near the center of the cemetery stands a small chapel — a place for reflection and prayer. Two inscriptions adorning the chapel walls read:

> *I give unto them eternal life and they shall never perish.*

> *Think not only of their passing, remember the glory of their spirit.*

Men and women, moved by values, join together in a common cause. The teams they represent are fearsome and formidable. The values they hold in their hearts are the beacons guiding the focus of their minds as they apply the strength of their muscles toward a worthy cause. The men and women, the politicians, the elected and appointed leaders who direct these forces, these teams of young, brave Americans, must not squander such a treasure as this. The purity of heart, the nobility of youth is an asset America should seek to preserve and sustain, for it rests with optimists and idealists to act for the greater good — for the benefit of mankind. Douglas MacArthur, oft quoted for his claim that «old soldiers never die, they just fade away,» points out the enthusiasm and idealism of youth, though tempered by experience, need not fade:

> *Youth is not entirely a time of life; it is a state of mind. Nobody grows old by merely living a number of years. People grow old by deserting their ideals. You are as young as your faith, as old as your doubt; as young as your self-confidence, as old as your fear; as young as your hope, as old as your despair.*

Youth need not fade; every day presents an opportunity for a new adventure.

America, though of late considered waning, still possesses potential, still commands the intensity of youth and the audacity to believe in a better future. It is time America takes a lesson from its Army and returns to its roots. For America to succeed and prosper once again it must be values based, focused on worthwhile objectives, and willing to act. Trying to succeed without these virtues, without self-discipline, commitment, and sacrifice is a fool's errand. A team is a powerful force. Coming together as a team and working for the greater good honors the sacrifice of millions who have come before, and is the only hope of realizing a better future.

When people are fed and dry and warm they seek first comfort, and then security. The security of America is only ensured because men and women stand strong, ready to risk everything — to give everything. Helen Keller, a woman who lived her life shut off from the brilliance of light and the melody of sound, a woman who had every reason to fear, expressed it most eloquently:

Security is mostly a superstition. It does not exist in nature, nor do the children of men as a whole experience it. Avoiding danger is no safer in the long run than outright exposure. Life is either a daring adventure or nothing.

Life is not secure; you might as well take your team to higher heights.

The remainder of this section of *Why America's Army Succeeds* is devoted to diverse examples of men and women who fought together, were tested, were pushed to the point of exhaustion and despair, but who endured and succeeded — Army units in action around the globe.

A team is a powerful thing. The actions of one man or woman can make a difference. The actions of many men and women can change the world. Every person possesses power. Every person controls energy and exhibits strength. Focusing that power, that energy, that strength forges a formidable team. America's Army is an example of one such awesome team.

Success is the outcome of action, which is the product of

focus driven by timeless, enduring, but elusive ideals. General George Patton pointed to this path when he said, «The secret of victory lies not wholly in knowledge. It lurks in that vitalizing spark, intangible yet evident as lightning.» That vitalizing spark focuses power and ensures victory for America's team.

A cohesive team represents decisive power.

CHAPTER 13

THE BATTLE AT COWPENS (1781)
WHEN ARROGANCE AND AUDACITY MEET

January 1781

The young American nation slipped into the fifth winter since the start of its war for independence. It was a tired nation, a confused nation, and some questioned if it had a right to call itself a nation at all. While the patriotic fervor still burned hot in each state, there was no effective central government that could marshal the resources to fight a coordinated battle against the enemy.

In 1780 George Washington lamented, "We have lived upon expedients till we can live no longer. The history of this war is a history of temporary devices instead of a system." General Nathanael Greene echoed Washington's sentiments while serving as the Quartermaster General. "The Congress have lost their influence. I have for a long time seen the necessity of some new plan of civil constitution. Unless there is some control over the States by the Congress, we shall soon be like a broken band."

As splintered as the war effort was on the part of the Americans, both parties found themselves in a stalemate in which neither had the men nor the resources to fight a decisive campaign. Unable to pin down Washington's main army in the North, the British decided in 1778 to change strategy and focus on the Southern states, where there were a significant number of Loyalists among the population.

A Change in Fortunes

Debarking from Philadelphia, the British commander General Henry Clinton sailed his army down the coast and took Savannah and Augusta, Georgia, in rapid succession. In May 1780 he attempted a second, and this time successful, siege of Charleston where 5,000 American troops surrendered. The surrender was the largest ever of American forces, and devastated the American military in the South.

Eighteen days after the fall of Charleston a small force of Americans consisting of raw recruits and militia, were attacked in an area of South Carolina known as Waxhaws, by elite British dragoons under the command of Banastre Tarleton. Overwhelmed, the Continentals threw down their weapons in an attempt to surrender. The dragoons, however, ignored the surrender and hacked and slashed the Continentals where they stood or lay. When the battle was over, the Americans suffered 117 dead and 147 wounded, and the term "Tarleton's quarter" became infamous.

The first two years of the occupation of the South saw significant gains for the British; however, their practice of indiscriminate hangings and shootings of any man, woman or child suspected of being disloyal to the King hardened the resolve of the population, including many Loyalists who otherwise might have supported the British, or at least would have remained neutral in the conflict.

But all the good fortune the King's army enjoyed was about to be reversed on a little patch of pastureland in the Thicketty Mountains of western South Carolina.

The Lead-up

In 1780 General Nathanael Greene was assigned as commander of the Southern Department, a badly bruised force of about 2,000 men camped in Charlotte. Green convinced the "Hero of Saratoga," Daniel Morgan, to come out of retirement to assist him in the maneuvering of the brigade.

It was after Morgan's arrival that Greene made a controversial decision. Faced with a far superior enemy force, Greene split his own army in two, an act that defied military convention of the time. Greene took most of the lame, sick and wounded and headed to Cheraw, South Carolina, to rest his men and find new recruits.

This left Morgan with a command of roughly 600 men, most of whom were professional, battle-experienced Continentals from Maryland and Delaware. Also included in his force was a detachment of the 1st Continental Light Dragoons commanded by George Washington's cousin William Washington, and roughly 200 veteran Virginia rifle militiamen. His orders were to proceed west to patrol the area between the Broad and Pacolet rivers and to engage the British, should they attempt to move into North Carolina.

By this time Lord Cornwallis had taken command of the British forces in the South and he did indeed plan to move north. When he learned of Morgan's brigade he dispatched Banastre Tarleton and his British Legion, the same group of dragoons that butchered the Continentals at Waxhaws, to track down Morgan and destroy him.

When these two forces met, it was to be a battle between a uniquely American mix of professionals and volunteers against the deadliest unit that the British could place in the field. More than that, it was to be a test of two leaders: Morgan and Tarleton, who had distinctly different backgrounds and styles.

Daniel Morgan

Little is known of Morgan's early life. He was born of immigrant parents either in Pennsylvania or New Jersey. By the time he was seventeen he had found his way to Virginia, where he worked as a laborer and had an affinity for drinking and brawling.

While he was uneducated and frequently in trouble with the local law, Morgan was also a model of industry, eventually saving enough money to purchase his own horse and wagon. It was as a freight hauler that he found himself heading north with the British army during the French and Indian War, and it was as a scout and messenger working for the British that he was shot in the neck, leaving a distinctive scar on the left side of his face.

Morgan's roughneck, backwoods behavior stayed with him while in service with the British army. Once, when he was insulted by a British officer, Morgan promptly responded with a powerful punch to the belly. The penalty for this act of insubordination was 500 lashes to his back. While this lashing often killed the unfortunate victim, Morgan survived — but his back was a mass of scar tissue and he developed a slight limp.

After recovering from his lashing Morgan returned to Virginia where he met and eventually married Abigail Curry. Abigail taught Morgan how to read and write. Morgan also became active in the local militia. When independence was declared he headed north to join Washington as a captain of the militia. Over the next two years, Morgan distinguished himself both for his leadership and for personal bravery, most notably in the ill-fated invasion of Canada and for his actions at Saratoga.

After Saratoga, Morgan felt snubbed when the command of a new light infantry unit was given to another officer. Suffering from sciatica, and his wounded pride, Morgan returned to Virginia on furlough.

While at home he kept track of the war's events, and when Greene called for him to be deputy of the Southern Department he was anxious to get back in the fight and avenge the losses at Charleston and Camden.

Banastre Tarleton

Born into privilege, Tarleton's wealthy merchant father saw to his son's every need, including an education to become a lawyer. Tarleton's father died unexpectedly, leaving his son a personal inheritance of 5,000 pounds, a small fortune by the standards of the time.

Like Morgan, Tarleton enjoyed his drinking and gambling. Unlike Morgan, Tarleton didn't frequent backwoods bars, but rather upscale public houses in London. He also gambled for real money, not for pennies, and as a result he quickly ran through his inheritance and burdened himself with gambling debts.

One way for a young English gentleman to rid himself of debt was to purchase a commission in the Royal Army. Tarleton finally convinced his reluctant mother to finance the plan and he became a lieutenant in the cavalry.

He sailed to the colonies with Cornwallis and discovered that the life of a cavalry officer agreed with him. Always arrogant and hot tempered, the speed and shock power of mounted combat suited him and he distinguished himself in the field. In fact, his actions merited him the fastest promotions seen in the army, a fact that did not endear him to his passed-over peers.

What truly differentiated Tarleton from officers on either side of the battle was his consistent use of brutality. He was not concerned with winning the war and then living in the country. He wanted to win the war and then return to England.

His view was that if someone was disloyal to the King, then he or she was a traitor — and the penalty for treason was death. He assembled and trained the British Legion, a mixed force unit composed of colonial Loyalists. He trained them and drilled them like regulars, and they become an excellent fighting machine with a code of brutality to match their commander's.

It was this legion of infantry and cavalry that made up the core of the force that met Morgan at Cowpens.

Morgan's Challenge

Seated in his saddle after his hasty departure from his camp on the Pacolet river, and with Tarleton's dragoons in hot pursuit, Morgan began to plan how best to engage the enemy. He didn't want this action to turn into a series of hit and run skirmishes; Morgan wanted to make a stand.

While at Pacolet, roughly 600 militiamen from North and South Carolina joined his group, nearly doubling the size of his force, but Morgan also knew that his mix of regulars and volunteers would be no match for the British in a set battle.

Morgan understood that few, if any, of his backwoods volunteers had any experience with conventional warfare. Their style of battle consisted of raids and ambushes where they could melt back into the countryside or, as they often did, stand up and run away once the British appeared to have the upper hand. Morgan knew that those men would not stand their ground against a determined British attack.

That left him with his 400 infantry regulars, and the detachment of 80 cavalry, who were battle hardened and led by two outstanding officers: Lieutenant Colonel John Howard of the infantry and Lieutenant Colonel William Washington of the cavalry. A better force could not have been found in the American army, but against 1,000 British regulars they had little chance.

And there was another issue.

While encamped at Pacolet it became obvious that there were difficulties between the volunteers and the Continentals. The regulars were painfully aware of the militia tradition of fleeing the battlefield, and had concerns of being left alone to fight the British. From the Carolinian volunteer perspective, all of the regulars were from "up north": Maryland, Delaware and Virginia, and they questioned just how hard the Continentals would fight for South Carolina.

The one thing that both groups shared was an unbounded hatred of the British. Morgan played to this common motivator, and encouraged his men to share stories, real or exaggerated, about the abuses and atrocities committed by the King's army. On more than one occasion Morgan fueled the fire by taking his shirt off in front of a group of troops to display the massive scars from his lashing.

As a result of his "common enemy" campaign, the group developed another common denominator, and that was a deep affection and respect for Morgan. He could relate to both groups, because he belonged to both groups. His service in the Continental army was known and respected by the regulars, and his backwoods speech and skill as an Indian fighter resonated with the militia.

But how could he use these two groups to the best advantage?

Morgan came upon an answer when he arrived at an area known as Cowpens and had a look at the terrain. In the fading light he spotted a hill that had a stream on the right and woods on the left. There was no time for a proper reconnaissance, so he gathered his commanders and sketched out his plan.

Morgan intended to place his Continentals in a line atop the hill. Near the base of the hill he would place the bulk of his militia and then send out 150 handpicked riflemen to act as a skirmish line in front of the militia. Washington's cavalry would be kept out of sight behind the hill and act as the reserve.

This deployment would leave both flanks wide open, but Morgan predicted that Tarleton would stay true to his style and attack up the middle.

Then he added a stroke of genius: knowing his militia wouldn't stand steady when the British attacked, he told them to fire two volleys, "Just two shots boys," and then withdraw to the left to reassemble behind the hill. Morgan figured that the British would view the withdrawal of the militia as a rout, rather than a planned movement.

To make sure that there wasn't a clever British officer who saw the movement for what it really was, Morgan told his skirmishers to "shoot for the epaulets" and kill as many officers as they could before withdrawing to the militia line.

Morgan's hope was that the skirmish line and the two volleys from the militia would significantly soften up the enemy, who would then have to fight uphill to get to the seasoned line of Continentals who held the top. While his regulars held the line, the militia would reform and reappear on the British right, while Washington's cavalry would attack its left — effectively completing a double envelopment.

When it was pitch black, Morgan and his officers placed the men in their positions. Each group knew the plan and the part that the others would play in it. Once in place, they settled in to doze before waking early for a cold breakfast.

When Arrogance and Audacity Meet - The Battle

Tarleton had pushed his men and horses hard through freezing winter rains to cut the distance between him and Morgan's encampment on the Pacolet. When he arrived and found that the rebels had departed, he rested his men only long enough for his scouts to pick up the trail once again.

During the five days it took to make contact with Morgan, Tarleton nearly marched his men and animals into the ground. Historian Lawrence Babits states that during the 48 hours preceding the battle, the British had run out of food and had less than four hours of sleep. On the morning of January 17th Tarleton awoke his troops at 2:00 A.M. to continue the push through thickets and bogs, boulders and trees, and threw them into battle some four and a half hours later.

When Tarleton arrived at Cowpens he immediately saw that his enemy appeared to be nothing more than rebel militia. He set his lines, assigning the infantry to form in the center while his dragoons formed up on the left and right flanks. He kept a detachment of the 71st Highlanders as reserve.

Tarleton had two three-pounder cannons with him, and he

used these to cover the advance of his troops as they moved on the line of militia.

There had to be a sense of relief for the exhausted British officers and men when they spied the ragged line of volunteers. They likely thought it would not be the hard-fought battle they had imagined, but rather a quick push to defeat the rebel rabble.

They were right about it being quick.

With their cannons booming, the British stepped off in perfect formation. Almost immediately bullets started cutting into their ranks, fired from riflemen hidden behind trees and boulders. The skirmishers started to withdraw to the militia line, firing as they went.

The British kept coming until they were in range of the militia, who cut loose with their first volley. In what was probably the fastest reload time in their lives, the militia readied for the second volley, took aim and fired.

The militia then left the field as planned; however, to the British this ragtag bunch in frontier shirts and floppy hats looked like the rabble they believed they were, and they assumed the militia was once again turning tail and running. Wanting a quick end to the fight the British broke ranks and started chasing the militia, when suddenly they received fire from a line of regulars atop the hill.

On the British right, Washington's cavalry appeared and attacked the British dragoons, sending them back in retreat. Tarleton quickly called for his Highlanders to exploit what he thought was a rout of the colonials, and ordered them into battle at double time.

Lieutenant Colonel Howard, having witnessed the advance of the Scots, ordered part of his Continentals to turn and face the new threat; however, the order was misunderstood and they started to withdraw instead. This absolutely convinced the British that a general rout was in progress, and all pretext of an organized assault disappeared as they charged pell-mell into the battle.

Morgan, having watched the Continentals withdraw, spurred his horse to their position and ordered them to about-face and fire. The British suddenly found themselves the hunted, rather than the hunters. At about the same time, the militia reemerged on the field, having circled around the hill, and appeared on the opposite side from where they had departed. To make matters worse, Washington's cavalry had reformed and started slashing at the British flank.

Meanwhile Howard, seeing the British in disarray, ordered his Continentals to "charge by bayonet" down the hill. The British literally threw themselves on the ground in surrender.

Tarleton was not one to give up and he tried to reengage, but at the end of the day he escaped with just 40 of the 1,100 men he had started with.

The battle was over in just under one hour.

Good News Bad News

While not involving near as many troops as other engagements, the American victory at Cowpens had a profound effect on the people of the nation. It was a rallying point. Militias swelled as hundreds of new recruits joined the fray armed with the knowledge that not only had the world's most powerful army been soundly beaten, but they were beaten by citizen soldiers.

For the regular Continental army news of Cowpens was a needed boost in morale, and Washington began planning for a move to the South to reinforce success.

For the British it was the beginning of the end. The English parliament was openly criticizing both the conduct of the war and the huge drain on its treasury. Cornwallis' stronghold in South Carolina crumbled as Loyalists switched allegiances and would no longer freely trade with or support the British military presence.

For Cornwallis himself, Cowpens was both a disaster and an embarrassment. The loss of 1,000 men, their horses and the two cannons put a serious dent in his forces, and he had to change his plan to dominate the South. Ultimately, his move northward would result in his fortifying Yorktown, where he would be defeated by the combined forces of the Americans and French.

It was also the end for Morgan, whose sciatica had returned along with hemorrhoids, making travel by horse excruciating. He returned to his wife in Virginia knowing he was responsible for bonding a diverse force, giving them a plan they could understand and inspiring them to execute that plan to the best of their ability.

Eight months later the war for independence came to an end and a new nation truly was born.

A Diverse, Effective Team

The American victory at Cowpens demonstrates clearly the veracity of the tenets of success: values based, mission focused, action oriented. The danger that Tarleton's British Legion represented for Morgan's unit was real...very real. Dangerous, but not indefensible. As Morgan demonstrated, a force that shares the same core values (in this case hatred of the enemy), employs an effective, focused plan maximizing the strengths of the group, and when executed with tenacity produces extraordinary results.

Every organization is made up of people, often times more diverse than Morgan's volunteers and regulars. Successful organizations actively promote values among all team members (like Morgan's back-baring pep talks). Successful organizations focus on and communicate how objectives will be met ("Just two shots boys"). Successful organizations are led by courageous leaders who act decisively, adapt and overcome (Howard's switch from defense to offense). Neither Morgan's regulars nor the militia could stand up to Tarleton's forces alone, but together they were victorious — an effective team is a powerful thing.

Engage people where they are; deliberately build a team; employ your people to exploit their strengths.

CHAPTER 14

THE BATTLE OF NEW ORLEANS (1814-1815)

NOT ON OUR SOIL

After defeating Napoleon in early 1814, the British were able to dispatch additional seasoned combat troops and commit more material to the war with the Americans. The British sacked the city of Washington, DC, in August and laid plans for one final strike to end the war on terms favorable to the empire.

The British never accepted Napoleon as a legitimate ruler, and therefore considered his sale of the territory of Louisiana to the United States as fraudulent. The British masterminds of the assault on New Orleans acted on three primary, although not all genuine, motives. First they intended to return the Louisiana Territory to its rightful owner: Spain (of course administered by Britain). Next they determined to sever the eastern states from the rest of the continent by seizing the entire Mississippi valley from Canada to the Caribbean. Lord Castlereagh, the British Foreign Secretary and architect of the Louisiana invasion, knew full well of the ongoing negotiations at Ghent to end hostilities. An overwhelming victory in the American heartland, however, would reshape the peace settlement, possibly bringing to an end the Americans' outlandish experiment in free democracy. Finally, as has been a timeless motivation for war, the invaders intended to make themselves rich by harvesting the "beauty and booty" available in the prosperous port city of New Orleans, and then the expansive territory beyond.

The entire war had been an economic and military disaster for the fledgling American nation. The British blockade and embargo had left American produce rotting on docks; the United States capitol had been occupied and burned; the nation had defaulted on its debt; parts of Maine were garrisoned by British forces; and states in New England were openly discussing succession and suing for a separate peace with Great Britain. The United States, though able to fight the British to a standstill, could not foresee victory in the struggle; the best the people could hope for was to avoid too devastating a loss.

The city of New Orleans itself in 1814 had an independent melting pot flair — a culture it sustains still. New Orleans was home to French, Spanish, African, Anglo and Creole peoples. The multi-ethnic, multi-racial population was dedicated to pursuing economic opportunism and the joys of life. The flourishing Crescent City stood as a tempting prize, both wealthy and militarily strategic, just 100 miles upstream from the mouth of the mighty Mississippi River.

Recognizing the vulnerabilities of New Orleans, the War Department appointed Major General Andrew Jackson as military commander of the 7th Military District headquartered in New Orleans. Jackson was fresh off of his victory in the Creek Indian War, having secured for the United States three-fifths of modern-day Alabama and one-fifth of Georgia. General Jackson's force of will was the predominant factor in bringing the Creek Indian War to a successful conclusion. Jackson intended to apply his iron will, his principle command characteristic, again at New Orleans.

Jackson's force at New Orleans was the most polyglot band to ever fight under the Stars and Stripes. Jackson's army mainly consisted of local New Orleans militiamen, a sizable contingent of African-American freemen, Kentucky and Tennessee frontiersmen armed with deadly long rifles, marines, sailors, Choctaw tribesmen, and a colorful band of outlaws led by Jean Lafitte — "pirates" Jackson had once disdained as "hellish banditti." This hodgepodge of 3,000 fighting men added to a core of Army regulars consisting of approximately 1,000 soldiers of the U.S. 7th Infantry Regiment. Many of those regulars were members of a hard-fighting nucleus of a few hundred men that had been together since the 7th was formed in 1808. At New Orleans, when the time came for a decisive showdown with the British invaders, Jackson would wisely assign the 7th Infantry to cover the most important positions.

The British contingent, though not huge by European standards, was a sizable and formidable force. The overall British commander of the North American station was Vice Admiral Sir Alexander Inglis Cochrane. He was a proud, stern, domineering Scot. Cochrane planned to exploit the success in the Chesapeake by ravaging the Gulf coast, capturing New Orleans and securing the Mississippi Valley.

Cochrane assembled the mightiest armada ever to sail North American waters. His naval flotilla, consisting of more than 50 ships, boasted such vessels as the triple-decked, 80-gun ship of the line, the HMS *Tonnant* (Cochrane's flagship), armed troop transports, frigates and sloops of war. The fleet transported over 14,000 ground troops, veterans of the Chesapeake and Napoleonic campaigns. Cochrane had intended for General Robert Ross, who had led the ground campaign in the Chesapeake and who had sacked the city of Washington, to command land forces. Ross, however, had been killed by a sniper in Baltimore. Cochrane instead appointed Lieutenant General Sir Edward Pakenham to lead the assault troops. Pakenham, the 37-year-old brother-in-law of the Duke of Wellington, and himself a highly decorated soldier, was considered one of the best officers in the army. The grand strategy was to capture Mobile, march along the coast to Baton Rouge, and from there seize New Orleans. Then the conquest of the Mississippi Valley would commence.

Taking the city of New Orleans looked deceptively easy; in reality, it was not. New Orleans was nestled in lowlands surrounded by a swampy morass. Narrow roads led into the city, roads which could be easily defended, given enough warning. The preferred avenue of attack was by way of an inland assault. The key to taking the city was to keep defenders guessing by moving fast and attacking from different directions.

An invasion of the scale needed to secure the Mississippi Valley took months to prepare. Anticipating his move from the Chesapeake to the Caribbean, Cochrane, in August 1814, sent Lieutenant Colonel Edward Nicholls to Pensacola in Spanish-held Florida. With a couple of ships and a small contingent of troops he was to establish a base of operations. Violating Spanish neutrality, Nicholls attempted to rally the Spanish and the Indians against the Americans.

While Nicholls was stirring up trouble on the mainland, the British were plotting yet other schemes. British officers landed at Grand Terre, the privateer base of Jean Lafitte. The British offered Lafitte a significant sum of money and other inducements to leverage Lafitte's assets and personnel for the invasion of the Louisiana territory. Lafitte met the British officers himself. After a cordial dinner, Lafitte left the British with the impression he had agreed to accept their offer and needed a couple of weeks to make preparations. He had, in fact, decided to throw his lot in with the Americans. The British learned of the double-cross weeks later. One possibility that would have greatly aided British prospects was out.

Initiating the grand strategy in September, Admiral Cochrane believed the fort defending Mobile was weak. He dispatched a small British force of 225 marines and Indians and a naval squadron to seize Mobile. When one of the ships, the *Hermes*, ran aground, the British assault failed. Since the land route from Mobile was the best invasion route to eventually roll up New Orleans, not taking Mobile was a costly setback.

Jackson recognizing the Americans' exposure to an overland invasion, and preferring offense to defense, invaded Florida. With a force of regulars and Indian allies, the Americans attacked and overwhelmed the defenders of the Spanish forts at Pensacola. This action forced the British to sail away. The deliberate American assault seriously disrupted British plans for the Gulf and forced the British to target New Orleans directly. Attacking simultaneously overland from the north and west, while the British fleet cut off supplies and reinforcements from the coast, was a sure way to victory at New Orleans. With this maneuver no longer an option, the British would have to execute a frontal attack through swampy south Louisiana — a distinct disadvantage, but a disadvantage they confidently (over-confidently) believed they could overcome.

The British used Negril Bay, Jamaica, as their staging port for Gulf Coast operations. Admiral Cochrane assembled his massive armada through the months of September and October. Delays in amassing the force allowed the Americans much-needed time to maneuver from New Orleans to Florida, and back to Louisiana

Chapter 14: The Battle Of New Orleans (1814-1815)

again, to prepare defenses at New Orleans. After spoiling the British opportunity for a cross-country assault, Jackson left Florida in mid-November. Cochrane in turn set sail in late November, intending to beat Jackson to New Orleans.

The mood was lighthearted and merry amongst the British sailing from Negril Bay to the American coast. So sure of victory were the British, they brought a complete civil governmental staff. This included the administrators and the equipment, and even printing presses, to rule "the Crown Colony of Louisiana." They sailed aboard an invincible armada. The British troops were considered the best in the world. Many of the British officers even brought their wives along. They ventured to meet, and presumably route, a ragtag band of American soldiers, misfits, and miscreants — a force that was short of ammunition, short of all manner of supplies, and the British believed, short of resolve. The latter belief was their ultimate undoing.

The British fleet arrived at the Chandler Islands on December 8th. To sail up the twisting Mississippi would have been a treacherous proposition, with becalming winds and shifting sandbars. On the 8th of January, the day of the main assault on New Orleans, the British did try to negotiate the Mississippi River, but were repulsed.

Cochrane proposed to attack New Orleans through Lake Pontchartrain, landing at Bayou St. John, just north of the city. To ferry troops and equipment to Bayou St. John required navigating shallow passes utilizing shallow draft boats. Though ordered for this operation, those shallow draft ferries never did arrive. The British then decided to land forces on Bayou Bienvenu on the western end of Lake Borgne. From there troops could advance quickly toward New Orleans, hopefully before the Americans could mount a viable defense.

Because of the deep drafts of the heavy ships and transports, the armada anchored near Cat Island at the mouth of Lake Borgne, about 70 miles from New Orleans. Assault troops would have to ferry from Cat Island to Pea Island at the mouth of the Pearl River, then conduct a grueling 40-mile row to disembarkation points at Bayou Bienvenu.

A small American flotilla commanded by Lieutenant Thomas Catesby Jones, consisting of five gunboats, guarded the access to the lakes. The British would have to destroy or capture the

American gunboats before troops could land. On December 14th, 1,200 British sailors and Royal Marines set out to attack the Catesby command. The British used longboats armed with lightweight cannons. After a brief skirmish, known as the Battle of Lake Borgne, the American vessels were disabled or taken. This was a disaster for the Americans, as now they would have no way of knowing where the British would land.

Free to navigate Lake Borgne, General John Keane, troop commander until Pakenham's arrival (Christmas Day), hustled thousands of Redcoats to Pea Island, to set up a garrison. On the morning of December 23rd, having scouted an unguarded waterway leading nearly to the east bank of the Mississippi River nine miles south of the city, a British vanguard of some 2,000 soldiers poled its way through the a maze of sluggish streams and traversed a boggy morass. Seemingly undetected, the British stood an easy day's march from their goal. Instead of immediately moving to attack, Keane set up camp at Lacoste's Plantation to await reinforcements.

At half past 1 o'clock in the afternoon, a sentry at the door of General Jackson's headquarters on Royal Street in New Orleans announced the arrival of three visitors. These men had just come galloping into town from the south, and they brought dire news. They informed Jackson of the British vanguard within striking distance of the city. Jackson was astounded at the British having reached so far, with such a force, without discovery. Realizing the enemy was at the gates, Jackson declared, "By the Eternal they shall not sleep on our soil."

That evening, Jackson led a force of 2,000 men against the unsuspecting British troops resting in their camp. The surprise attack was a three-pronged assault from the north under the cover of darkness. The American soldiers moved quickly and struck their British adversaries hard. Having set the British on their heels, the Americans withdrew north to Chalmette Plantation on the banks of the Rodriguez Canal, about four miles south of New Orleans. The bold move startled the British. Keane decided to defer any advance toward New Orleans until all the troops could be brought in from the fleet.

The American force used the time well. The Rodriguez Canal was a wide, dry ditch that marked the narrowest strip of solid land between the British camp and New Orleans. The Americans, working together tirelessly, built a fortified mud rampart, more than half a mile long. They anchored the fortification on its right to the Mississippi River, and on its left to an impassable cypress swamp.

On December 25th General Sir Edward Pakenham arrived on the battlefield. Irate over the position of the army, Pakenham met with General Keane and Admiral Cochrane. Pakenham had intended to use Chef Menteur Road along the northern bank of Lake Borgne as the attack route to New Orleans, but he capitulated to Admiral Cochrane. Incensed, Cochrane insisted that his boats provided everything needed for the assault. Cochrane was convinced the British force could easily eliminate the ramshackle American contingent. He asserted that if the Army did not take the lead on this action, his sailors would.

Pakenham immediately ordered a reconnaissance-in-force for December 28th against the American earthworks being defended along the advance to New Orleans. In addition to the cannons on the battlements, the defenders had aid of the guns on the American ship, the *Louisiana*, grounded in the Mississippi. The light British advance was blasted from the left flank with broadsides from the river. The reconnaissance-in-force was beaten back. As soon as the British troops fell back, the Americans reinforced their earthworks with batteries of artillery. A few days later the British attempted to bombard the Americans with an artillery barrage of their own. The American cannoniers fought valiantly, and though nearly dislodged, they ultimately held their ground.

Fresh British troops arrived the first week of January, 1815. These reinforcements gave the British new hope. Pakenham decided to outflank the American defensive works by sending a strong force across the Mississippi to then overwhelm the thin line of American defenders on west bank opposite the Rodriguez Canal. In a coordinated motion, under the cover of the early morning fog, the redcoats would pour flanking fire at the Americans from across the river. Heavy columns of British infantry, employing ladders and other scaling equipment, would storm each end of the American line and overrun the ramparts. The British would then pursue the insolent defenders six miles into the heart of New Orleans. The final assault was set for January 8th at dawn.

The British plan was solid in conception, but fell apart in execution.

On a damp and foggy Sunday morning, veteran soldiers of the U.S. 7th Infantry Regiment, along with the motley crew of laborers, French and German mercenaries, Haitians, farmers, artisans and frontiersmen cobbled together to defend New Orleans were severely outnumbered. As the first streaks of dawn began to pierce the night sky, an ominous reality began to permeate the rank-and-file American soldiers. At any moment would come the attack from the heavily armed British army, recently returned from a thorough thrashing of Bonaparte at Waterloo.

The men amongst the ramparts fought back the trepidations of battle. Focus took the place of fear — a calmness of invincibility. Each man placed his faith in the men to his right and to his left. These men of wildly disparate heraldry, of contrasting loyalties, and in most cases of usually conflicting goals for now were on the same team. They became one solid immovable corps.

Then began low, rumbling sounds. It was the British, as yet unseen, moving. Soldiers, cannons, horses, and just then, the explosion of battle — and time stopped.

Rockets began, one followed by another, soaring from behind the British line and hanging in midair for moments, each moment seeming like an eternity, before discharging over the arena below. British officers ordered an advance; the hardened veterans of the Duke of Wellington's army rushed forward to put down the ragtag band of miscreants — a ragtag band that was focused on and committed to the task at hand: defending their homeland.

Pakenham had ordered a two-pronged strike against the American position. Colonel William Thornton of the 85th Regiment was to cross over the Mississippi during the night with his brigade, move quickly upriver and attack the American batteries opposite the canal. Upon neutralizing that position, the British assault would commence in earnest.

For days the British had been working on a canal to facilitate their crossing of the Mississippi. They were going to float longboats by way of the canal to the river, and then ferry troops across. The canal collapsed, forcing sailors to drag the heavy boats for the west bank attack through deep mud, causing a long delay. Thornton's force did not reach its intended goal until well after dawn. The British soldiers of the main attack force waited anxiously.

As the British bombardment began and the British advanced, the fog lifted. Deprived of their misty cover the British troops were exposed to withering artillery fire and the long rifles of the defending frontiersmen. The main British columns had no choice but to advance across the open fields toward the Americans, who waited expectantly behind their mud and cotton-bale barricades. To make matters worse, the British forgot their ladders and scaling equipment, so they had no easy means to mount the ramparts protecting the Americans.

The British assaulted in two columns: General Keane led the column closest to the river, while General Samuel Gibbs commanded the swarm line. One British brigade, commanded by General Lambert, remained in reserve. The Americans had planned and prepared their defenses well. Anticipating the main thrust of the British, American commanders arrayed their forces. It so happened that the main point of the British attack against the earthworks was manned by the veteran 7th U.S. Infantry.

Possibly because of Thornton's delay in crossing the river, and the crushing artillery fire from across the river, the British 93rd Scottish Highlanders were ordered to leave Keane's assault column moving along the river, and advance across an open field, to join the main force on the right. The American sharpshooters had a broad expanse of bright red targets to engage. The Highlanders were decimated. General Keane himself fell wounded while crossing the field with the 93rd.

Keane's primary column managed to reach and overwhelm the Americans' forward-most redoubt (reinforced shelter) next to the river, but the tenacious defenders responded. Elements of the American force immediately began to move forward. They fired on the British, who without adequate reinforcements could not hold the position. The Americans took back the redoubt and restored their line. The British assault along the river floundered.

In the main battle on the right, the American fire was so intense and so well directed that many British soldiers flung themselves to the ground in defenseless surrender. Soldiers who had survived the advance in open skirmish order ahead of the main assault force concealed themselves in a ditch below the parapet, unable to proceed further without support. Others huddled behind any cover they could find. For most, however, a combination of musket fire and grapeshot mowed them down. A few managed to scramble to the top of the parapet on the right, but death or capture was their eventual fate. Within half an hour, most of the senior British officers were either killed or wounded.

Pakenham's assault was doomed from the beginning. His men made perfect targets as they marched precisely across a quarter mile of open ground. Hardened veterans of the Peninsular Campaign in Spain fell by the score, including nearly 80 percent of a splendid Scottish Highlander unit that tried to march obliquely across the American front. Both of Pakenham's senior generals were shot early in the battle. With most of their superior officers killed or wounded, the British soldiers received no orders, either to advance or retreat. As they stood out in the open, rifle bullets and grapeshot tore them apart. Pakenham himself suffered two wounds before a shell severed an artery in his leg, killing him in minutes. His successor, General Lambert, who had held the British reserve, wisely disobeyed Pakenham's dying instructions to continue the attack; he ordered a retreat, pulling the British survivors off the field.

In the weeks leading up to this defining encounter, and most notably in the din of battle, the American command and control should have been greatly handicapped by language problems. The American forces were comprised of a number of French, German and Haitians who spoke no English. Despite every hardship and challenge, this force, greatly outnumbered but motivated by a powerful cause, drew together. The Americans overcame every obstacle, and severely defeated an army known to be among the most powerful and disciplined fighting forces in the world.

For the British, in summary, just about everything that could go wrong, did so. The battle was nothing short of a massacre. The British suffered 2,042 casualties: 291 dead (including Generals Pakenham and Gibbs), over 1,267 wounded (including General Keane) and a reported 484 were captured or missing. The Americans casualties numbered 13 dead, 39 wounded and 19 missing. General Jackson, reflecting on the battle, observed, "It appears that the unerring hand of providence shielded my men from the power of balls, bombs, and rockets, when every ball and bomb from our guns carried with them the mission of death."

Chapter 14: The Battle Of New Orleans (1814-1815)

The Battle of New Orleans was a major British defeat. An experienced, well-equipped British invasion force, 18,000 men strong, was rebuffed by a disparate, cobbled-together American contingent. The decisive American victory at New Orleans, the last major battle of the War of 1812, restored American confidence in their new republic and made Jackson a popular hero.

How does a largely outnumbered ragtag patchwork of regulars and polyglot militia soundly defeat the world's most powerful, disciplined, well-equipped and experienced military force? They did so by acting as one team — bound by common values, focused on a worthwhile mission, fighting tenaciously, aggressively, and decisively. This is how America's Army succeeds.

Ensure everyone knows the mission; employ limited resources carefully for maximum impact; commit - act decisively when you must.

CHAPTER 15

THE BATTLE OF SAN JUAN HILL (1898)
BUFFALO SOLDIERS' VICTORY

The heat was already beginning to sear as Friday, July 1, 1898, dawned on the outskirts of the city of Santiago de Cuba on the island's southeastern shore. The sun rose over a bay that lay as flat and still as a mirror. Silhouettes of battleships and troop carriers appeared to float like gray ghosts on the horizon.

The mood was restive in the encampments along the coastline, less than a mile from the base of the San Juan Heights, the low ridge that encompassed what the American soldiers called "Kettle Hill" and "San Juan Hill." These hills together formed a natural barricade for the city beyond. The word was going down the line to prepare for the assault at long last.

For the soldiers of the 9th and 10th Cavalry and 24th and 25th Infantry Regiments, the moment had been a long and hard time coming. The battle would provide another opportunity for glory that had been mostly denied them, because the enlisted men and officers of these particular cavalry and infantry units were African-Americans, better known as "Buffalo Soldiers."

Descended from slaves or born into slavery themselves, they had been allowed to join the military under Reconstruction. After enlisting, they were dutifully stationed to various outposts west of the Mississippi. Their service on the frontiers and been both vilified and embraced. Political leaders of certain racist stripes preached furiously against Negroes serving in the military — unless they were cooking or cleaning latrines. At the same time, white citizens who had at first bridled at the thought of African-Americans stationed in their frontier communities came to appreciate the security these same troops provided and to gain respect for their dedication to the military.

Whatever the reception to their presence, there had never been any question about the courage the troops displayed in campaigns against the Kiowa, Comanche, and Sioux. Indeed, with the west essentially tamed and occupied, it was Buffalo Soldiers' reputation for duty and bravery that earned them orders to leave their outposts and report to Florida in early 1898 in preparation for being sent to the front in Cuba.

There was another, less-authentic factor in the Buffalo Soldiers' selection for the assignment. Commanders had made presumptions based on supposed racial characteristics that deemed these troops uniquely qualified to endure the intense heat and the variety of diseases that ravaged white soldiers serving in the tropics. In fact, the blacks were no more immune to tropical diseases than any other races, and would pay a price for the fallacy.

Seventeen thousand soldiers, almost a fifth of them African-American, had been gathered at a staging area around Tampa, on Florida's west coast. The black officers and enlisted men found themselves thrown abruptly back into a segregated and at times openly hostile region, a South they thought they had left behind. In short order, they were met with a series of rude, sometimes violent shocks from Southerners repelled by the thought of Negroes in uniform. One hostile incident in the surrounding communities followed another. When it was finally time to ship out, the black soldiers were only too happy to leave and, as one wrote later, "Hoping never have cause to visit Florida again.» The troop ships set sail from Tampa Bay in mid-June.

As eager as the black and white infantry and cavalrymen were to engage, it's doubtful that many of them understood the grander political designs that had placed them in that particular theater of war. After a hundred years of westward expansion, the America continent was now occupied and secure from coast to coast. The last of the Indian tribes had been subdued — in some cases, all but exterminated — to make way for this manifest destiny. With that task completed, the nation's leaders had turned sometimes wary and sometimes covetous eyes beyond American shores and to the east, west, and south.

It was the cusp of what would later be called "the American Century," and politicians and newspaper editors joined in a feverish effort to convince the populace that the future belonged to this new world power, pushing the premise until it became a national obsession. The British and French had seen their once-grand empires wane everywhere in the world. German power had not yet begun its ascent. Only the Spanish remained, with one foothold in the Far East—the Philippines—and two on America's southern doorstep: Cuba and Puerto Rico.

All the islands had been engaged in bloody rebellions against their Spanish rulers for the entire latter half of the 19th century, with insurgencies growing more desperate as the 1890s passed. Closest to home, the brutality of the repression of the Cuban rebellion had fueled outrage in the United States. American leaders, recognizing an opportunity to rid the Caribbean as well as Southeast Asia of foreign influence, overtly supported the uprisings, infuriating the Spaniards.

American warships heightened the international tension by sailing south in late December 1897, affecting a blockade of Cuban ports that lasted until February 15th, 1898, when the *USS Maine* exploded and sank in Havana Bay. Headlines screamed that the sinking of the ship and the deaths of its 260 crewmembers were the result of direct hostilities by the Spanish, charges that were only slightly tempered when it was announced that the ship might have strayed off course and struck a Spanish mine. The discovery that the actual cause was likely an accidental explosion on board the ship would not come until decades later. With "Remember the Maine" as a battle cry, on April 25th, the United States declared war on Spain and an invasion of Cuba was set in motion.

The first confrontation in what would be named the Spanish-American War occurred on a more distant front. On May 1, 1898, in the Battle of Manila Bay, the Americans engaged and destroyed the Spanish fleet that was defending the Philippines, leading Spain to surrender the islands. Having lost that part of their empire, the Spanish were determined to hold on to Cuba and Puerto Rico, their last bastions in the New World, and readied for the American invasion.

That invasion force, including the four regiments of Buffalo Soldiers, boarded troop carriers that set sail on June 19th and came ashore on the beaches at Daiquiri and Siboney on the 22nd.

Three of the units: the 1st Regular Cavalry, the Buffalo Soldiers of the 10th Cavalry, and the 1st Volunteer Cavalry — the regiment soon to be commanded by Colonel Theodore Roosevelt and known forever after as "the Rough Riders"–began a march north to Las Guasimas. The Buffalo Soldiers got their first taste of action at Las Guasimas in the Cuban campaign–and their first awareness of a pattern of rewriting history to diminish their contributions, one that would be repeated time and again through this conflict and beyond.

The 10th had been brought along to Las Guasimas to act as a reserve unit for the 1st Regular Cavalry, but when Roosevelt's troops ambushed Spanish infantry and then found themselves under attack from a second side, the 10th jumped into the fray and fought to drive the Spaniards into retreat. Though the black regiments were the equal of their white counterparts in the midst of the battle, their part in the victory was swept aside. Roosevelt's promotional crusade, which included efforts by a publicist brought along to feed real and exaggerated tales of the Rough Riders' combat glories to the stateside newspapers, dominated the coverage.

After the rout at Las Guasimas, the troops returned to the staging area to join the other units for the march west toward Santiago de Cuba, where a Spanish army of over ten thousand soldiers was garrisoned. On June 31st, the full American contingent encamped on the low ground that followed the Caribbean shoreline at the bottom of San Juan Heights.

The troops woke the next morning and prepared to take part in a battle that would advance one great empire, and mark the downfall of another.

The Americans went into the conflict with an almost two-to-one numerical superiority, not the preferred three-to-one ratio of attackers to defenders. The American odds were, however, improved by a pair of stunning errors, one strategic and the other tactical, committed by Spanish General Arsenio Linares. The first was the commander's decision to position only a quarter of his troops on the San Juan Heights as a defense against the American advance. General Linares chose to keep the remainder of his infantry, cavalry, and artillery in a ring around the city.

Even so, the assault on the two hills promised to be tortuous — and deadly. The new day was growing hotter and the small bursts of rain barely cooled the air before it sweltered again. The soldiers were faced with crawling through a steaming, insect-infected palm jungle and then making a long uphill climb as 2,500 Spanish infantrymen rained down fire from their Mauser rifles (referred to by the American troops as «Spanish Hornets») and artillery batteries showered them with shells.

At seven o'clock, with the sun just breaking over the palm fronds and mist rising from the damp earth, General William Shafter ordered one of his generals, Brigadier General Henry Lawton, to lead the 2nd Division, which included the 12th and 25th Infantry Regiments, to carry out a preliminary attack on the Spanish stronghold of El Caney, some seven miles to the north. The plan was for the division to overrun the much smaller enemy contingent and then return to join the primary assault over San Juan Heights and into Santiago de Cuba.

Since it was impossible for horses to maneuver the steep and rough terrain, the 10th and the other cavalry units dismounted and fought as infantry. While the assault on El Caney was in progress, the other units advanced northwest through the palm forest to the San Juan River, where they were ordered to halt and wait for the return of the rest of the cavalry and infantry. For the next three hours, the Spanish riflemen in their trenches on the hills had a clear view of the American soldiers below and fired at will. The veterans of the battle would later refer to the valley where they were pinned down as "Hell's Pocket" and "Bloody Ford."

When ten o'clock arrived and the 2nd Division had still not returned from El Caney, the officers and troops at the base of the Heights, wearied by the searing July heat and the non-stop rifle and artillery barrages from above, were agitating to get into the fight. A young lieutenant named Jules Ord petitioned General Shafter to allow him to lead the 10th Cavalry in an assault.

By this time, American artillery had been rolled to the peak of nearby El Pozo Hill. When the guns began firing on the Spanish position, General Shafter gave Ord permission to mount the attack. The lieutenant led the 10th out of the palm jungle and up the first yards of the incline of San Juan Hill. Seeing their brethren emerging from the palm forest to begin the charge, the black soldiers of the 24th Infantry Regiment let out a raucous cheer. They were ordered to join the assault, followed by the rest of the infantry on the left flank. Ord, the officer who had led the charge, took a bullet in the throat and became one of the first Americans killed.

Though the fire from the Spaniards' Mausers continued unabated as the troops advanced, it was for a time less intense. General Linares had made a major tactical error by placing his rifle trenches on the geographical peak of the Heights, rather than the lower "military" ridge, which would have provided far better sight and firing lines at the advancing infantry. For a few hundred yards, the Americans had clearer going, though the harsh heat and the brutal climb disabled more infantry than the Spanish rifles.

The Buffalo Soldiers, preferring the advance even under these conditions to being shot at like fish in a barrel, were focused and tenacious. They knew exactly what the objective was, and they were acting as one well-synchronized team to press every advantage.

By this time, the American units from the assault on El Caney had arrived back to join the fray. As the combined attack progressed on San Juan Hill, Colonel Roosevelt led his Rough Riders and the rest of the 10th Cavalry on a charge up Kettle Hill, the lower peak to the north on the right side of the line.

The volleys from the Spanish trenches on that side of the Heights were met by the rapid covering fire from a Gatling gun nest at the bottom of the hill. As the American troops here also advanced through the blistering heat and the chaos of rifle and cannon volleys, soldiers fell from wounds or from heat exhaustion. The American infantry forces intermingled so that the Negro and white troops were fighting shoulder-to-shoulder.

John J. "Black Jack" Pershing, who would later lead the American Expeditionary Force in World War I, was at the time a lieutenant serving in the Cuban campaign. He would later describe how in the midst of the battle the soldiers advanced up Kettle Hill "unmindful of race or color, unmindful of whether commanded by ex-Confederate or not, mindful of only their common duty as Americans." Indeed, a Buffalo Soldier was the first to reach the crest and pull down the Spanish flag. After a brief hand-to-hand skirmish in the trenches, the Spaniards retreated down the other side of the ridge, heading west toward Santiago de Cuba to regroup and stage a counterattack.

Back on San Juan Hill, with the Buffalo Solders leading the charge, the first line of infantry reached the lower crest of the hill as the Spanish rifle fire resumed its accuracy. The distance between the attackers and defenders was now reduced to a number of paces. A ripple of shock and confusion shuttered through the trenches as the Spanish infantrymen laid eyes on the mix of faces rushing at them. The bulk of the American force fought the rest of the way up the slope in the midst of the whistle of bullets, the boom of artillery rounds shaking the earth, and smoke that all but blinded them.

When the first line of attack reached the Spanish trenches, the 10th and the other units made quick work of the assault. They captured the blockhouse that had served as the key defensive position on the southern end of the heights and drove the Spanish troops into a gradual retreat down the other side of the rise.

Roosevelt, still on Kettle Hill, caught sight of the fierce action engaging the black and white infantries on San Juan Hill. Desperate for more action, he called out for a charge across the gorge and onto the opposite slope. He started off, only to find that a mere handful of soldiers had heard the call and followed him. The future president raced back across the gorge to round up a larger force to lead up San Juan Hill. By the time this newly reconstituted force could start up the slope, the fighting was nearly over. General Shafter ordered Roosevelt back to Kettle Hill in anticipation of the Spanish counterattack from the north.

When the assault came, the Rough Riders caught it full force. Responding once again the Buffalo Soldiers jumped into action. Adding to the Americans' power was a lone Gatling gun mowing down Spanish attackers. The Spanish were driven back for a second time, but as one of Roosevelt's corporals claimed, "If it hadn't been for the black cavalry, the Rough Riders would have been exterminated." With the noonday sun high over the ridge, the sound of rifle and cannon fire faded and then died off. Medics and fellow soldiers scrambled to save the wounded and retrieve the bodies of the dead. The Battle of San Juan Hill was over.

As in Las Guasimas, both the Buffalo Soldiers' bravery in battle and their losses would be diminished, and indeed all but forgotten, until almost a century later. It was the infantry and cavalry units composed of black and white soldiers working as a cohesive team, rather than the Rough Riders alone, who captured both hills on San Juan Ridge.

In terms of hostilities, the Spanish American War was over in a matter of days. After the San Juan Hill and Kettle Hill retreats, General Linares' depleted and overmatched forces were pushed back into Santiago de Cuba and surrounded. On July 3rd, the U.S. Navy engaged and completely destroyed the Spanish fleet in Havana harbor. The American fleet then sailed directly to Puerto Rico, where the troops took the island with barely a shot fired. Two weeks later, Spain formally surrendered, ceding Puerto Rico, Guam, and the Philippines to the United States and giving Cuba independence.

With the combat over, the diseases of the tropics proved to be far deadlier than the bullets. Once again, the Buffalo Soldiers affected a rescue at their own peril. Yellow fever had run rampant among the black and white troops. Of the occupying force kept in Cuba after the hostilities ceased, almost three thousand men died of Yellow fever and other diseases, compared to the two hundred lost in combat.

When the staff at the hospital in Siboney was unable to manage the multitudes who had come down with the disease, the commander made a request for volunteers to assist with the ailing patients. After eight white regiments turned down the call, the 24th Infantry responded. As a war correspondent wrote of the Buffalo Soldiers in the aftermath, "They were at the front at Las Guasimas, at El Caney and at San Juan, and what was the severest test of all, that came later, in the yellow fever hospitals." The Buffalo Soldiers honored timeless American principles. They chose to bear the burden, focused on the mission at hand, and acted. In short order, dozens more men were infected, but they persisted and soldiered on.

Though the Spanish American War for all purposes ended with the Battle of San Juan Hill and the destruction of the fleet a few days later, the official treaty was not signed until December of that year. Spain had lost the last of its possessions, and an empire that had lasted four hundred years was finished.

The African-American troops found themselves lauded throughout the summer of 1898, but the praise faded in the face of the realities of racism, and was soon overshadowed by the constant drumbeat of praise from Roosevelt's admirers. Emphasizing the glory of the Rough Riders, advocates used Roosevelt's biography to help get him elected as governor of New York later that same year. He was William McKinley's vice-presidential pick in 1900, and when McKinley was assassinated, became the 26th president.

The racism that the soldiers encountered back home became more, rather than less vicious. Though African-Americans served with distinction in every war in the 20th century, during those same decades the lot of most of black America remained appalling. Racism swelled all the more in the first decades of the century, and black soldiers and civilians were routinely ostracized and attacked throughout the Depression and into World War II. Though the Army was officially integrated in 1948, the legacy of bravery in battle still did not earn the Buffalo Soldiers their full due. Human beings can be contentious, but if the ideals are still kept alive, eventually Americans will move in the right direction. That shift, however, can be a long time coming.

In 1992 a monument recognizing the contributions and accomplishments of America's Buffalo Soldiers was dedicated at Fort Leavenworth, Kansas, the original home base of the Buffalo Soldiers. The duty, commitment, and sacrifice that it honors were no more striking than during those twelve hours on a distant rise of land called San Juan Hill.

A team proves itself by its deeds; be willing to take on the hard jobs; the honor of doing a difficult task ultimately rests with the doer.

CHAPTER 16

BATTLE OF THE BULGE - BASTOGNE (1944)

"NUTS"

There are many roads to choose from: roads that lead to life, roads that lead to death. Whichever road is being traveled, the specific route itself is vital to the outcome of whatever task is to be accomplished. The sights surrounding such routes often go unnoticed. The details, overlooked, blend in and become a part of the greater whole. But without those trappings — the terrain, the structures, the people — the journey would be much different; the outcome would be much different.

By October 1944 the rapid Allied advance into Germany that followed the breakout from the Normandy beaches had slowed to a crawl. Allied forces had advanced so far, and so fast, they had outrun their supplies. The Germans, backs to the wall, were preparing to fight for their homeland. As the advance pressed in on two fronts, Adolph Hitler realized that Germany was close to losing the war. Dreading defeat, he believed that his only option was to try and slow the Allied advance on the Western Front. If he could counterpunch effectively and make the cost severe enough, he could possibly divide the United States and Great Britain from Russia. He could negotiate for peace in the west and then concentrate his efforts on the Eastern Front. Delaying the Allied advance would also buy time, possibly allowing for a game-changing technological breakthrough.

Hitler considered a variety of options until he arrived at a devious gambit to halt the Allied forces. He intended to strike at the heart of the advancing armies. Antwerp was the Allies' main port of supply, and Bastogne was a key crossroads and communications hub. By seizing Antwerp and controlling Bastogne, Hitler believed that he could, at least for a time, cleave apart the sinew holding the Allies together.

Hitler settled on the Ardennes Forest as the route to make his counterattack a success. Against the advice of his generals, Hitler wagered three factors were enough in his favor to risk the mission: the blistering cold, rugged and difficult terrain, and the fact that he was attacking so near the Christmas holiday. Hitler was confident that if the Allies' northern forces were surrounded, and their supplies cut off, then the southern forces would have no option but to withdraw. He anticipated the Americans would not stand for a bloody fight.

By first seizing Antwerp he would reduce Allied air power and sever supply lines to the Western Front. Then, in a bold move, he would surround Canada's 1st and Britain's 2nd armies, as well as the United States' 1st and 9th armies. The surprise of such a powerful counterattack would divide Allied forces, causing them to stall — if not crumble. Either way, Hitler thought he could secure enough time for his secret weapons projects to bear fruit.

Under control of Field Marshal Von Rundstedt, the German strategy aiming to divide the Allied forces was put into motion. Hundreds of tanks from the Sixth Panzer Army attacked. Newly constituted German divisions rammed into Allied territory, hoping to destroy all of the gains realized in the last six months since the Allies swept across the beaches of Normandy. The Panzer Army was followed by SS troops, Wehrmacht units and rogue members of the Volksgrenadier. For a time, the road that Hitler had chosen gave him an advantage. For a moment, the element of surprise had supplied the Germans with a false sense of hope. For an instant, United States and Allied forces reeled back.

Major General Troy H. Middleton, commander of the U.S. VIII Corps, had set up headquarters in Bastogne, Belgium, and occupied the southern sector. This line of defense and communication stretched out from Losheim, Germany, to a point where the Moselle River crossed the Franco-German border — a front of about 88 miles. Extremely rugged terrain, littered with hills and deep valleys, as well as a restricted road net, was the hub of communication for the Allied troops. The VIII Corps had a single mission: to hold the line. The best intelligence they had was that the enemy force opposing them was thin and weak... the intelligence was very wrong. Near the outskirts of Duren, the 83rd division rested after a trying battle in the Hurtgen Forest just weeks before. A new, untested division, the 106th Infantry, had recently arrived to join two battle proven divisions: the 4th and 28th, rounding out the Corps; the latter, however, had sustained a crippling number of casualties during the First Army drive to the Roer. The veteran soldiers were tired, homesick, and unsuspecting of the battle they were about to engage in, unaware that the United States Army would pull together, and with the help of storied heroics, defeat Nazi forces in an epic battle that would echo throughout history.

American soldiers along the front sat frozen in the forest, many recovering from the loss of their brothers, desperately trying to restore their bodies. The ice was a bitter reminder of the dark, cold tyrant that they were trying to defeat. There came a time when finding beauty in a snowflake seemed to be an impossible dream. As soldiers shivered at their posts, the ground, the one thing that could warm their freezing blood, had turned into a concrete demon. The only way to settle into a foxhole was by figuring out how to bust open a crack in the hardened earth, and then exploding a grenade in the crack. The thawed earth offered a fleeting chance to generate some kind of warmth in a freezing hell. There was no option for air cover; mother-nature had clouded that hope. The soldiers' M1 rifles routinely froze to the point where the bolt would not recoil. In a fire fight, sometimes the only way to keep the M1s operating was to urinate on them, freeing the action.

Soldiers, preparing to advance into the gates of hell, waited quietly, yearning for an end to the torture. Then came the news — overnight, upon receiving the reports of Hitler's attack, the troops began to push south. There was one road that they had to choose, literally and metaphorically. Defeat was not an option. These men had already chosen to fight. Allied troops began to move, taking action, strategically preparing to devour the enemy, down one road.

Against the advice of trusted advisors, who had recommended that Bastogne was a vital crossroads needing to be controlled, not captured, Adolph Hitler went forward with his plan to seize the city. When commanders tried to convince Hitler to follow another course, he is said to have asserted, "Bastogne must be captured, if necessary from the rear. Otherwise it will be an abscess in the route of advance and tie up too many forces. Bastogne is to be mopped up first; then the bulk of the corps continues its advance." The mission of the XLVII Panzer Corp was to attack through Bastogne, and then cross the Meuse River. On the 16th of December, 1944, the Germans launched their audacious assault. The German high command was counting on the Americans, the British, and the Canadians to break, surprised by the sheer weight of numbers and ferocity of the attack — it was a desperate hope. A heavy artillery barrage was followed by tank and infantry attacks. As soon as Allied commanders recognized Bastogne was threatened, they acted.

Initially stunned by the scale of the counteroffensive, the Allies were astonished by Hitler's desperate play. General Eisenhower saw the German assault as an opportunity, not a setback. Holding together a patchwork defense, the Allied command devised a plan to respond. In the southern sector of the German advance, operatives had obtained documents showing the panzer corps' objective was Namur, to gain control of the roads and railroads leading to the Meuse River. Armed with this information the Allies realized the enemy needed a system of roads greater than those in the area that they were currently threatening. A plan was set in motion, requiring the cooperation of men who had endured the sting and trial of combat and those who had virtually just arrived. The Allies were summoning the power of the team.

For the plan to work, Allied forces must execute as perfectly synchronized teams. Each soldier must protect the lives of his comrades, each ensuring another's freedom. Some would have to withstand the withering blows of the Nazi savagery, while others maneuvered for advantage. The initial phase of the defense was to delay by holding in place along the original Allied line. Leaders realized that both the extensive front and minimal reserves might not allow this phase to last very long, and so the second phase of the defense was to deny vital road nets to the enemy by building strong defenses at St. Vith, Houffalize, Bastogne, and Luxembourg as rapidly as possible. Prompt assistance from the

First and Third Armies would build up the defenses of St. Vith and Luxembourg, and the attachment of two airborne divisions would make the defense of Bastogne possible.

The 101st Airborne Division rested at Camp Mourmelon in France. The soldiers looked forward to spending a quiet Christmas there after their trials in Holland. The division commander was back in the United States, while the assistant division commander was giving a lecture in England on the airborne operation in Holland. One day after the attack on Bastogne, the 101st Airborne was on the move. Composed of 805 officers and 11,035 enlisted men, this unit of battle-hardened veterans was led by the artillery commander Brigadier General Anthony McAuliffe. With no time to waste, McAuliffe gathered his leaders and informed his men, "All I know of the situation is that there has been a breakthrough and we have got to get up there."

With McAullife, his G-3 (operations officer) Lieutenant Colonel H. W. O. Kinnard, and his aide 1st Lieutenant Frederic D. Starrett near the head of the column, the division drove as quickly as possible toward Bastogne. Allied tanks pulled over to the side of the road in order to let the 101st pass. To keep speed, the division drove with full lights blazing — a risky move. Had the Luftwaffe (German Air Force) recognized this movement, the defense of Bastogne may have turned out very differently. Luckily, the weather that was assisting the German advance could be leveraged by the Allies as well.

General McAuliffe arrived at Bastogne ahead of the Germans. He reported to General Middleton immediately. Colonel Roberts, commander of Combat Command B, 10th Armored Division, interrupted the generals' meeting to inform them that the remainder of his command would be arriving in Bastogne within hours. "How many teams can you make up?" General Middleton asked. Roberts replied, "Three." General Middleton directed, "You will move without delay in three teams to these positions and counter enemy threats. One team will go to the southeast of Wardin, one team to the vicinity of Longvilly and one team to the vicinity of Boville. Move with the utmost speed. Hold these positions at all costs." Colonel Roberts did not appreciate the motivation of the general; however, understanding that General Middleton must know more than he did, he followed orders. This decision by General Middleton is said to have been

the initial tactical step that saved Bastogne. Roberts' men immediately prepared to meet the German onslaught. For eight hours
they withstood the blows of the Nazi panzers alone.

General Middleton turned over responsibility for Bastogne
to General McAuliffe and left the city. The first combat element
of the 101st Airborne Division to arrive in Bastogne was the
501st Parachute Infantry Regiment, arriving just after midnight
on December 19th. The 501st commander, Lieutenant Colonel
Ewell, notified Brigadier General McAuliffe of their arrival and
requested orders. By chance, young Lieutenant Colonel Ewell
had taken a holiday just weeks before and had visited Bastogne.
McAulliffe instructed Ewell to seize the road junction east of
Longvilly. McAulliffe issued orders with confidence in Ewell as
a commander. McAulliffe was unaware of how capable the 501st
would be — he put his faith in Ewell and the American soldiers
under his command. What McAulliffe did not know was that
Ewell had extensive knowledge of the area, and was fully capable
of using that knowledge to defend Bastogne. McAulliffe's in-
stincts suggested the enemy would most likely attack from the
east, but this was all that he knew. So, he pointed to the map,
moved his finger and basically told Ewell, "Go this way." Lieutenant Colonel Ewell's only response to this vague order was "Yes,
Sir."

After the battle, while recalling the defense of Bastogne, General McAulliffe is quoted as saying, «There were many men and
commanders in my operation who did outstanding things. But
Ewell's was the greatest gamble of all. It was dark. He had no
knowledge of the enemy. I could not tell him what he was likely
to meet. But he has a fine eye for ground and no man has more
courage. He was the right man for the spot I put him in." While
Ewell followed his orders, and the other supporting units pro-
tected their posts, McAulliffe chose to sit on Bastogne; this was
ground he would not give up.

The 101st Airborne Division was designed as a light infantry
division. To properly defend Bastogne, the 101st Airborne was
transformed into a massive firepower threat. In addition to Combat Command B of the 10th Armored Division with its M4 Sherman tanks on the ground, ten artillery battalions could support
the 101st at any one time. The combination of artillery, anti-tank,
and anti-air assets allowed for a robust, flexible defense. With-

out the prospect of an "airborne" mission, the soldiers of the 101st changed their normal strategy. They reconfigured their loads, packing additional ammunition, far more than they would normally have the ability to carry. Headquarters were dismantled and supplies were allocated to fighting units. Anticipating the worst, General McAullife determined that the best type of defense would be a static one. He evenly distributed artillery, anti-tank, anti-air and tank forces around Bastogne to create an impenetrable 360-degree perimeter. Responding to German threats, defending units were able to reinforce each other on interior lines. The intent was to prevent any German penetration at all.

More than ten different divisions of the United States Army were constantly communicating - working together, shifting forces, responding to threats and changing priorities - to ensure the defense of Bastogne.

One additional asset proved vital to the defense of Bastogne. This asset was a battalion led by Lieutenant Colonel Clifford D. Templeton — the 705th Tank Destroyer Battalion. En route to Bastogne, the 705th headquarters element encountered a German force armed with heavy machineguns and several anti-aircraft batteries. The battle that ensued lasted about twenty minutes and wounded three American soldiers. The 705th headquarters element was forced to abandon a vehicle and withdraw. Templeton radioed the rest of his battalion, informing them of the roadblock, and warning them to be prepared. He pressed on. He was confident that the M18 Hellcat tank destroyer, the battalion's main weapon system, would be sufficient to defeat any enemy tank or infantry that they may come across during the trek to Bastogne.

Templeton arrived at Bastogne with his battalion late on the evening of the 19th. He quickly dispersed his teams to bolster the defensive perimeter. Close coordination between the 101st infantry and the men in the tank destroyers proved to be a formidable adversary to the German panzers.

When not assaulting into the city, the Germans tried to keep their tanks out of range of the American artillery, but without success. The Americans were eager to take out any German target within range. They were tenacious and focused on the task at hand. It has been said it was the attitude of the soldiers, more than anything else, which defined the defense of Bastogne. Bit-ing cold, rations from World War I, little sleep — all were of minor consequence. Throughout the turmoil, American soldiers vowed to defend their posts. This was not a tactical struggle; the battle for control of Bastogne was a test of wills, a test of resolve.

From December 19th, 1944, through Christmas Eve, the Germans repeatedly attempted to break the impenetrable barrier McAulliffe had placed around Bastogne. Sure of the hopelessness of American's position, the Germans offered McAulliffe an opportunity to surrender. McAulliffe countered with one word: "Nuts."

On the 23rd of December, the besieged defenders received an early Christmas present: the frigid weather broke. Clearing skies allowed much-needed air support for perimeter defenses and provided an opening for resupply. From the bulwarks on the ground the hum of Allied airplane engines above were like church bells on Sunday morning. Those planes brought help, hope, and the glimmer of a new day — support needed to continue the fight.

The 101st's signal company maintained unfailing communications during the siege and facilitated that much-needed aerial support. Landlines, antennas, and wires were constantly being severed and communications systems destroyed by the fighting. Signal soldiers worked tirelessly around the clock to keep the vital lines of communication open. Continuous communication allowed the harried defenders to work in unison, responding to threats from any and all directions.

On Christmas day, seven days into the siege, the Germans tried attacking again. American infantry, artillery, tanks and tank destroyers operated in unison to stymie the advance. The 5th Panzer Army forces regrouped and attacked again on the 26th, this time with battalion-sized combined arms teams, but again they were beaten back. While the Germans attempted to breach the perimeter, American artillery targeted, attacked and disbanded other German units staging to mount further attacks. By now, with Bastogne still in American hands and the Nazi advance along the entire front waning, any German hope for success of the Ardennes offensive had faded. An American submission at Bastogne or an Allied capitulation at large was not in the cards. The Germans launched several more half-hearted assaults against Bastogne on the 27th and 28th of December, but soon all activity towards the beleaguered city ceased. Bastogne remained firmly and resolutely in American hands.

Bastogne was defended successfully, not by a large force overpowering the enemy, but rather by a number of small units, determined men working together as an integrated, cohesive team. Working collectively they were able to defeat overwhelming odds. Each separate action worked toward a common objective and served as another nail in the coffin of the Panzer armies. Like fingers of a hand, one alone makes little impact, but when grouped together as a fist, they possess power magnified more than tenfold.

The defenders of Bastogne, the 101st Airborne and its supporting battalions, came together as a team of circumstance and became a family of devotion — a group of brothers who would be connected for life. They displayed unbreakable resolve and resilient spirit.

Upon recognizing the threat of the Nazi counteroffensive, or when called into action, American soldiers moved swiftly and engaged decisively. Leaders and soldiers alike focused on the mission at hand. A huge, disparate force coordinated all available assets to ensure the defense of a critical crossroads. Teamwork and the ability to adapt and overcome proved to be indispensable qualities. The soldiers were disciplined, well trained, and worked effectively as synchronized teams. They were determined to succeed, or were willing to die trying. By necessity they came together, they supported each other, and they acted.

Hitler wanted Bastogne because of the seven roads leading into and out of the city. Hitler picked his route, but the Americans employed the trappings — the terrain, the structures, and the men — to their advantage. For some it was a road to death, for others a road to life. The American force was completely surrounded. The soldiers endured an incessant pounding — a barrage of steel and lead. They fought back with everything they had. Ultimately, America's Army relied on the strength of soldiers' convictions and the nobility of their cause. American soldiers held their ground. Striving to liberate a continent, they determined to never give up, never surrender.

Know your environment - the lay of the land; trust your people; over communicate and react as one.

CHAPTER 17

THE BATTLE OF CHIPYONG-NI - KOREA (1951)
OVERWHELMING NUMBERS

Prelude

On the 3rd of February, 1951, Colonel Paul Freeman, commander of the 23rd Regimental Combat Team (23RCT), surveyed the little crossroads town of Chipyong-ni, which his forces had just taken, chasing out a few Chinese riflemen. There wasn't much to look at: just a beaten-over podunk village with a mill (now demolished), a school and a Buddhist temple (both now destroyed), but whoever held Chipyong-ni controlled roads running west, northeast, and south, as well as the railroad line running from the important supply depot at Wonju. Additionally, if the Chinese controlled the village, they could threaten to enter the Han River valley and roll up the flank of the Eighth Army; and if the Eighth Army held it, they could threaten to envelop the Chinese forces to the West.

The 23RCT was a tough, battle-tested regiment that had fought on the Pusan Perimeter, chased the North Koreans to the Yalu, and fought a delaying action at Kunuri after the Chinese entered the war. It had three infantry battalions (each with three rifle companies and a heavy weapons company), as well as the Headquarters Company, the Regimental Tank Company (14 M4A3 Shermans), heavy mortar company, service company, and medical company. Additionally, a French Battalion, mostly tough, experienced Foreign Legion troops, had been attached since December 11th.

Colonel Freeman was confident the Chinese would fight to regain control of Chipyong-ni, and he began to make preparations to hold it.

Preparation

Freeman was just the man for the job. He had begun to think that the best way to deal with the Chinese was to find the enemy, dig in to good positions on high ground within easy range of his artillery, and let the enemy come to him, and now he had a chance to prove it. Chipyong-ni was nestled in a little bowl of small bare hills, surrounded by rice paddies and higher hills further out. While Freeman would have liked to occupy the higher ground, he simply did not have the bodies to man a line that long. So, he occupied the lower hills around the town, giving him a perimeter about two miles long east-west and about a mile deep.

His supply line to the south was open and he trucked in what he could for the defense of this position, including rations and more ammunition than he had ever seen in Korea. The 23RCT spent the time between the 3rd and 10th of February digging in automatic weapons, mortars, and artillery; laying barbed-wire and mines; setting trip flares and booby traps; working out interlocking fields of fire; registering mortars and artillery on likely enemy assembly areas, lines of approach, and points of attack; filling gaps in the line with tanks and automatic weapons; building a small airfield; and patrolling daily to the higher hills looking for the enemy. The team worked in unison to prepare for what was to come.

Corps thought Freeman needed more muscle to do the job, so on February 3rd the 1st Ranger Company was attached to the 23RCT; the 37th Field Artillery Battalion (18 105mm howitzers) arrived on the 5th; Battery B, 82nd Anti-aircraft Artillery Automatic Weapons Battalion also joined, adding six M16s (quad-.50 calibers mounted on a half-track) and four M19s (twin 40mm mounted on a light tank chassis). Several days later, Battery B, 503d Field Artillery Battalion (six 155-mm howitzers) was attached, along with Company B of the 2nd Engineer Battalion. The 23RCT was now a formidable formation of about 5,000 men.

Freeman placed his units clockwise around the perimeter: the 1st Battalion to the north with C and A Companies; the 3rd Battalion on the east with L, I, and K Companies; the 2nd Battalion on the south with E, F, and G Companies; and the French Battalion on the west. He retained B Company and the 1st Ranger Company as Regimental reserve north of the town behind A and C Companies, and placed his artillery south of the town behind the little hill occupied by G Company.

As the 23rd prepared, patrols came into contact with sizable Chinese forces more and more frequently. Several times those patrols had to be rescued by tanks and infantry, so Freeman was not very surprised when, on the 11th of February, the Chinese launched their Fourth Phase Offensive with major attacks toward the towns of Hoengsong and Wonju, east and southeast of Chipyong-ni. The Chinese overran the South Korean (ROK) III Corps, annihilating the ROK 8th Division; overran the U.S. 15th Field Artillery Battalion (attached to the 9th Regimental Combat Team); mauled the 38RCT in "Massacre Valley;" and caused UN troops to fall back toward hastily formed defenses around Wonju.

As the Chinese swept south and then turned west, threatening to cut off the supply road to the 23RCT, Freeman, painfully aware that he was about to be isolated miles from the nearest friendly unit, requested that the 23RCT be withdrawn south to tie in with other friendly troops. His Corps commander flew out, looked the situation over, and concurred, bumping the request up to Eighth Army, but Lieutenant General Matthew B. Ridgway, newly installed as commander of the Eighth Army, would have none of it. He promised to resupply Freeman by air and send the entire Eighth Army to relieve them, if necessary, but he agreed with Freeman that well-dug-in and supported American troops could defeat Chinese light infantry. Ridgeway wanted Freeman to fight and he ensured the 23rd would not go it alone.

The First Night, 13/14 February

On the night of the 12th of February and into the morning of the 13th the perimeter received indirect artillery fire and the Chinese probed C Company on the north and the 3rd Battalion on the east. The next day the 23RCT readied itself for the inevitable battle, as the Air Force flew 40 sorties against Chinese positions around Chipyong-ni.

By late afternoon and early evening flares were seen on all sides, enemy movements were heard, and small arms and mortar rounds began to fall inside the perimeter from the northwest, north, and southeast. At about 2000 hours an intense mortar and artillery barrage crashed into the perimeter. When the barrage lifted, twenty minutes later, the Chinese attacked.

Hundreds of Chinese — blowing whistles, banging gongs, and yelling —rose up and advanced on C Company's position in the north, K Company in the east, and E Company in the southeast. Despite the racket, the Americans were not startled into giving away their positions but held their fire until the Chinese hit the wire. Then rifle and machinegun fire laced into the attackers as tracers crossed and ricocheted in the dark and flares lit the eerie scene. Mortar and artillery fire rained down on the regimental command post and the artillery positions, while the artillerymen answered with their own preplanned fires.

The Chinese probed for weak points, withdrawing only to probe again. The G Company position in the south was soon found to be the soft spot in the line. Although there was a double apron of barbed-wire in front of G Company's First Platoon, on the right of the company position, the wire had run out before they got to Lieutenant Paul McGee's Third Platoon in the center. Then there was the terrain. A spur of the hill McGee was dug into ran out toward one of the higher hills that surrounded Chipyong-ni: Hill 397, which the Chinese occupied, providing a natural avenue of approach into his position. Additionally, a dry stream bed about four feet deep ran south from where his position tied into the First Platoon before turning west. This provided the Chinese with cover almost up to the American lines. At 2230 hours, McGee's Platoon was hit by a squad of Chinese, who crawled along the spur. Another squad of Chinese took advantage of the dead ground provided by the stream bed and climbed the hill to attack at the juncture of the First and Third Platoons. But these were merely probing attacks, and the Chinese withdrew after a few minutes. McGee saw the danger, but all he could do was cover the spur and the dry stream bed with machineguns and preplanned mortar fire, keep an eye on them, and hope for the best.

First Battalion, in the north, beat off three Chinese probing attacks during the night. In the east, the Chinese made limited penetrations. At about 2300 hours Chinese infiltrators ambushed a jeep and an M16, capturing the jeep driver, and at about 0230 hours on the 14th, the Chinese penetrated K Company's position, cutting off a portion of the company. Responding to the incursion, reinforcements rushed to K Company's aid, repelled the Chinese and restored the line.

In the west, the Chinese ran up against the French battalion. The French fended off probing attacks with machinegun fire for about three hours, when a platoon-sized group of Chinese with fixed bayonets suddenly jumped up a couple of hundred yards in front of the French position and charged up the hill, blowing whistles and bugles and yelling like crazy. A French squad promptly jumped out of their holes, fixed bayonets, and charged down the hill throwing grenades left, right, and center while yelling and cranking a Chinese siren of their own. The two groups ran at each other until they were about twenty yards apart, when the Chinese hesitated and broke, running for their own lines. The French tackled those Chinese they could and dragged back fourteen prisoners.

After repelling multiple attacks all around the perimeter, penetrations and infiltrations were cleaned up by dawn of February 14th. At about that time, Colonel Freeman, who had spent the night shifting around the perimeter, checking on his units and managing the fight, laid down on his cot for a few minutes' rest. He had just swapped ends, his head now where his feet had been, when a Chinese 120mm mortar round exploded right next to his tent, wounding several officers and mortally wounding Major Harold Shoemaker, the regiment's intelligence officer. A jagged piece of shrapnel ripped into Freeman's left calf and left a painful, though not serious wound. The regimental surgeon, Captain Robert Hall, bandaged the wound and gave Freeman two aspirin. The colonel then hobbled off to look after his men.

Two Long Days, 14-15 February

Daylight during the 14th was busy. High winds made evacuating the wounded difficult, but H-5 helicopters of the 3rd Air Rescue Squadron succeeded in bringing in medical supplies and taking out the seriously wounded. In addition, C-119s from the 314th Troop Carrier Group managed to parachute in 87 loads of supplies. General Ridgway himself helicoptered in, and told

Freeman he would have to hold for another 24 hours. Ridgeway promised to start relief forces forward that day and to have flare-ships overhead that night.

But there was bad news that day, too. Poor flying weather and the demands of supporting the defense of Wonju meant that Chipyong-ni got only three close-air support missions. Also, interrogation of the prisoners taken in the previous night's attack revealed that the 23RCT had been assaulted by four regiments representing four different divisions from three different Chinese armies. Last night had merely been probing attacks looking for weaknesses. The next attacks would be much larger, and for real.

The worst news was that the commander of X Corps used the pretext of Freeman's wound to relieve him of command, sending Colonel Jack Chiles, X Corps operations officer, to take command of the 23RCT. Freeman was understandably angry. To be pulled in the middle of a battle smacked of a reprimand and Freeman protested vigorously. He was assured by General Ridgeway that nothing of the sort was implied, but he still managed not to be at the airstrip when Colonel Chiles arrived. The strip was under Chinese mortar fire and the pilot couldn't wait to take Freeman out, so he loaded some wounded and took off. Freeman told Chiles to find shelter and stay out of the way. Chiles was smart enough not to press the issue and Freeman continued in command until the morning of the 15th. Even then Chiles allowed the regimental executive officer, Lieutenant Colonel Frank Meszar, to run the battle, as Meszar knew the capabilities of the subordinate commanders.

For the troops, it was a relatively quiet day. They were in good spirits, they got hot food, and anyone who wasn't doing something else, dug holes — bigger holes, deeper holes, better holes, using railroad ties and bags of rice found in the village to fortify aid stations, command posts, fire-direction centers, and supply dumps. They had a sense that they could not be too well dug in.

The Chinese opened the battle at dusk, far earlier than the night before, as if they knew they had a long job ahead of them, and they added an unnerving touch: just before the initial assault a Chinese bugler blew taps. The American and French soldiers steeled their resolve. Then it came.

In the west, the French were attacked by an overpowering onslaught. They were forced to pull their southern-most company back to defend themselves from pressure from the south. In the north, First Battalion was assaulted three times but held its lines. In the east, Third Battalion was probed then massively assaulted after midnight - I Company was penetrated and K Company had to give ground. Elements from L Company, held in battalion reserve, rallied to help restore the line by daybreak.

The Chinese, while attacking from multiple directions, had clearly determined that the southern perimeter was weakest, and that was where their main push came. Early in the assault a regiment-sized force came down from Hill 397 and crashed into G Company's little piece of the perimeter.

Using the dry stream bed, the Chinese hit the seam between McGee's Third Platoon and the First Platoon to his right. They quickly overran two First Platoon foxholes, emplaced machineguns, and began to rake McGee's position. The Chinese also came up the spur of the hill, hit McGee's position head-on and pushed hard to evict Third Platoon. Their tactics were crude, but effective. The Chinese tied a stick of dynamite to a long pole and crawled toward a foxhole. If that soldier was shot, another picked up the pole. If he was shot, another picked it up, and another and another, until the stick of dynamite was over the foxhole. Then the dynamite was detonated and the foxhole occupied by the Chinese. It was a terribly costly and bloody business, with the Americans firing carefully so as not to waste ammunition, and the Chinese always having one more man to pick up that pole.

Each foxhole lost meant a new Chinese position, allowing more Chinese to come up the hill and making more foxholes vulnerable, but things held together mainly because a machinegun being fired by Corporal Eugene Ottesen in Second Platoon, to McGee's left, covered the spur of the hill the Chinese crossed to reach Third Platoon positions. The Chinese targeted that gun from the beginning, and had killed one gunner before Ottesen took over. Ottesen stood fast, holding up the Chinese even though he knew he was a marked man. Sometime around 0200 hours the Chinese lobbed a couple of grenades into Ottesen's hole; the gun fell silent and G Company's perimeter began to break up.

There were just too many attacking Chinese and too few defenders to hold them back. The Chinese had overrun First Platoon on the company right, forcing the French to pull back a company and refuse their flank, and sometime during the early morning the Second Platoon on the company left was forced to pull back. This left McGee and his Third Platoon in an exposed salient under assault from three sides. As Ottesen went down, and with daylight still hours away, McGee knew he couldn't hold out much longer.

McGee sent his runner, Private First Class John Martin, to tell Lieutenant Thomas Heath, his company commander, that they were going to lose the hill unless he got reinforcements and supplies. Heath telephoned Lieutenant Colonel James Edwards, the battalion commander, who ordered a squad from F Company, in battalion reserve, to reinforce McGee. Sergeant Bill Kluttz, McGee's platoon sergeant, guided the men west toward the enemy-occupied foxholes and they immediately got into a fire fight that wounded or killed the entire Company F squad in ten minutes.

Heath also borrowed fifteen men from an artillery unit and directed Martin to lead them up the hill, but just as the artillerymen reached the crest, a mortar round killed one man, wounded another, and panicked the rest, who fled back down the hill. Heath gathered some of them at the bottom of the hill and led them back up himself. At the crest they met the Chinese and fled back down again. A frustrated Heath yelled, "Goddamn it, get back up on that hill! You'll die down here anyway. You might as well go up on the hill and die there." Martin rallied a few men, picked up some ammunition, and went back up the hill.

By about 0300 hours, McGee knew it was over. He was firing a Browning Automatic Rifle (BAR) in a foxhole with Bill Kluttz, who was firing a machinegun. There were only a couple of Third Platoon survivors still firing nearby. "Kluttz," McGee yelled over the din, "I believe they've got us." "Well, let's get as many of the sons of bitches as we can first," Kluttz yelled back, blasting away. Then the machinegun jammed. "Let's try to get out," McGee yelled. They threw the last of their grenades, gathered up the two other men, and walked back over the crest. Of the forty-six men in Third Platoon, these four were the only ones to walk out under their own power. The Chinese had taken McGee's hill, but it cost them the better part of three regiments. McGee was told later that more than 800 Chinese dead were counted immediately in front of his position.

When the Chinese finally occupied the crest, they brought Battery B of the 503rd Field Artillery under fire. The 503rd artillerymen fell back into the 37th Field Artillery Battalion's position. Defensive fire from the 105s discouraged the Chinese from trying to exploit their advantage, but they could be heard digging on the reverse slope.

Lieutenant Colonel Edwards, the battalion commander, released a platoon from F Company, the total remaining battalion reserve, and Freeman released a platoon of rangers from the regimental reserve, to try to restore the southern perimeter. There were 36 men in the ranger platoon, 28 in the F Company platoon, six or seven mortarmen, two machinegun crews, and four or five men left from G Company, all under the command of Captain John H. Ramsburg of the regiment's staff. Supported by mortars and machineguns, they attacked about 0540 hours and took the crest. A Chinese counter-attack threw them back.

At dawn the Americans expected the Chinese to withdraw, as they usually did with the coming of daylight and American aircraft. Instead, they continued to fight. The 23RCT had only 230 rounds of 81-mm and 4.2-inch mortar ammunition remaining. The situation was grave enough that at 0800 hours Freeman released B Company and the remainder of 1st Ranger Company from regimental reserve. This committed all available troops, with the exception of the engineer company, to restoring the southern perimeter. At 1000 hours, behind a mortar barrage and supported by direct fire from tanks and anti-aircraft artillery, B Company tried to take McGee's hill. B Company was kept off the crest by fire from the Chinese dug in on the southern slope. The Americans tried several more times to retake the hill in the following hours, and each time they were thrown back by the Chinese.

By late morning Colonel Freeman was evacuated under protest, and only after assurances from Lieutenant Colonel Edwards that the battle was in hand. But the Chinese stubbornly held on to the southern slope of McGee's hill, evidently hoping to use it to destroy the American position in the coming night.

Requested air support was on station at around noon. The Air Force flew 131 ground attack missions that afternoon, and dropped desperately needed ammunition and other supplies. Colonel Edwards decided that the only way to deal with the Chinese on the hill was by direct fire from the rear. He ordered three tanks, accompanied by rangers, to move south on the road past the perimeter. This would put them behind the Chinese and in a position to fire northeast into their positions.

After the engineers lifted mines and cleared barbed wire from the road, the tanks and rangers rolled past the perimeter. In co-ordination with artillery and air strikes, they pounded the Chinese positions late in the afternoon. After the preparatory shots were fired, B Company stormed over the crest and the Chinese position began to crumble. Just as the Chinese defense fell apart, a column of tanks appeared down the road to the south. After a moment of nervous surprise, Edward's men realized it was the relief force that had started for Chipyong-ni the day before. The Cavalry had arrived.

And they did so with a bang. The 5th Cavalry tanks fired on Chinese positions on Hill 397 to the west while the Air Force napalmed the surrounding hills. This reinforced assault, com-bined with the retreat already underway from McGee's hill, was just too much for the Chinese. The entire force began to run. It suddenly seemed as if thousands and thousands of Chinese just jumped up out of the ground and started running in the open. The Americans rained artillery and tank rounds and napalm canisters down upon them, killing hundreds. For the members of the 23RCT it was great relief, but also a terrifying prospect, as it became obvious just how badly they had been outnumbered.

In five months of fighting, Chipyong-ni was the first ma-jor battle the Chinese lost. Word of the victory spread quickly throughout Eighth Army, boosting morale as the men of the Eighth began once again to have confidence in themselves and their leaders. And lessons were learned. Experienced American units, well trained and well led, dug in with a sound plan of de-fense and adequate support from air and artillery, fighting te-naciously and tirelessly, could defeat any attempt by light infan-try to overrun them. The power of a cohesive team was proven against an enemy with overwhelming numbers. Chipyong-ni was a resounding victory, and set the pattern for future battles in Korea, and later in Vietnam.

Face fear and it will back down; use your assets to maximum advantage; rely on each other and the team will persevere.

CHAPTER 18

OPERATION DESERT STORM (1991)
THE SABRE

In the oppressive desert heat, members of the United States Army's 82nd Airborne Division, XVIII Airborne Corps, sat and waited for G-Day. Their rifles and lightly-armored M551 Sheridan Airborne Assault Vehicles were the only obstacles standing between the Iraqi army sitting at the border of occupied Kuwait, and the possibility of an Iraqi invasion of Saudi Arabia. "Speed bumps," the 82nd jokingly called themselves, despite the truth of the matter. Iraqi tank divisions a few hours to the north of their position could have rolled right over them at any moment, but still the 82nd waited, for they formed the vanguard of Operation Desert Shield.

Back in the States, the naysayers, the detractors, the antiwar protestors — all claimed that a swift war with Iraq was an impossibility. According to them, ground conflict would result in horrific casualties and a protracted occupation that would devolve into an unwinnable war of attrition. After Iraq invaded the sovereign nation of Kuwait, and allied coalition troops began guarding the Saudi border against possible Iraqi incursion, the entire world held its breath in anticipation.

The critics' concern was not unwarranted, for the 82nd Airborne soldiers who waited in the desert heat shared many of the same fears, and for the same reasons. Aside from a few minor deployments during the 1980s in Grenada and Panama, the Army hadn't seen a real wartime operation since Vietnam. Most of the Vietnam vets had long since retired, and only a scant few still served on active duty. Despite countless years of training drills and teamwork exercises, the Army could rely only on military theory. Any veteran would attest that real, live-fire combat against an enemy force couldn't compare to a training exercise. Training occurred in a controlled environment, whereas real combat could turn unpredictable at a moment's notice.

Also, training budgets had been cut in recent years, which left most Army soldiers unable to train long enough with some of the more sophisticated anti-tank weapon systems — mainly TOW, Dragon, and Hellfire missiles — due to the cuts and the sheer hardware expense. Because a single Hellfire missile cost the military $10,000, most Army personnel had never live-fired one before their deployment to the Persian Gulf. Ground troops and helicopter pilots could only lean on what training the Army could afford to give them, and hope the missiles performed up to spec at crunch time.

Lack of combat experience wasn't the biggest problem, however. Recruiting was down, by design. The U.S. military was shrinking. What soldiers President Bush could deploy to the Gulf would spend several months in an oppressive desert heat that few were adequately prepared for. Staunch military critics spoke ill of the Boeing AH-64 Apache attack helicopter, its laser-guided Hellfire missiles, and the M1A1 Abrams Main Battle Tank, decrying the equipment as too costly and without any real track record to justify the expense. Then, looming over the whole U.S. deployment was the ever-present threat of Iraqi troops employing chemical weapons, deployed either by ground troops or by Al-Hussein ballistic missiles — modified, Soviet-manufactured Scuds.

By mid-February 1991, the coalition force buildup consisted of two corps of U.S. Army soldiers, two divisions of U.S. Marines, various Saudi forces, and a host of other allied troops. Together they faced the fourth-largest military in the world. At the outset, the Iraqis appeared to have the home-court advantage. In addition to their army comprising roughly the same number of troops as the allied coalition, the Iraqis possessed intimate knowledge of their home territory, and they had dug into defensive positions. Sand berms and natural terrain would hinder any allied attempt to advance into Kuwait or onto Iraqi soil, and amongst the Iraqi forces, allied intelligence had identified at least five reserve divisions of Saddam Hussein's elite Republican Guard.

The most fearsome opponent thus far has been the waiting, and the 12,000 soldiers of the 82nd Airborne had suffered the worst. Their Division Ready Brigade had been in Saudi Arabia since August 7th, 1990: nearly seven whole months. Normally stationed at Fort Bragg, North Carolina, the 4,000 men of the 82nd's Ready Brigade had trained for years for this kind of mission. Within eighteen hours of receiving deployment orders, their boots were on the ground in the Saudi desert at Dhahran. They began immediately to establish an airhead for the growing contingent of allied forces.

The irony was, by G-Day the members of the 82nd were already considered the veterans of the campaign to liberate Kuwait, and yet they hadn't even fired a shot except in target practice. But, like every other American soldier, when G-Day arrived they had only their training, their leaders, and each other to rely on. Fortunately, the U.S. armed forces in the Gulf had proof positive that their soldiers' assets, both material and immaterial, could withstand the crucible of combat.

On January 29th Iraqi forces had pushed south through the border of Kuwait and attacked the Saudi border town of Khafji, overrunning the Saudis' observation posts. Two days later, a joint task force of Arab troops, U.S. Marines, and U.S. Army Special Forces drove the Iraqis back across the border, with few allied casualties. Coalition leaders saw the Battle of Khafji as a successful test run for the upcoming operation, and the outcome bolstered the confidence of all 400,000 American troops poised to displace Iraqi forces from Kuwait. Morale remained as high as the desert heat would allow, and the air sorties across the Iraq border continued.

The United Nations had given Iraq until the 15th of January to withdraw from Kuwait. Once Saddam Hussein allowed the deadline to expire, Operation Desert Shield officially transformed into Operation Desert Storm. For the past several weeks, allied air sorties had pounded Iraqi infrastructure as best they could, taking out bunkers, aircraft, aerial defenses, and bridges. Missiles, smart bombs, and U.S. Navy-launched Tomahawk cruise missiles had struck strategic targets throughout Iraq and had "prepared the battlefield" in accordance with the Pentagon's Air-Land Battle doctrine.

But Hussein refused to capitulate. The White House agreed with the Joint Chiefs: ground war had to commence. Then it was the Army's turn — all that waiting and training in the desert the 82nd had been doing would finally be worth something.

On February 17th, the members of the 82nd moved to the Saudi town of Rafha, nearly 200 miles west of Wadi al Batin, the dried-up riverbed marking the Kuwait/Iraq border. They met up with the French 6th Light Division, with whom they would work alongside in the first phase of the invasion. The soldiers of the 82nd quickly established observations posts — allowing them to see down the valley across the border — and set up possible ambush points.

Then they dug in and waited some more, just like they had been doing since August. They had gotten pretty good at it by then.

Further east, the rest of the Army soldiers had been keeping busy. The 24th Mechanized Infantry Division, another unit of the Army's Rapid Deployment Force also assigned to Lieutenant General Gary E. Luck's XVIII Airborne Corps, arrived in Iraq near the end of August to reinforce the 82nd Airborne's defensive line with a bit more muscle. Their standing orders were to patrol the highways right at the Saudi/Kuwait border with more than four hundred M1 Abrams tanks and M2 Bradley Armored Fighting Vehicles. They were instructed to remain as visible to the enemy troops as possible. The goal was to maintain a large display of force, to trick the Iraqi army into thinking the 24th had more hardware in their pocket than they actually did. The allied forces even used buried dumpsters and large cardboard boxes to fool radar and reconnaissance into artificially inflating Iraqi perception of the coalition's total force strength.

On the night of January 17th, Apache attack helicopters from the 101st Airborne Division — also assigned XVIII Corps — flew beneath radar coverage and destroyed two important Iraqi radar installations across the border. This blinded Iraqi troops to allied military traffic, which made the 24th Infantry's mission of maintaining a blatant show of force even more important. To further confuse Iraqi intelligence, the 1st Cavalry Division, which was assigned to the Army's VII Corps, began light scouting raids up Wadi al Batin during the second week of allied air strikes. These maneuvers were intended to convince the Iraqi army that when the coalition ground troops attacked in force, they would move north through the wadi to invade Kuwait. Concurrent raiding operations by Marines into southern Kuwait diverted Iraqi attention eastward, where the occupying troops anticipated an amphibious assault would come at any moment. These elaborate ruses had kept more than eight Iraqi divisions pinned in place, right where the allies wanted them.

The 82nd Airborne and the rest of XVIII Corps were slated to attack, but not where the Iraqis were expecting. The whole corps was situated along a stretch of Iraqi border far to the west of Kuwait, with VII Corps at their right flank. February 22nd saw every XVIII and VII Corps division scouting across their 300-mile front to search for the best avenues through difficult terrain for the imminent G-Day invasion.

In the early hours of Sunday, February 24th, 1991, something changed in the desert air amongst the assembled soldiery, something imperceptible. Electricity passed through the line of allied troops as Commanding General "Stormin' Norman" Schwarzkopf announced G-Day had arrived. The balloon was up. The mission clock for Operation Desert Sabre began counting.

The shield had become a sword.

For the 82nd Airborne, the time they had been waiting for had finally arrived. Of the whole U.S. Army, they had been waiting the longest, and their anxiety was mixed with a healthy injection of trepidation. The plan for Operation Desert Sabre, the ground offensive to push the Iraqi army from Kuwait, was straightforward in theory, but a thousand and one things could have gone wrong. A month earlier General Colin Powell, Chairman of the Joint Chiefs of Staff, distilled the plan into layman's terms for the press. "Our strategy for dealing with this army is very, very simple," he told them at a Pentagon briefing. "First we're going to cut it off, then we're going to kill it."

The perfect task for a proper sword.

Accomplishing all of the campaign's objectives would require a never-before-seen level of coordination, cooperation, and synchronicity across the whole allied front. Army training and constant drilling had given the American soldiers the tools and the foundation upon which to make this operation work, and it was time to put the plan into effect.

At 0400 hours GMT, the 2nd Brigade of the 82nd Airborne Division accompanied the French 6th Light Division north into Iraq. Their primary goal was an airfield at As Salman nearly 100 miles into Iraq. After taking As Salman, the 6th would create a screen on the western flank of the battlefield to prevent any Iraqi reinforcements from threatening the allied advance. Working in concert, the French troops and the soldiers of the 82nd converted their years of training into a swift, decisive victory over elements of the Iraqi 45th Mechanized Infantry Division. Together they took nearly 2,500 enemy soldiers prisoner, and both the French and the 82nd suffered extremely light casualties, far fewer than predicted — a sigh of relief to the weary soldiers of the 82nd.

So far so good.

Further east along the XVIII Corps battle line, the 82nd's fellow airborne division, the 101st, commenced, at 0800 hours, the largest helicopter assault in history. Flying just fifty feet above the desert sand to avoid radar and possible anti-aircraft defenses, hundreds of the 101st's CH-47 Chinook and UH-60 Blackhawk helicopters ferried 2,000 troops north, on a line parallel to the 82nd's advance. The remainder of the 101st followed closely behind in ground vehicles. Both the 82nd and 101st linked up at As Salman and cleared small pockets of infantry. As soon as the objective was secured, fifty Chinooks immediately airlifted refueling supplies to an area just east of the airfield. Within three hours, XVIII Corps had established a fully functioning Forward Operating Base, codenamed Cobra, which effectively doubled the operational range of allied helicopters and provided a staging area for further assault into Iraq.

The 82nd and the rest of XVIII Corps were one step closer to their ultimate goal of cutting off the Iraqi army, and with surprisingly few casualties. Either the coordinated AirLand Battle blitzkrieg had shattered the Iraqi resolve, or the feared Iraqi forces were not as formidable as their reputation.

By 1300 hours, Marine and coalition success in moving towards retaking Kuwait City allowed the 24th Mechanized Infantry Division to cross the Line of Departure into Iraq and begin their assault nearly fifteen hours ahead of schedule. The 24th held XVIII Corps' rightmost flank as they moved into position for phase two of the attack. This division had spent the last several years training specifically for desert missions, yet their northward assault occurred during wind and rain. Like the 82nd, the soldiers of the 24th had waited far too long and trained too much for these conditions to let a little inclement weather delay their advance when other divisions were counting on their success.

By the end of G-Day, the whole operation had performed far beyond expectation. Army divisions achieved their 24-hour objectives within a mere twelve hours. American and allied casualties from enemy action were exceptionally light, far below even the most conservative projections.

Critics of military operations in the Persian Gulf no longer had a leg to stand on. Coordination between the many divisions on the battlefield had thus far prevented Desert Sabre from turning into a quagmire of attrition.

Monday morning, February 25th — G Plus 1 — the 1st Cavalry Division of VII Corps sent thirty-six Apache helicopters up Wadi al Batin to scout for a safe attack route for their ground forces, a risky daytime action for these aircraft. The much-maligned Hellfire missiles performed exactly as expected, despite the pilots' lack of live-fire experience, and were responsible for destroying several tanks, artillery batteries, armored personnel carriers, and bunkers. But not all went according to plan. Iraqi anti-aircraft fire downed one of the helicopters. Fortunately, the Apache "crashes well" due to its reinforced chassis, which is designed to absorb the impact of the crash and protect the two-man crew in just this kind of incident. Both of the pilots survived without injury. As soon as they abandoned the disabled rotorcraft, another Apache from the 1st Cavalry landed nearby to pick up them up, all while still under enemy fire. For their bravery and teamwork, the rescuing crew's commanding officer recommended they be awarded the Army's Bronze Star with Valor.

One $10-million helicopter was lost in the maneuver, but zero personnel casualties. The Apaches — and their worthy crew complements — had already demonstrated their inherent value contributing to the coalition effort.

As the rest of VII Corps advanced north into Iraq, the soldiers of XVIII Airborne Corps still had their work cut out for them. The 24th Infantry continued heading north through rapidly deteriorating weather conditions. Departing from the Cobra FOB, the 82nd and the 101st kept on their spearhead deep into Iraq, while the French patrolled their westernmost flank for any surprises. Aside from individual military objectives, XVIII's overall mission defined the essence of General Powell's overall military strategy. They were to isolate the Iraqi army within Kuwait, to "cut it off" from the main body in Iraq, while VII Corps, the Marines, and the coalition forces "killed it" within Kuwait's borders. However, if XVIII arrived too late to cut off the Iraqis, the rest of the plan would fall apart and the enemy would then be able to easily withdraw, regroup, and return in force at a later date.

The 101st air-assaulted their way to the Euphrates River Valley and were the first to reach the road south of the river, a four-lane highway that runs east-to-west from Basra in south Iraq all the way to Baghdad. This Main Supply Route (MSR) formed one of the major arteries of the Iraqi military. Cut the MSR, and Iraqi reinforcements and supplies coming from the capital would not be able to reach the beleaguered troops inside Kuwait. Also, if the rest of the allied troops executed their mission well, any Iraqi forces retreating from Kuwait would have nowhere to go. With this goal in mind, the 82nd and the 101st set up roadblocks along the MSR and used their ordnance to reduce sections of pavement to craters, thus preventing any further travel by enemy forces in either direction. The strategy quickly paid off when the 101st destroyed a supply truck heading east, towards Basra.

To support the roadblock, the 24th Infantry Division advanced towards objective "Gray" through rough terrain consisting of wadis, steep cliffs, and swampland. The enemy infantry they encountered immediately surrendered without firing a shot. The 197th Infantry Brigade, an independent unit that was operationally attached to the 24th Division, screened the VII Corps flank. This task force quickly cut off another route known as "Scud Road," a position from which the Iraqis would often launch Al-Hussein missiles.

Past midnight on February 26th — G Plus 2 — it began to rain. The 24th were caught in what members of the 197th accurately dubbed a "mudstorm." Visibility was extremely poor, forcing them to halt for a time, but they pressed on eastward, toward Tallil Airbase, fighting with Mother Nature for every inch of ground they negotiated. By early morning, tanks and Bradleys were getting stuck in the mud. Progressing forward required a brutal team effort to find traversable spots through the terrain. Each vehicle drove until it got stuck, then the next vehicle tried a different spot until a stable path was found through the muck. Eventually, they pushed through. Just as their vehicles were about to run out of gas, supply trucks arrived in the nick of time with 25,000 gallons of fuel. The offensive toward Jalibah Airfield continued. The 197th softened up the airbase with artillery before launching a "textbook" assault amidst the worst sandstorm of the whole operation — an overwhelming success.

By midday, the armor of VII Corps had surrounded Republican Guard divisions near the Kuwait/Iraq border. The massive, coordinated flanking maneuver of XVIII and VII Corps blocked all Iraqi force escape routes. The hammer of Marine and allied advance from the south had pushed the withdrawing enemy into VII Corps' anvil. Allied forces and air strikes then pounded retreating columns of Iraqi armor down Highway 80 in Kuwait, effectively ejecting Iraqi forces from the nation's capital. After midnight on February 27th — G Plus 3 — the Pentagon declared that allied troops controlled Kuwait City.

But the job was still not quite finished. If the retreating Iraqi troops could successfully withdraw and regroup, little would prevent them from attempting to reinvade Kuwait once the coalition troops returned home. In a coordinated assault, tanks from the 1st Armored Division, Apache attack helicopters, and Air Force A-10 Warthog ground attack aircraft engaged the Republican Guard's elite Medina and Hammurabi tank divisions. The ensuing conflict resulted in the largest tank battle since the clash of Soviet and German forces at Kursk in 1943. The Republican Guard tanks attempted a fighting withdrawal, but they had neither the weapon systems nor the strategy to prevail against overwhelming force.

The sabre had successfully cut off the enemy before running it clean through.

The next morning, February 28th — G Plus 4 — President Bush announced that allied troops had achieved the war's primary objective — the ejection of Iraqi troops from Kuwait — and Saddam Hussein has acquiesced to UN resolutions. At 0800 hours local time, the ground campaign was declared complete exactly 100 hours after it began. During that four-day period, the U.S. Army and its allies had killed or captured tens of thousands of Iraqi soldiers and destroyed over 2,000 tanks, nearly 1,800 armored vehicles, and more than 2,100 pieces of artillery. American casualties for the entire Gulf War amounted to 147 battle deaths and fewer than 500 wounded as a result of combat.

Despite all the negative assumptions impugning the U.S. Army's ability to wage a short campaign, the soldiers' training, teamwork, and esprit de corps more than made up for a lack of combat experience. The coordination between and synchronization with disparate Army, Marine, and coalition commands across a massive battlefield culminated in a ground offensive that ended far, far sooner than any initial forecast. America's Army served to preserve liberty. The soldiers focused on clear objectives and acted decisively to get the job done.

For the 82nd Airborne Division, however, the cessation of hostilities means the end of a long, yet satisfying haul. Of all the American soldiers that participated in the defense of Saudi Arabia and the liberation of Kuwait, the boots of the 82nd were on the ground longer than anyone else's. With the sovereignty of Kuwait restored and any further Iraqi threat neutralized, the airborne soldiers had earned their trip back home to Fort Bragg for some well-deserved R&R.

Great rewards demand great risks; when you have momentum exploit it; if you are doing the right things for the right reasons trust your team to see the task through.

CHAPTER 19

AAR - LESSONS LEARNED

To continually improve capabilities the Army has established a formalized After Action Review (AAR) - Lessons Learned process. This process, employed after every training exercise and mission, is an opportunity for participants to review and evaluate what happened. They discuss what went well, what went poorly, and how individuals and the team as a whole can improve future performance. The Army even goes so far as to gather lessons learned across the entire institution and has established a centralized digital repository for soldiers and leaders to draw on to better prepare for whatever the future might hold. This final chapter serves as my attempt to fulfill my obligation to review and emphasize the main points. The quality and impact of my presentation throughout is left for you to determine.

We have covered a lot of ground in *Warriors, Diplomats, Heroes, Why America's Army Succeeds.* My purpose with this effort, using America's Army as the example, is to help you glean some insight as to what it takes to succeed in any aspect of life. I've shared some of my personal story, presented relevant and battle-tested doctrine, discussed the principles of leadership, illustrated the impact of individuals, and offered examples of cohesive teams striving valiantly to survive and succeed. I don't claim to have presented all the answers I just hope to have given enough to help you and your organization move in the right direction.

America's Army strives valiantly to uphold the ideals upon which America is built — ideals of liberty, justice, equality, and opportunity. American soldiers take on the hard challenges at the behest of the people, so that society might prosper. American soldiers are warriors, diplomats, and heroes — leaders, thinkers, and doers. Warriors are aggressive, action-oriented men and women — men and women who prepare themselves to endure tremendous hardships and who willingly meet audacious adversaries anytime, anywhere. Diplomats endeavor to grasp the big picture and then focus on the most important elements, so as to do what is right and best for the team, for society, for humanity. Heroes make the hard choices. They do what is needed, what is right, despite the cost. Heroes act so that others might survive, might grow, might live and might love. Heroes do the things most people are unable or unwilling to do.

America's Army succeeds because it is ***Values Based, Mission Focused, and Action Oriented***. Army leaders inspire. They lead by example. They stir people to action by means of a compelling vision and powerful motivation. America's Army is a cohesive, capable team - a team that routinely accomplishes the seemingly impossible. America's Army applies the principles you must apply to succeed in business and in life.

Though not all the lessons one can draw from examining the legacy of America's Army or the example of American soldiers are captured here, following is a list of insights we have covered:

Part 1

♦ The key to success - in battle, in business, and in life - is being values based, mission focused and action oriented.

♦ Build on a solid foundation of enduring values.

♦ Focus on the objective, not obstacles.

♦ Act with enthusiasm, with commitment.

♦ Individuals lead and contribute; teams win!

♦ Nothing brings people together like shared hardship.

♦ Life presents challenges, prepare yourself and your team to endure hardship.

♦ Failure is often a symptom of lack of will.

- Values guide; lose your values, lose your way.
- Test your limits; you and your team are more capable than you know.
- Clearly define and understand your mission and your team's mission.
- Business, like life, is constantly changing - manage change.
- Prepare to deal with distractions.
- Design and employ effective systems for personal and professional success.
- Determine tasks, conditions, and standards for your organization; then adhere to them.
- The surest route to success: disciplined people applying effective processes.
- Think through your circumstances; consider all viable options then choose the best one.
- Task and purpose (what to do and why) are the most important aspects of success.
- Health and fitness matter.
- Working together people can do what seems impossible.
- Fear limits you only when you allow it to.
- Success demands you take risks.

Part 2

- We all follow, we all lead; like it or not.
- While every individual influences the team, the team leader influences most.
- Nothing worth having comes easy.
- To lead is to inspire; to provide vision and or motivation.
- Successful leaders are competent and caring; they care about their people and about the mission.

Chapter 19: AAR: Lessons Learned

- ◆ Leadership matters - your leadership.
- ◆ You possess the potential of an outstanding leader; you are one heroic act away from greatness.

George Washington
- Remain grounded in values
- Discipline yourself and your team
- Offer an inspiring vision

Meriwether Lewis
- Know yourself and the members of your team (capabilities and limitations)
- Adapt to whatever circumstances you face
- See the task through despite the challenges

Joshua L. Chamberlain
- Leadership requires conviction
- Courage demands a willingness to assume risk
- Honorable men are empathetic

Alvin C. York
- Rely on your moral compass (enduring values)
- Focus in the moment on the task at hand
- Act for the greater good

George C. Marshall
- You are responsible for yourself
- Focus on the big picture; understand what resources are available and what can be done
- Live so that others might prosper and you will lead a full life

David H. Petraeus
- Never settle for mediocrity
- Discipline prepares for excellence
- Flexibility and creativity are seeds of success

Part 3

- ◆ Business and life are team sports.

- ◆ Success requires discipline, tenacity, and a willingness to take risks.

- ◆ Trust is the ultimate bond.

- ◆ We succeed or fail together - all of us.

- ◆ Youth need not fade; every day presents an opportunity for a new adventure.

- ◆ Life is not secure; you might as well take your team to higher heights.

- ◆ A cohesive team represents decisive power.

Cowpens (1781)

- Engage people where they are
- Deliberately build a team
- Employ your people to exploit their strengths

New Orleans (1814-1815)

- Ensure everyone on your team knows the mission
- Employ limited resources carefully for maximum impact
- Commit - act decisively when you must

San Juan Hill (1898)

- A team proves itself by its deeds
- Be willing to take on the hard jobs
- The honor of doing a difficult task ultimately rests with the doer

Bastogne (1944)

- Know your environment - the lay of the land
- Trust your people
- Over communicate and react as one

Chapter 19: AAR: Lessons Learned

Korea (1951)

- Face fear and it will back down
- Use your assets to maximum advantage
- Rely on each other and the team will persevere

Iraq (1991)

- Great rewards demand great risks
- When you have momentum exploit it
- If you are doing the right things for the right reasons trust your team to see the task through

Power and fear are the two most compelling aspects of the human condition. Power and fear are the domain of warriors, diplomats, and heroes. Every human being yearns for power. Every individual longs to master his or her circumstances and choose his or her own way. To overcome inherent weaknesses and multiply power, we individuals band together. But, no matter how powerful we become, we recognize limitations and feel threats. We are limited by time and by a failure of will. We are haunted by the specter of pain or loss, feelings of fear, which destroy the promise of individual lives and inhibit the potential of society.

America's Army is an institution established and maintained to manage power and address fear. America's Army though far from perfect is a bastion of values, courage and discipline. We can learn much from America's Army.

Warriors, Diplomats, Heroes, Why America's Army Succeeds offers lessons for business and for life. Learn the lessons. Take yourself, your family, and your team to new heights. You can be a warrior, a diplomat, a hero. Do the right things, for the right reasons and your success is guaranteed.

AFTERWORD

America's Army succeeds because the institution collectively, and soldiers individually, are values based, mission focused and action oriented. America's Army succeeds for the same reasons anyone succeeds at anything. The Army and its soldiers don't always win — they get beat up, suffer horrendously, and endure catastrophic loss. But soldiers press on; they persist and they try again until they give the last full measure of devotion.

America's Army is your Army. The challenges the Army faces are the challenges you face. An individual can have an impact — can make a difference. From the strength of individuals comes the power of a team. Learn from the Army's experience.

Choose the hard road, as the hard road is the only road that leads somewhere worthwhile. Do what is right, discipline yourself, focus, and most importantly ACT. Know, even as you face trial and tribulation, that you never advance alone — soldiers past, present, and future guard that road.

SUMMARY LESSON:
Life is not a spectator sport.
Make hard choices.
Focus on challenging tasks.
Get in the game; play to win.

ABOUT THE AUTHOR

Colonel Scott F. Paradis retired at the end of 2011 from active service after 31-plus years with the United States Army. He lives with his beautiful wife of 26 years, Lisa, in Alexandria, Virginia. Together they have two extraordinary children, Merideth and Mitchell. Following is a brief military bio (headlines serve as a civilian translation/summary).

Diverse assignments around the world.

Completed two tours with Department of the Army at the Pentagon focused on strategic communications and congressional affairs; helped stand up the Multi National Corps - Iraq (MNC-I) Improvised Explosive Device Task Force in Baghdad; served as a National Security Fellow at the John F. Kennedy School of Government at Harvard University and as a National Defense Fellow in the United States Senate working with the Armed Services and Government Affairs Committees. Served in various infantry assignments with the 187th Separate Infantry Brigade in New England; as operations officer with the Kansas City Recruiting Battalion and later with the 21st Theater Army Area Command in Europe and in the Balkans during Operation Joint Endeavor. Served as aide-de-camp to the commanding general of Fifth United States Army in San Antonio, Texas and as Deputy Commander of Fort Dix, New Jersey.

Broad military and civilian education.

Senior Service College, National Security Fellow, John F. Kennedy School of Government, Harvard University; Congressional Fellow, Georgetown University and the United States Senate; Masters of Science in Administration, Central Michigan University; Bachelor of Arts in Sociology, University of New Hampshire; Command and General Staff College; Combined Arms and Services Staff School; the Civil Affairs Qualification, Infantry Officer Advanced, Infantry Officer Basic, Airborne, Air Assault, and Northern Warfare Instructor courses.

Recognized for excelling at challenging tasks.

Military awards and decorations include the Legion of Merit, the Bronze Star, five Meritorious Service Medals, three Army Commendation Medals, two Army Achievement Medals, Army Reserve Components Achievement Medal, National Defense Service Medal, Iraq Campaign Medal, Global War on Terrorism Service Medal, Armed Forces Service Medal, Armed Forces Reserve Medal, Army Service, Overseas Service, and Army Reserve Component Overseas Training Ribbons, NATO Medal, Parachutist Badge, Air Assault Badge, and Royal British Parachutist Wings.

Contact Scott F. Paradis at Success101Workshop.com for help training your team to excel.

ACKNOWLEDGEMENTS

Everything I have done, everything I do, and everything I am yet to do is made possible by the loving and supportive people that surround me and by those that are drawn into my awareness. It is their genius and their generosity that make my accomplishments possible.

For Lisa, my wife, and my two terrific children, Merideth and Mitchell, and all my family and friends I am forever grateful. I am truly blessed having wonderful people in my life.

Warriors, Diplomats, Heroes, Why America's Army Succeeds is not a singular achievement. It takes a team of focused, dedicated, professionals to put something like this together. I owe many thanks to great people, some mentioned here and others for contributions that though not singled out are no less important. First I have to recognize all the Soldiers I have encountered, worked with, and been inspired by over the term of my career of service and for the countless Soldiers who have sacrificed to give me the opportunities I enjoy today. Thanks go to contributing researchers and writers for the constructive combination of detail and creativity: Peter Gerardo (George Washington), Anthony Chatfield (Meriwether Lewis), Norma Jean Lutz (Joshua Chamberlain), Bob Hanover (George Marshall), Stephanie Pierce (David Petraeus), Chris Smith (Cowpens), Terence O'Connor (New Orleans), David Fulmer (San Juan Hill), Rebecca Bugger (Bastogne), David Brooks (Korea), and Philip Lee (Desert Storm). I am grateful to pre-publication readers, confidants, and

Acknowledgments

friendly critics who took the time to offer beneficial feedback and advice: my sister Renee and Colonel (Ret) Joe Follansbee, Mr. Janko Jackson, Mr. Ron Adolphi, and my informal council of retired colonels: Corrina Boggess, Kevin and Renee Finnegan, and Charles "Rocky" Stone. Thanks go to my diligent and exacting editor Stephanie Pierce for weeding through the detail and smoothing over rough spots; to the professional design team at Archer-Ellison led by the capable Kim Leonard; and to the creative vision of the cover design team at The Brand4U.

People's courage, commitment, and sacrifice inspire me. I pray that the words etched on these pages might inspire others to take on laudable challenges, endure worthwhile hardships, and fulfill what I know to be limitless potential.

SELECT SOURCES

Chapters 1 - 5 and 12

United States Army Field Manual 1, *The Army*, June 2005, Headquarters, Department of the Army, Washington, DC

United States Army Field Manual 3-0, *Operations*, February 2008, Headquarters, Department of the Army, Washington, DC

United States Army Field Manual 5-0, *The Operations Process*, March 2010, Headquarters, Department of the Army, Washington, DC

United States Army Field Manual 6-0, *Mission Command: Command and Control of Army Forces*, August 2003, Headquarters, Department of the Army, Washington, DC

United States Army Field Manual 6-22 (FM 22-100), *Army Leadership*, October 2006, Headquarters, Department of the Army, Washington, DC

United States Army Field Manual 22-100, *Military Leadership*, October 1983, Headquarters, Department of the Army, Washington, DC

United States Army Field Manual 7-0, *Training for Full Spectrum Operations*, December 2008, Headquarters, Department of the Army, Washington, DC

Select Sources

United States Army Field Manual 27-10, *The Law of Land Warfare*, July 1956, Headquarters, Department of the Army, Washington, DC

Chapter 6 George Washington

Ellis, Joseph J. *Founding Brothers.* New York: Alfred A. Knopf, 2001.

Ellis, Joseph J. *His Excellency George Washington.* New York: Alfred A. Knopf, 2004.

Thomas Paine. "The Crisis," December 23, 1776.

Stazesky, Richard C. "George Washington, Genius in Leadership." Presentation to the George Washington Club of Wilmington, DE, February 22, 2000.

George Washington: American Revolutionary. The Biography Channel.

http://www.history.org/almanack/life/manners/rules2.cfm

"New Jersey and Trenton." http://www.usahistory.info/Revolutionary-War/Trenton.html

Chapter 7 Meriwether Lewis

Ambrose, Stephen. *Undaunted Courage: Meriwether Lewis, Thomas Jefferson, and the Opening of the American West.* New York: Simon and Schuster, 1996.

Danisi, Thomas C. *Meriwether Lewis.* New York: Prometheus Books, 2009

DeVoto, Bernard. *The Journals of Lewis and Clark.* New York: Houghton Mifflin Co., 1953

http://xroads.virginia.edu/~HYPER/JOURNALS/toc.html

Fritz, Harry. *The Lewis and Clark Expedition.* Connecticut: Greenwood Press, 2004.

Lavendar, David. *The Way to the Western Sea*. Nebraska: University of Nebraska Press, 2001.

"Lewis and Clark: The Corps" PBS.org. Lewis and Clark. http://www.pbs.org/lewisandclark

Woodger, Elin and Toropov Brandon. *"Encyclopedia of the Lewis and Clark Expedition"*. Infobase Publishing, 2004.

Chapter 8 Joshua L. Chamberlain

Chamberlain, Joshua Lawrence. *Joshua Lawrence Chamberlain Collection 1817 - 1914*, Maine Historical Society, Portland, Maine and Bowdoin College, Brunswick, Maine.

Chamberlain to Fanny, Oct. 26, 1862, *Chamberlain Letters*, in possession of Miss Rosamond Allen.

Chamberlain, "Through Blood and Fire at Gettysburg," *Hearst's Magazine*, XXIII, 898-899.

Deans, Sis Boulos. *His Proper Post : A Biography of Gen. Joshua Lawrence Chamberlain*. Kearny, NJ: Belle Grove Publishing Co., 1996.

Desjardin, Thomas A. *Stand Firm Ye Boys From Maine : The 20th Maine and the Gettysburg Campaign*. Gettysburg, PA: Thomas Publications, c1995.

Pullen, John J. *Joshua Chamberlain : A Hero's Life and Legacy*. Mechanicsburg, PA: Stackpole Books, c1999.

Chapter 9 Alvin C. York

Birdwell, Michael E. *Celluloid Soldiers: The Warner Bros. Campaign against Nazism*. New York: New York University Press, 1999.

Capozzola, Christopher. *Uncle Sam Wants You: World War I and the Making of the Modern American Citizen*. New York: Oxford University Press, 2008.

Lee, David D. *Sergeant York: An American Hero*. Lexington, Kentucky: University Press of Kentucky, 1985.

Perry, John. *Sgt. York: His Life, Legend & Legacy*. Nashville, TN: B&H Books, 1997.

Toplin, Robert Brent. *History by Hollywood: The Use and Abuse of the American Past*. Chicago: University of Illinois Press, 1996.

Wheeler, Richard (editor). *Sergeant York and the Great War*. Bulverde, Texas: Mantle Ministries, 1998.

Williams, Gladys. "Alvin C. York". York Institute. Archived from original on March 26, 2005. http://web.archive.org/web/20050326202450/http://volweb.utk.edu/Schools/York/biography.html.

Chapter 10 George C. Marshall

Alter, Jonathan. *The Defining Moment: FDR's Hundred Days and the Triumph of Hope* New York: Simon & Schuster, 2006.

Ambrose, Stephen E. *The Victors: Eisenhower and His Boys: The Men of World War II* New York: Simon & Schuster, 1998.

Diggins, John Patrick. *The Proud Decades: America in War and Peace, 1941-1960* New York: W.W. Norton & Company, 1988.

Evans, Harold, Gail Buckland, and Kevin Baker. *The American Century* New York: Alfred A. Knopf, 2000.

Gavin, James M. *On to Berlin: Battles of an Airborne Commander 1943-1946* New York: Bantam Books, 1985.

Light, Paul C. "Government's Greatest Achievements of the Past Half Century," *Brookings*, (December 2000) http://www.brookings.edu/papers/2000/11governance_light.aspx.

Marshall, George C. "My Early Life in Uniontown." Interview by Forrest C. Pogue, Tape 1M, 21 February 1957, http://www.marshallfoundation.org/library/pogue.html (accessed April 7, 2012).

Parker, R.A. C. *Struggle For Survival: The History of the Second World War* New York: Oxford University Press, 1989.

Pogue, Forrest C. *George C. Marshall*, New York: Viking Press, 1963-87. http://www.marshallfoundation.org/about/timeline/between.html (accessed April 7, 2012).

Walker, Martin. *The Cold War: A History* New York: Henry Holt and Company, 1995.

Chapter 11 David Petreaus

Atkinson, Rick. *In the Company of Soldiers: A Chronicle of Combat.* New York: Henry Holt & Co., 2004.

Bumiller, Elisabeth. "Petraeus Retires, With a Warning." *The New York Times Online.* August 31, 2011. Available from http://atwar.blogs.nytimes.com/2011/08/31/petraeus-retires-with-a-warning/?ref=us.

Cloud, David and Jaffe, Greg, *The Fourth Star: Four Generals and the Epic Struggle for the Future of the United States Army.* New York: Crown Publishers, 2009.

Dozier, Kimberly. "Headed for CIA, Petraeus Leaves a Revamped Warzone." *ABC News Online.* July 19, 2011. Available from http://abcnews.go.com/Politics/wireStory?id=14102691.

Chapter 13 Cowpens

Babits, Lawrence E. *A Devil of a Whipping: The Battle of Cowpens.* Chapel Hill: University of North Carolina Press, 1998.

Bearss, Edwin. C. *The Battle of Cowpens: A Documented Narrative and Troop Movement Maps.* Johnson City, Tennessee: Overmountain Press, 1996.

Moncure, John. The Cowpens Staff Ride and Battlefield Tour. Fort Leavenworth, Kansas: Combat Studies Institute, 1996. http://usacac.army.mil/cac2/cgsc/carl/download/csipubs/moncure.pdf

Roberts, Kenneth. *The Battle of Cowpens: The Great Morale-Builder*. Garden City: Doubleday and Company, 1958.

Chapter 14 Battle of New Orleans

Brown, Wilburt S. *The Amphibious Campaign for West Florida and Louisiana, 1814-1815*, Tuscaloosa: University of Alabama Press, 1969.

Groom, Winston. *Patriotic Fire: Andrew Jackson and Jean Laffite at the Battle of New Orleans*. New York: Vintage Books, 2006.

Hickey, Donald R. *The War of 1812 : a forgotten conflict*, Urbana: Univ. of Illinois Press, 1989.

Patterson, Benton Rains. *The Generals, Andrew Jackson, Sir Edward Pakenham, and the road to New Orleans*, New York: New York University Press, 2008.

Quimby, Robert S. *The U.S. Army in the War of 1812: an operational and command study*, East Lansing: Michigan State University Press, 1997.

Remini, Robert V. *The Battle of New Orleans*, New York: Penguin Putnam, Inc., 1999.

Rowland, Eron. *Andrew Jackson's Campaign against the British, or, the Mississippi Territory in the War of 1812, concerning the Military Operations of the Americans, Creek Indians, British, and Spanish, 1813-1815*, Freeport, NY: Books for Libraries Press, 1971.

Battle of New Orleans, http://battleofneworleans.org/

Chapter 15 San Juan Hill

Field, Ron and Bielakowski, Alexander. *Buffalo Soldiers: African American Troops in the US forces 1866-1945*, Oxford, United Kingdom: Osprey Publishing, 2008.

General Kent's Report: Official Account Of The Three Days' Fighting Around Santiago de Cuba, *The New York Times*, 22 July 1898.

Konstam, Angus. *San Juan Hill 1898: America's Emergence as a World Power*. Oxford, United Kingdom: Osprey Publishing, 1998.

Powell, Anthony L. *"Black Participation in the Spanish-American War"*. The Spanish-American War Centennial web site: http://www.spanamwar.com/.

Schubert, Frank N. *Black Valor: Buffalo Soldiers and the Medal of Honor, 1870-1898*. New York: Rowman & Littlefield, 1997.

Schubert, Frank N. *"Buffalo Soldiers at San Juan Hill,"* Paper delivered at the 1998 Conference of Army Historians, Bethesda, Maryland.

Schubert, Frank N. *Voices of the Buffalo Soldier: Records, Reports, and Recollections of Military Life and Service in the West*, Albuquerque: University of New Mexico Press, 2009.

Chapter 16 Bastogne

Arnold, James R. *1944: Hitler's Last Gamble in the West*. Oxford, United Kingdom: Osprey Publishing, 1990.

Brim, R.J., Klingel, T.D., Perkins, D.L., & Blevins, L. Battle of the Bulge. USASMA Digital Library, 2004, http://cgsc.contentdm.oclu.org/cdm/singleitem/collection/p15040coll2/id/5111/

Hayhow, Ernie (Ed.). *Thunderbolt Across Europe*. Nashville, TN: Battery Press, 1997.

Historical Section, E.T. *Siege of Bastogne. World War II Operational Documents*. Combined Arms Research Library Digital Library, http://cgsc.contentdm.oclc.org.

Mitchell, R.M. *The 101st Airborne Division's Defense of Bastogne*. Fort Leavenworth, Kansas: Combat Studies Institute, 1986.

Oden, D. *"The 4th Armored Division in the Relief of Bastogne"*. Fort Leavenworth, Kansas: Command and General Staff College Military Review Volume XXVII, Number 10, January 1948. http://cgsc.cdmhost.com/cdm/search/searchterm/Ardennes

Select Sources

Chapter 17 Chipyong-ni, Korea

23d Infantry Regimental Combat Team After Action Report, 29 January-16 February 1951. http://www.usfk.mil/usfk/Uploads/120/23dInfRCAAR.pdf

G Company, Second Battalion, 23rd Regimental Combat Team. After Action Report and Interviews, 1951. http://www.usfk.mil/usfk/Uploads/120/GCompany2ndBN23RCTAAR.pdf

UN Forces Task Organization (Order of Battle) at Chipyong-ni, First UN Counteroffensive, 25 January-21 April 1951. http://www.usfk.mil/usfk/Uploads/120/OrderofBattleUNForces.pdf

Catchpole, Brian. *The Korean War: 1950-1953*. New York: Carroll & Graf, 2000.

Freeman, Paul. "Wonju Thru Chipyong: An Epic of Regimental Combat Team Action in Korea." unpublished manuscript, 1951. http://www.usfk.mil/usfk/Uploads/120/COLPaulFreemanAccount.pdf

Gugeler, Russell A. *Combat Actions in Korea: Infantry, Artillery, Armor.* Combat Forces Press, 1954. http://www.history.army.mil/books/korea/30-2/30-2_8.htm

Halberstam, David. *The Coldest Winter: America and the Korean War.* New York: Hyperion Books, 2007.

Mossman, Billy C. *Ebb and Flow, November 1950-July 1951: United States Army in the Korean War.* Washington, D.C.: U.S. Army Center of Military History, 1990. http://www.history.army.mil/books/korea/ebb/fm.htm

Toland, John. *In Mortal Combat: Korea, 1950-1953.* New York: William Morrow and Company, 1991.

Chapter 18 Operation Desert Storm

Allen, Thomas B., et al. *War in the Gulf.* Atlanta: Turner Publishing, Inc., 1991.

Halberstadt, Hans. *Desert Storm: Ground War*. Osceola, WI: Motorbooks International, 1991.

Morrow, Lance, et al. *Desert Storm: The War in the Persian Gulf*. Boston: Little, Brown & Company (Time Warner Publishing), 1991.

Hiro, Dilip. *Desert Storm to Desert Shield: The Second Gulf War*. New York: Routledge, 1992.

Steed, Brian. *Armed Conflict: The Lessons of Modern Warfare*. New York: Ballantine Books, 2002.

INDEX

A

Abrams, Creighton 51
Act 12, 55, 205, 207
Action Oriented 9, 12, 205
After Action Review 204
Aristotle 20
Armed Forces 213
Army Leader 66, 67

B

Bastogne ix, 175, 176, 177, 178,
179, 180, 181, 182, 183, 208,
214, 222, 223
Bill of Rights 19
Bonaparte 39, 51, 162
Bonaparte, Napoleon 39, 51
Buffalo Soldiers 166, 167, 168, 169,
171, 172, 173, 174, 221, 222
Bush, George H.W. 195

C

Cato 74
Chamberlain, Joshua Lawrence ix,
91, 92, 93, 94, 95, 96, 97, 98,
99, 100, 101, 207, 214, 218
Character 66, 80
Chipyong-ni, Korea 184, 185, 186,
187, 189, 193, 223
Churchill, Winston 59, 112, 116,
117, 120
Cicero 20
Clark, William 84, 85, 86, 88, 89,
90, 217, 218
Clausewitz, Klaus Von 17, 25, 43
Cochrane, Alexander Inglis 157,
158, 159, 161
Command 40, 50, 51, 52, 65, 69,
123, 127, 179, 180, 212, 213,
216, 222
Constitution 3, 10, 18, 19, 24, 60
Corps of Discovery 82, 84, 85, 86,
87, 89, 90
Course of Action 36, 37, 38
Cowpens ix, 145, 149, 150, 151,
153, 154, 208, 214, 220, 221
Cromwell, Oliver 50

D

Davis, Wynn 51
Desert Storm ix, 52, 122, 128, 194,
196, 223, 224
Diplomats iii, vi, xi, 204, 205, 209,
214, 226

E

Eisenhower, Dwight D. 39, 112,
117, 118, 140, 178, 219

F

Focus ix, 11, 26, 28, 35, 39, 41, 52,
55, 126, 162, 205, 207, 210
Focused Power 140
Fort Benning 5, 46, 114
Franklin Delano Roosevelt 112
Freeman, Paul 184, 185, 186, 188,
189, 192, 223

G

Gaulle, Charles de 112
George W. Bush 126
Greene, Nathanael 77, 145, 146,
148

H

Hamilton, Alexander 19

SUCCESS101WORKSHOP.COM

The **Success 101 Workshop** helps individuals and teams succeed in business and life. Through insightful messages, hands-on workshops, and focused courses and presentations **Success 101 Workshop** helps businesses prosper and people live full and fulfilling lives. **Success 101 Workshop** programs help people uncover their foremost desires, develop their innate talents, and leverage their personal power to create and live the lives of their dreams.

Scott F. Paradis, founder and principle trainer of the **Success 101 Workshop,** trains individuals and teams to excel.

Success in business and in life is not a matter of employing overwhelming resources and commanding irresistible power, it is a matter of doing the best you can with what you've got. By learning and leveraging the fundamental principles of leadership and success you can change your mind, your business, and your life.

Through hands-on workshops and focused presentations the **Success 101 Workshop** broadens people's perspectives so they see with greater clarity and come to understand what is most important. Armed with that knowledge they can act with greater confidence to succeed and prosper.

AVAILABLE AT:
SUCCESS101WORKSHOP.COM

Books:

Success 101 How Life Works
Know the Rules, Play to Win
Scott F. Paradis, Cornerstone Achievements, 2012

E-book (.PDF) with Volume 2, Words and Deeds, and audio and audio-visual bonus materials at Success101Workshop.com

Hard Cover, Soft Cover, E-Readers - available where books are sold

Warrior, Diplomats, Heroes:
Why America's Army Succeeds
Lessons for Business and Life
Scott F. Paradis, Cornerstone Achievements, 2012

E-book (.PDF) with audio, and audio-visual bonus materials at Success101Workshop.com

Hard Cover, Soft Cover, E-Readers - available where books are sold

Promise and Potential
A Life of Wisdom, Courage, Strength and Will
Scott F. Paradis, Cornerstone Achievements, 2008

E-book with bonus material and Hard Cover - at Success-101Workshop.com

Self-Study Courses:

Success 101 How Life Works

Warriors, Diplomats, Heroes - Leading from the Front

CPSIA information can be obtained at www.ICGtesting.com
Printed in the USA
BVOW011547081012

302423BV00001B/1/P

9 780979 863875